Exploring Unequal Achievement in the Schools

Exploring Unequal Achievement in the Schools

The Social Construction of Failure

George Ansalone

LEXINGTON BOOKS

A division of
ROWMAN & LITTLEFIELD PUBLISHERS, INC.
Lanham • Boulder • New York • Toronto • Plymouth, UK

LEXINGTON BOOKS

A division of Rowman & Littlefield Publishers, Inc.
A wholly owned subsidary of The Rowman & Littlefield Publishing Group, Inc.
4501 Forbes Boulevard, Suite 200
Lanham, MD 20706

Estover Road
Plymouth PL6 7PY
United Kingdom

British Library Cataloguing in Publication Information Available

Library of Congress Cataloging-in-Publication Data

Ansalone, George Edward, 1944–
  Exploring unequal achievement in the schools : the social construction of failure /
George Ansalone.
     p. cm.
  Includes bibliographical references and index.
  ISBN-13: 978-0-7391-2468-0 (cloth : alk. paper)
  eISBN-13: 978-0-7391-3515-0
  1. Children with social disabilities—Education—United States. 2. School failure—
Social aspects—United States. 3. Discrimination in education—United States. I. Title.
  LC4091.A73 2009
  306.43—dc22   2008048314

Printed in the United States of America

∞™ The paper used in this publication meets the minimum requirements of American
National Standard for Information Sciences—Permanence of Paper for Printed Library
Materials, ANSI/NISO Z39.48-1992.

To Mary Jo, Laurie, and Karen

Contents

Preface

As a young man growing up in New York City, I believed that schooling was essential for social and economic advancement, and that access to education was available to all. I believed that class, status, and occupational level were meritocratic and that ability and effort were relied upon more readily than privilege and inherited status. As far as I was concerned, schooling provided the means of socializing young adults into roles required by society; it ensured social cohesion and harmony by moving us closer to equity and social justice, and, above all, it accomplished this without prejudice to race, gender, or class. Today, many still subscribe to this *functionalist perspective of education.*

As I grew older, my perspective changed. The post-modern era had begun; the civil rights movement became a hard fact of life, and the Brown decision (*Brown v. Board of Education*) was beginning to inscribe an indelible mark on the American character. In time, it became clear to me that less-advantaged youth from America's inner-cities were being left behind. Large segments of the American population failed to complete their education and many, mostly minorities, could not even read or write on grade level.

While many blamed the students themselves, it seemed apparent to me that American education was at least partly at fault. Clearly, schools were failing in their attempt to effect change in the lives of students.

For over a half century and without much success, educational sociologists have debated the cause of this failure. Some point to families and insist that they, too, must bear responsibility for the success or failure of their children. But, can families, especially those from disadvantaged backgrounds, be held *totally* responsible?

Others have offered more radical explanations for this troublesome disparity. Jensen's (1969) claim of an 80 percent variation in intelligence due to heritable factors continues to rear its ugly head, and more recently, has found support in the work of Herrnstein and Murry (1994). While seriously misleading, the simplicity of this theory is key in maintaining its intermittent popularity. But rather than moving us toward practical solutions, this theory seems only to focus blame on the innocent victims themselves.

As an educator and sociologist, I failed to be impressed with these inadequate explanations. I continued to search for an alternative explanation to explain the seemingly guaranteed success of children from advantaged families and the frequent failure of others. More than three decades have elapsed and my professional career has gone full circle, from college lecturer to academic dean and more recently, to professor once again. In each of these positions, I have taken the opportunity to observe, inquire and collect my thoughts. This work rejects the tired theories of genetic hereditability and cultural deficiency and represents the theoretical explanation that has evolved from my ongoing inquiry. Unlike other explanations, it employs a theoretical synthesis resting on macro and micro sociological theory. A macro-level orientation enables us to focus on the social structures that shape our society and permits us to view children in schools as full-fledged members of the American social system, taking into account the issues of *race, gender, and class.* On the other hand, the addition of a micro-level orientation, specifically a symbolic interactionist approach, permits us to build theory that views academic success as the result of the everyday interactions of individuals and processes that take place within classrooms. Further, it suggests that educational practices and policies operating within the schools (testing, tracking, and teacher expectations) play an exacting role in the construction of success or failure by identifying and labeling children as achievers or underachievers. In turn, these measurements impact the development of a hidden curriculum, students' self-concept, and the manner by which teachers present subject matter to their classes.

Furthermore, this approach underscores the plight of the disadvantaged family that lacks the political clout to *negotiate* a different image for their children. As a result, the new student identity which emerges begins to effect a change in the manner by which students perceive themselves and helps to create a new "definition of self" as achiever or underachiever. Finally, as expectations are communicated to students by members of the school community, they soon learn to accept this academic perception of their abilities. In so doing, schooling becomes a crucial factor in the social construction of academic success or failure.

This book is about schooling and how it impacts on equity, excellence and social inequality in America. The work has progressed as a result of my frustration with the lack of reading material available in this area. It has been designed especially for the educational practitioner, students of sociology and education, policy makers and parents. Essentially, the material is presented in an understandable manner devoid of complicated statistical procedures and terminology. *Chapter 1* explores some of the major challenges and issues facing schools today. It presents the sociological approach to the study of education and examines the role of theory in understanding what is happening in schools. *Chapter 2* explores macro-theories of unequal achievement and presents the pros and cons of each. *Chapter 3* considers the role that family and status characteristics play in explaining unequal achievement and explores the impact of different family configurations, aspirations and interactions on the development of student academic success. The impact of socio-economic status, gender and race are also examined. *Chapter 4* examines the role of the school as a possible cause of unequal achievement and assesses how various characteristics *between schools* including resources, school size, school SES, single gender vs. coeducational and private vs. public may play a role in unequal achievement. *Chapter 5* focuses on how differences *within* schools contribute to the construction of success or failure. Beginning with the research of Coleman and Jencks, it explores the most recent studies in this area and suggests how educational structures and practices facilitate academic success for some and failure for others. *Chapter 6* presents a theoretical synthesis utilizing a social constructionist approach that offers an explanation for unequal achievement in the schools. It examines closely the day-to-day interactions of students and teachers and how they may explain the success of some students and the failure of others. Finally, *Chapter 7* suggests what schools, families and governments can do to begin to solve the problem of unequal achievement; implications for educational policy are also discussed. A useful Glossary of terms is also included to assist the reader.

The schooling experience is formidable in the everyday lives of our children, yet we lack detailed and reliable data on how it affects their self-concept and their ability to learn. This book provides a beginning in this area. I promise that after reading this book, you will no longer think about schools and schooling in the same way—*ever again*!

Part I

INTRODUCTION

Chapter One

Perplexing Problems in American Schooling

. . . if there was ever a time and a country in which the sociological point of view was important for educators, it is certainly our country and our time. It is not because sociology can give us ready made procedures which we may use, but because it may provide us with a guiding framework of ideas that may be the core of our practice.

Emile Durkheim, *Education and Sociology*

SCHOOLS IN CRISIS

Even though there is no mention of education in the U.S. Constitution, schooling in America has always been considered important and is often extolled as an avenue of upward mobility. In fact, an integral part of the American dream has been the belief that education can transcend divisions of race, gender, and class and can be effectively utilized as a tool of social and economic advancement. Faith in our educational system; has been supported not only by our historical belief that education is valuable in and of itself, but by our commitment since the early nineteenth century to schooling as an instrument of social engineering. Clearly, the importance of schools and schooling in our society is reflected in the vast number of schools, the increasing enrollment, as well as the high level of education completed by the general population. This faith in education has led our nation to allocate over $600 billion dollars each year to develop one of the most extensive educational systems in the world; a system that enables most citizens to complete both an elementary and secondary education. Almost 90 percent of all American school age children and over half of the youth falling in the age category 18 to 21 are in some type of educational institution (U.S. Bureau of the Census 2000).

3

But when asked to comment on the overall quality of American education, today, Americans fail to give it a passing grade (Bennett et al., 2006). Many perceive schools to be ineffective. Much of the contemporary research underscores how little some students learn and the media continues to draw our attention to the increasing episodes of violence and student misconduct. In fact, many parents and educators actually believe that the system is in crisis and that American schooling cannot provide even the most fundamental education for students. Some, now even question its ability to enhance social and economic equality.

Christopher Jencks was among the first to suggest that although educational opportunities have become more equally distributed, social inequalities persist. His controversial study, *Inequality*, concluded that educational attainment, while related to occupation, can do little to improve financial success. Rather, the considerable income variation of workers with similar educational backgrounds can only be attributed to chance (Jencks, 1972, 1993). Still others have suggested that educational structures and policies within schools might act as determinants of educational outcomes and serve to limit the academic and affective development of some students (Ansalone, 2006; Gilbert, 2003; Ginorino and Huston, 2000).

Confidence in schools and education has declined in recent years and the criticism comes from all sectors of the American community. The growing perception among Americans is that our educational system is broken and that American schools are facing a crisis of unparalleled proportions. A recent Gallup Poll uncovered that only 35 percent of Americans expressed confidence in public schools—a drop of 23 percent since the mid seventies (Public Agenda, 2000). More and more, key stakeholders in the process, parents, students, and teachers are expressing the belief that schools are ineffective and that some alternative strategy is needed to educate our youth.

Schools should provide children with basic life-skills. Yet, employers point to the increasing number of job applicants who cannot complete an application or write a paragraph. They should develop students' intellectual abilities and facilitate the creation of new knowledge and technology. Instead, studies suggest that a large percentage of high school graduates cannot read a map and lack even the most basic knowledge of geography. Education should foster a common culture and convey values. Instead, critics point to low test scores and even lower rates of literacy among students, a deteriorating infrastructure, high rates of violence and an increasing achievement gap between the rich and the poor. In Virginia, for example, only 40 percent of white students were able to pass the American history exam required for graduation; less than 15 percent of black students were able to pass the same exam (Bracey, 2000). Ironically, at the same time, parental groups argue that school boards have appreciably "dumbed down" the curriculum and lowered academic standards making it possible for students to graduate without the ability to read and write.

Today's teachers are also confronted with far different challenges than their predecessors. Issues of cultural and religious diversity challenge the heart of the educational system. An increasing number of students and their parents cannot speak English, members of some religious groups will not salute the American flag, and Muslim students are often treated with distrust and suspicion. Still another challenge facing the schools is employing enough teachers to staff the growing system. Increasingly, qualified and experienced professionals are becoming frustrated by regulations, bureaucracy, and the growing number of disinterested students. Many are actually leaving the profession while others have expressed the wish that they had selected another profession!

In order to address these issues, a number of systematic reforms including charter schools, high-stakes testing, school choice, and site-based management have been suggested. Regretfully, when attempted, some of these have only intensified the debate on school effectiveness and exacerbated an already bad situation. More recently, the Congress of the United States passed the "No Child Left Behind" (NCLB) legislation. This bill mandated the development of standards and testing procedures to evaluate what students know by the end of each grade level. School success is evaluated annually and parents are permitted the option of withdrawing their children from failing schools. Schools with high failure rates lose Federal funding and also face the possibility of a complete restructure (Wallis and Steptoe, 2007).

The reviews on NCLB are mixed. In its assessment of forty-nine states, the Center on Education Policy reported some increase in test scores in about three-quarters of the states (Ripley and Stephoe, 2005). But many are concerned that exams have been made easier to guarantee the continuation of federal funds. Critics also argue that the NCLB legislation will do little to promote equity and excellence in schools since academic success is measured by standardized tests. Still others have noted the gender and class bias inherent in these exams. Thus, the testing utilized in NCLB may actually place women and poor students at a further disadvantage. Reliance on increased testing may also cause teachers to "teach to the test" and eliminate many valuable and enriching activities in music and the arts since they fear that these subjects will not be evaluated by the tests. Thus, economically disadvantaged and minority students will suffer even more.

The purpose of this book is to provide an understanding of why some students underachieve in school. It employs a sociological approach. Chapter 1 reviews some of the most critical problems facing schools today, and some of the strategies that have been developed to solve them. It addresses the need for educational sociology and the application of the sociological approach to schooling. It explores the unique theoretical approaches utilized by sociologists to understand the process of schooling, the Functional, Conflict and Symbolic Interactionist, and how each contributes to our understanding of underachievement. It provides a Functionalist and Conflict perspective on the development of schooling in order to shed light on the original and contemporary functions of schooling. Finally, it presents the unique relationship between schooling and life-course events in testing the assumption, Do Schools Really Matter?

But before we begin, let us examine more closely some of the perplexing problems and issues facing education today.

Functional Illiteracy

One of the most troubling issues in America, today, is that almost 30 million Americans are functionally illiterate. Functional illiteracy refers to an individual's inability to read and write well enough to carry out everyday activities (National Center for Education Statistics, 2003). But being functionally illiterate in the United States means much more than not knowing how to read or write. It affects virtually every aspect of living. The functionally illiterate cannot write a letter to challenge a bill. They find it difficult to read a newspaper with any real understanding and cannot follow directions on a prescription label. For the most part, it is almost impossible for them to engage in the everyday activities that you and I take for granted.

Almost twenty-five years ago, a presidential panel warned Americans of a "rising tide of mediocrity" in education that threatened the very future of our nation. The report, *A Nation at Risk*, revealed that verbal and math scores were on a dramatic decline and that functional illiteracy, the inability to engage in everyday reading and writing, was dramatically increasing in our nation (National Commission on Excellence in Education, 1983). In spite of this warning, almost two and a half decades later, these scores remain relatively unchanged. Seven out of ten fourth graders in disadvantaged neighborhoods cannot read a simple children's book. More recently, the Department of Education reported that almost 30 million Americans fell below the basic literacy level while only 63 million (29 percent) could be placed at the Basic level (Table 1.1). Scores for women tend to be lower than those of men and racial minorities lag behind the white middle-class. Clearly, the available evidence underscores the need for dramatic improvement in this area.

Many issues influence the learning of reading and writing and schools alone cannot be held totally responsible for this depressing problem. But they,

Table 1.1. Prose Literacy in the United States

Below basic	30 million	14%	(no more than the simplest literacy skills)
Basic	63 million	29%	(simple everyday skills)
Intermediate	95 million	44%	(moderately challenging literacy activity)
Proficient	28 million	13%	(complex literacy activity)

Source: U.S. Dept of Education, National Assessment of Adult Literacy (NAAL), 2003.

too, must bear some blame if they continue to graduate students who cannot read and write. Many relate this problem to social promotion, the policy of promoting students who have not satisfied the requirements for the lower grade. Today, social promotion is common and many educators suggest that it may be better to create some emotional trauma in students now, rather than relegate them to living life as functional illiterates. Others point to the increase in grade inflation and the growing complacency of schools in reaching educational goals. Today, approximately 46 percent of all entering college freshmen graduate high school with an overall grade point average of "*A*" and this percentage has more than doubled since the 1970s (Higher Education Research Institute, University of California). Many also attribute the decline in literacy to the hodgepodge of programs currently employed in the schools to teach reading as well as the declining involvement of the family in the education of their children.

School Violence

Violence in American schools remains a grave concern for parents and educators alike. Americans report the lack of discipline, blatant violence and use of drugs as some of the most serious problems facing schools today (Rose and Gallup, 1999). Our nation's schools, once considered safe harbors for learning and teaching, have become settings for theft, rape, aggravated assault and homicide (National Center for Education Statistics, 2006). Uniformed guards, metal detectors, and surveillance cameras, unheard of years ago, have become commonplace in many schools across our nation. In fact, some inner-city schools have even replaced the traditional fire drills with "drive by shooting" alerts. Perhaps most startling is that educational institutions in quiet, middle-class suburbs like Blacksburg, Virginia, and Littleton, Colorado, have become settings for mass killings. Televised images of young children fleeing school buildings have generated worldwide media coverage that has initiated a national debate on school security capturing the attention of a troubled nation.

Of an estimated 54 million students attending elementary and secondary schools in the United States during the 2004–2005 academic year, the National Center for Education Statistics reported a total of twenty-eight violent deaths (twenty-one homicides and seven suicides). Students were also victims of about 1.4 million nonfatal crimes including 863,000 thefts and 583,000 violent crimes—107,000 of which were serious violent crimes including rape, sexual assault, robbery, and aggravated assault. Additionally, the percentage of public schools reporting one or more violent incidents increased between 1999–2000 and 2003–2004, from 71 percent to 81 percent. Approximately 6 percent of students in grades 9-12 admitted to carrying weapons (National Center for Education Statistics, 2006).

Teachers also report the fear of being attacked by their students. During the 2003–2004 school year, 8 percent of teachers in secondary schools and 6 percent of teachers in elementary schools were threatened with bodily harm by their students. Elementary schoolteachers were more likely than secondary schoolteachers to suffer a physical attack (4 percent vs. 2 percent). Clearly, the presence of weapons in schools interferes with the creation of a positive learning environment (National Center for Education Statistics, 2006).

The presence of gangs in schools is also alarming to Americans. Gang presence is pervasive in many inner-city schools. The percentage of students reporting the presence of gang members in their schools increased from 21 to 24 percent between the 2003 and 2005 school years. Schools in urban areas reported an increase of from 31 to 36 percent for this same time period (National Center for Education Statistics, 2006). Yet, some minority parents remain ambivalent about prohibiting members of local gangs from attending neighborhood schools. While they dislike the violence and unnecessary force, many still believe that gangs provide better protection than do the local police (Karcher, 2002).

Schools should be free from crime and violence. Violence in schools not only harms students but disparages the purpose of education. Educational sociologists have identified a number of social and cultural factors that may contribute to the escalating violence in schools. Among these are the popularity of violent video games, music that glorifies excessive violence, and the general level of violence in the media. The perception of gender roles has also been significantly influenced by popular music and cinema. Rock-music videos often depict women as deceitful and illogical while men are portrayed as domineering and aggressive. These popular forms of media often display sexual images combined with acts of violence. Heavy metal and rap also employ violent lyrics in which women are represented as sex objects on whom violent acts are perpetrated (McLeod, 2001). Each of these portrays excessive violence as an acceptable and normal event in everyday life.

The American response to school violence has included a number of diverse approaches. Some schools have opted for the addition of metal detectors and cameras, while others have incorporated conflict resolution programs. Another popular approach has been the adoption of a school uniform dress code. Proponents of this policy assert that school uniforms promote order, ease peer pressure, enhance self-esteem and curb truancy. While there is little research to support their claims, some schools have reported fewer incidents following the adoption of a school uniform policy.

Some associate the increase in school violence with the massiveness of contemporary schooling and suggest that smaller and more personal schools might also alleviate some of the alienation that leads to school misbehavior. Mosteller (1995) suggests that we can effectively "humanize" schools by reducing both school and class size. He argues that the typical urban school tends to be large and impersonal with little opportunity for teachers and students to interact on a more personal level. Proponents of smaller classes also argue that a reduction in class size will facilitate discipline and increase academic achievement. Providing teachers with the opportunity to know more about their students by reducing class and school size can possibly bring a more human element to what is often an impersonal process. Small school proponents also suggest that the inclusion of art, gardens, and even greenhouses will create a more personal and sensitive school environment.

Schools cannot be effective if they do not provide an orderly and secure environment. Although schools are relatively safe when compared with other institutions in society, any amount of undisciplined behavior and violence in schools reduces their effectiveness and limits student learning. Considering the level of violence and the emphasis being placed on security, it is no wonder that an increasing number of students are dropping out of schools.

School Dropouts and Truancy

Dropouts and truancy represent another persistent problem in contemporary schooling. Students drop out of school for a variety of reasons. Some may be highly skeptical about the value of an education and question its ability to increase their job opportunity. Others become pregnant or leave to support a family. Still others may become disenchanted with a system of education they cannot understand or to which they cannot relate. Students may also become discouraged with the learning environment and by the educational policies followed by schools. It is highly possible that some policies and practices may polarize students' attitudes toward school into pro and anti-school positions. Tracking, the separation of students into different ability groups for the purpose of instruction, represents one such policy. Research suggests that assignment to a lower track may lead to student's boredom, frustrations and eventual withdrawal from school (Ansalone, 2000; Oakes, 1985).

Although the dropout rate has declined slightly in recent years, slightly over 10 percent of all students between sixteen and twenty-four drop out of school before earning a high school diploma. As might be expected, minority students are more likely to drop out than others. The rate of Black students leaving school (1 out of 6) has slightly declined in recent years but it is still higher than that of white students (1 out of 8) (Statistical Abstract of the United States, 1999).

Sociologists have suggested a number of interesting and controversial programs for decreasing the dropout rate in American schools. Programs designed to identify early signs associated with withdrawal (chronic lateness, truancy, poor grades, etc.) have been around for years. More innovative and controversial programs that offer cash incentives to remain in school and encourage parents to become more involved in their children's education are more recent. A cash incentive program is currently being considered by the New York City public school system. Some question the logic of coercing students with financial rewards to remain in school and doubt that it will enable them to achieve the minimum level of academic competency. Finally, at the other end of the spectrum are those who suggest that education is not for all and that many will be better off in the workforce. Permitting them to do so will eliminate many of the frustrations associated with keeping dropouts in school and eliminate much of the stigma that students experience upon leaving school.

Creeping Credentialism

The amount of formal education that is required to apply for and gain even a menial job has increased over the past few decades. Thus many believe that the steady rise in educational credentials required for employment, often referred to as "creeping credentialism," is a serious problem for the poor who have difficulty affording the required education. It also provides an edge to those who are economically advantaged in securing better jobs and thereby perpetuating their class status. Regardless of how hard the disadvantaged try to secure a life better than that of their parents, educational requirements continue to remain far beyond their reach. Credentialism also results in educational inflation since the education required to perform a job remains the same while the educational requirements increase from year to year.

Because of the strong positive correlation between class and educational level, some educational sociologists suggest that credentialism is, in fact, an instrument of discrimination against minorities and disadvantaged populations (Collins, 1979; Marshall, 1997). In his research, *The Credential Society*, Randy Collins argues that schools do little to increase knowledge required for jobs. Instead, they provide a credential, a kind of *currency* that enables the holder to purchase different types of status. Inequalities of social class are actually reproduced within the educational setting and reproducing the existing class structure is an important function of education. Collins argues that schools provide the credentials that enable children of the middle-class to obtain middle-class jobs. Similarly, Meyer suggests that education provides a sorting and selecting mechanism to some individuals. It classifies them into distinct categories (college grad, MBA, dropout, etc.), those who are entitled to elite positions and those who are not (Meyer, 1977). These classifications, he argues, may not actually correspond to differences in the actual ability of the person to perform a job, but the important thing is that society believes that they do. The ceremonies and graduations associated with completing these credentials go far in convincing credentialed people of their right to high-status positions. Thus a type of self fulfilling prophesy takes place in which holders of the appropriate credentials begin to accept and believe in their entitlement. This also empowers them to develop the appropriate attitudes and state of mind associated with the performance of these careers; while dropouts become increasingly convinced of their worthlessness. The most significant value of education therefore rests in its ability to legitimate differences between groups rather than its ability to effect change in abilities. This difference and perception also acts as a justification and rationalization that people without these credentials should not hold these advantaged positions. In spite of this, employers will continue to insist on a certain educational level, even though it may not be related to the actual ability of the candidate to fill the job.

Unequal Funding

One of the most critical issues facing American education is the problem of unequal funding of schools. Although many Americans believe that unequal funding represents a serious source of inequality in education, most also continue to subscribe to an inconsistent educational philosophy. They agree that schools should provide equal opportunity to all; yet, they concede to the problem of unequal funding.

Ninety percent of all American students attend public primary and secondary schools funded by the State. But not all public schools are equal. Even within the same city, differences in funding between rich and poor districts result in unequal resources for the various schools. These funding differences can result in dramatic differences as advantaged districts often spend appreciably more on their students. The result is that children in advantaged areas generally attend schools with better resources and more qualified teachers.

Per-capita spending on education varies from state to state and the geographical inequality in tax assessments and school funding becomes evident when we consider what different states spend for education per student. States like Massachusetts, New York and New Jersey spend about two times more per student than South Dakota, Mississippi and Utah (Table 1.2). A general rule of thumb is that the Eastern states rank highest for per capita expenditures while most of the Southern states fall in the bottom half (National Education Association, 2003).

Unequal funding is also a problem between school districts within the same state. This is primarily due to the fact that school districts are generally funded by a local property tax assessment. Complicating the situation is that many children living in inner-cities attend public schools in districts where tax assessments have been eroded by an exodus of middle-class families to the suburbs. For decades, Americans have funded schools through property taxes. Since poorer districts have an abundance of less-expensive real estate, which results in lower property assessments, these districts receive less state funding. Because of this practice, schools in economically advantaged areas have greater resources to provide better schools and higher paid teachers for their students. The current system of funding schools almost always benefits white middle class districts and has contributed to what many term a "savage inequality" in school resources between poor and rich districts (Kozol, 1992). The situation is further exacerbated by the fact that inner-city schools often experience less family support (parental involvement) and greater situational problems (dropouts, underachievers) which require more funding than do schools in higher socio-economic areas.

Table 1.2.   Current Expenditures ($) per Student in Public Schools of Selected States

Rank	State	2001–2
1.	District of Columbia	$13,993
2.	New York	$11,023
3.	New Jersey	$10,869
4.	Connecticut	$10,825
5.	Massachusetts	$10,190
19.	Georgia	$ 7,824
20.	Oregon	$ 7,804
29.	South Carolina	$ 7,012
32.	Texas	$ 6,850
38.	South Dakota	$ 6,540
47.	Mississippi	$ 5,469
48.	Alabama	$ 5,210
50.	Utah	$ 4,674
51.	North Dakota	$ 4,612

Source: National Education Association. Washington D.C. 2003.

School funding determines the quality of the educational experience within the school. It determines the availability of computers, new textbooks, well-equipped labs, and the overall conditions of classrooms. It impacts on the hiring of experienced teachers and goes a long way in determining class size. More recently, taxpayers have voiced their concern about increasing property taxes and state legislatures have become reluctant to increase the level of funding if it necessitates an increase in taxes. However, strategies employed by the various states to effectively improve educational financing have been limited. In an attempt to solve this difficult problem, Michigan recently voted to eliminate property taxes in place of a higher state income tax. Another response has been to divide money equally across a state as was done in Vermont. Equal funding of this type is often accompanied by accusations of unfair tax burdens being placed on only some residents. Some districts have also initiated a policy of *Busing*—transporting students to achieve a balance in race and equity in schools. This policy remains highly controversial and many claim that it challenges the concept of the neighborhood school. Still others assert that it can only be effective if children are bussed from the inner-cities to the suburbs.

But higher spending alone will not guarantee quality education and some argue that spending more money on schools will not necessarily mean that children will receive a better education (Coleman, 1990). Yet, unequal funding is tantamount to stacking the decks against poorer areas of the country especially inner-city school districts. Because U.S. schools are a microcosm of the nation, children attending schools in advantaged neighborhoods are more likely to continue to gain acceptance to better high schools and colleges. Accordingly, unequal funding of the nation's schools contributes to long-term social consequences for the disadvantaged and the perpetuation of the social class system.

School Choice

Closely related to the overall issue of unequal school resources is the debate over exactly how and where federal funds should be spent and whether parents have the right to choose their children's school. The idea of *school choice* or permitting parents to decide where their children attend schools, first surfaced in the 1960s and was based on the idea that *competition* among schools would enhance equity and excellence in education. This typically American idea gained strength during the conservative wave that swept the nation after the 1994 elections and the development of the Contract with America.

The *Contract with America* included strong support for school choice and privatization in public education. The idea of school choice seemed to provide an appropriate response to many of the problems plaguing the public school system. Clearly, most parents believed that it would promote the element of competition and thereby enhance excellence. Middle class parents also saw in it the opportunity to provide their children with a safe and academically challenging educational experience. Disadvantaged families argued that *choice* would finally enable their children to attend better schools with better teachers and more resources (Gallup, 1991). Perhaps the strongest supporters of the Choice movement were the religious schools. These private schools believed that this alternative might break the monopoly of the public schools and also provide them with an opportunity to enhance their religious ideology.

But not everyone favors Choice and the movement against it has been led by the various teachers associations around the country. These strong unions and associations advanced the idea that school choice would eventually alter the fundamental structure of education. They waged an effective campaign against it by arguing that it was a surrender of the nation's commitment to public education and that it would eventually deteriorate the already bad conditions in poor school districts. Additionally, they argued that the plan would lead to greater economic and racial segregation (Morse, 2002). Essentially, School choice options fall into the following categories: school vouchers, charter schools, home schooling and magnet schools.

School Vouchers

The concept of school vouchers first surfaced in the 1990s. A Voucher entitled parents, in neighborhoods where schools were considered to be inadequate, to enroll their children in the private school of their choice. Parents, not schools, would receive public money, which could be used to pay for tuition. The underlying idea was to force the public schools to compete with each other. Good schools would thrive and poor schools would be forced to improve.

The U.S. Supreme Court upheld the use of vouchers in *Zelman v. Simmons-Harris*, 2002. At present, most students attend schools in their own neighborhoods. A voucher system would enable parents to select from a wider range of choices and provide them with tax dollars to pay for the education. Voucher programs are more often supported by poor and minority parents who view the choice they provide as a chance to enhance the educational opportunities of their children. Supporters of the program insist that it is the only sure way to improve the school system, since it increases competition for students among the various schools. On the other hand, opponents believe that it will direct finances away from public education and into the hands of private schools, many of which are religiously sponsored. This, they argue, will further deteriorate public education and also act as a violation of the "separation" principle.

The widespread adoption of the school voucher program was impeded by the passage of the "No Child Left Behind" legislation. This legislation guaranteed the right to special tutoring or a school transfer to those low income students who continued to underachieve. From all of the available research, there is no evidence to suggest that Vouchers help to close the achievement gap between White and Black students. Some also attribute the failure of vouchers to gain widespread popularity to the increase in popularity of Charter and Magnet schools.

Charter Schools

Charter schools are public schools managed by private parties (parental groups or educational corporations) operating under a special charter from the state. These schools are designed to support educational innovation and are given more liberty to explore new programs and innovative approaches to instruction. To many, they represent a middle position between public and private education and afford parents the opportunity to exercise some control over the educational experiences of their children. The charter permitting the schools to operate is an official contract which outlines the school's mission, goals, and programs and includes the methods to be used to evaluate the success of its students. Charter Schools offer programs to students-at-risk and provide support for programs not adequately available in the regular schools, that is, communications, computer science, performing arts. In 2005, slightly over 3,000 charter schools were operating in forty states and serving over one million students (U.S. Department of Education, 2006).

Regretfully, Charter schools have not enrolled the most disadvantaged youth and these schools have not improved the grades of those who have attended them. They are also expensive to operate and many struggle to raise funds (Carnoy et al., 2005).

Magnet Schools

Similar in purpose to Charter schools, Magnet schools attempt to attract White students to predominately minority schools. They are public schools with high academic standards with specialized curricula such as math and science. There are approximately 5000 magnet schools in the United States.

Homeschooling

Homeschooling refers to the education of children within their own homes under the supervision of their parents. It has become an increasingly popular form of Choice. There are an estimated one and a half million homeschooled children in the United States and the number continues to grow at an estimated

10 percent each year (U.S. Department of Education, 2006). Essentially the requirements for home schooling are quite simple. Instruction must be equivalent to that provided by the local school and the qualified adult providing the instruction must offer a minimum numbers of hours per day. Additionally, about 65 percent of the states now require that the homeschooled must be tested periodically for academic progress (Mawdsley, 2000).

The concept of homeschooling is not new. Soon after the establishment of public schools in the 1800s, families with strict religious views and those living in isolated environments chose to school their children at home. More recently, home-based education has been facilitated by the need to provide stronger moral training and limit the child's exposure to the negative socializing impact of peer culture in public schools. The perceived lower quality of the public schools and the fear of increased violence in the schools have also caused many concerned parents to homeschool their children.

At the center of the debate over home schooling is the belief that America's schools can no longer provide a values-oriented education. Some parents argue that the delicate question of religion in schools has been interpreted by recent Court decisions as attacks on morality in general. While the relationship between school and religion has always been controversial, maintaining the "wall of separation" between Church and State has often been difficult. Some contend that the desire for separation has paved the way for a loss of values in education. The homeschooling movement grew as these parents were joined by others who believed that the academic quality of the educational experience in the public schools was deteriorating.

But how effective is homeschooling? Most proponents argue that children can perform as well, if not better, when schooled at home. Comprehensive studies suggest that the academic achievement of homeschooled children is higher than that of those attending public schools. They argue that a natural advantage of homeschooling is its ability to provide an individualized curriculum for each child (Cloud and Morse, 2001; Ray, 1997).

On the other hand, The National Education Association claims that homeschooling lacks the ability to properly socialize children. It fails to allow students to learn and compete (extracurricularly) together as members of the same community. Neither does it allow them to come in contact and work with children of diverse backgrounds. Additionally, opponents of the homeschooling movement claim that this type of choice represents a rejection of some of the fundamental reasons for public schooling, that is, learning to get along with others and experiencing a common culture. The idea of providing for the education of children within their own home has both popular and political appeal. While it is difficult to discard a 200-year commitment to public education, how can one argue for less choice? In all likelihood, the contentious debate will continue for some time.

THE NEED FOR EDUCATIONAL SOCIOLOGY

Education has changed dramatically during the past half century. Teachers at all levels face far different problems and issues than their predecessors only a decade ago. Classroom diversity, school violence, issues of cultural and functional literacy, as well as the knowledge that the educational structures and policies of a school can influence achievement present challenging and even daunting problems for American educators.

The field of Educational Sociology is concerned with how schools face these challenges and how they can best meet the constantly changing needs of society and individual learners. Additionally, since sociology is concerned with the impact of groups and institutions on individuals, the sociological approach can add a new dimension to the study of education. It permits us to study schools as dependent and independent variables. When we consider the school as a dependent variable, we are able to understand and appreciate the impact that groups have on it. As an independent variable, we focus on how schools affect others—especially students. For students entering the field and for in-service professionals this perspective can provide practical information about their chosen career.

The application of sociology to the field of education is recent and sociology of education courses are relatively new additions to the curriculum. During the past half century, a greater awareness has developed about the role that schools play in the creation and perpetuation of certain social issues. For example, what is the role of the school in perpetuating social inequality and unequal achievement? Does education affect income? Can schools promote equality? Research in educational sociology can provide answers to these questions and some of the most commonly asked questions about education and schooling.

Consider some of the issues that face American schools today:

How much can family influence student achievement?

Does ability grouping enhance academic outcomes?

Is equity and excellence possible in schools or is inequality facilitated in pursuing academic excellence?

Is social reproduction a natural outgrowth of current schooling?

Are Catholic schools better than public schools and, if so, why?

Do teachers' expectations influence students' achievement?

Does integration affect student learning?

What is the relationship between academic achievement, social class, and parental education?

How may family structure, size, and single parent status affect student achievement?

Today, Sociologists distinguish between the terms *education* and *schooling*. *Education* refers to the process of learning, which extends over the span of one's lifetime. Education may take place in a variety of formal and informal settings. When this learning takes place in a formal setting by an agency that is entrusted with the socialization of specific groups in the society, it is referred to as *schooling*. Therefore, schooling refers to the more formal, institutionalized aspects of education, often with some political agenda or overtone.

Lester Ward, one of the founding fathers of American Sociology, considered schooling to be one of the most important institutions in American society and the principal source of human progress. Through schooling, we could foster a new moral commitment that would ultimately improve society. He was among the first to refer to the field as *educational sociology* and looked to it to examine practical problems and formulate policy decisions for change and improvement. The name *sociology of education* was not introduced until some years later by Robert Angell, a former President of the American Sociological Association. He argued that sociology should not attempt to solve educational problems; rather, it should gather data and explore the field of education since schools were excellent sources of scientific data. This book deals with the study of schools, educational policies, and structures operating within schools. It attempts to draw useful implications for educational practice and policy especially about one of the most perplexing issues of our time—*unequal achievement*. After years of schooling, many students continue to fall behind the learning curve and fail miserably in their attempt to complete an education. Educational sociology addresses this issue and helps us to understand why. In this regard, I consider it to be a work in educational sociology.

APPLYING SOCIOLOGICAL THEORY TO EDUCATION

The word *theory* comes from the ancient Greek term "theoria" which conveys the idea of looking at or contemplating something (Gutek, 2004). Therefore, to theorize is to form a set of loosely held generalizations that attempt to explain why something happens. In everyday language, we use the word to refer to a particular conviction or state of mind we employ to view the world or to suggest that we have an opinion about something.

Sociological theories about education and schooling are generally closely related to many commonsense notions about education and its functions. Sociological theory has looked at and made major contributions to understanding education and how it affects the individual and society. It permits sociologists to organize their thoughts on education and schooling. Whether it is a large-scale macro level analysis focusing on education and its functions or a micro level analysis focusing on the daily interactions of students and teachers, theory provides us with a better understanding of how education impacts society. In sum, a theoretical approach provides us with a unique perspective on a particular issue. It helps us to formulate the questions that we ask as well as the manner by which we organize our research and present our findings.

While sociologists agree on many things, they often subscribe to different theoretical perspectives in order to explain the issues and functions of education and schooling. For the most part, sociologists have employed three major theoretical perspectives to explore education and schooling, *the functional, the conflict and the symbolic interactionist.* Each provides a unique viewpoint or special way of looking at the various issues. Each also offers an interesting set of assumptions that frame our research questions and determine our method of analysis. Both the functional and conflict perspectives provide macro-level views of the school, its culture and social relations. The structural functional perspective also referred to as functionalism or the functional approach focuses on social structure and order. It views society as a system of interrelated parts, each fulfilling a specific function thereby contributing to the functioning of the whole system. On the other hand, the conflict perspective looks at society as being composed of diverse groups with conflicting interest, each with differential access to power and economic resources. In each ensuing confrontation, the dominant group attempts to force its ideology and values on the less powerful. By contrast, the symbolic interactionist approach views social meaning as arising through the process of social interaction. It focuses on small-scale micro level analyses, which describe the interactions of students and teachers as individuals and members of small groups operating within the school. Each of these three perspectives offer a different view and often different explanation for schools and schooling. Yet, each provides us with a better understanding of the important issues. Let us examine each perspective more closely.

The Functionalist Perspective

Why do we need schools? What is the function of education in society? Functional theory provides unique answers to these questions. It considers education as one of the most important components of any society. It argues that schools and the education system perform functions that are critical to the survival of society. According to the functionalist view, schools incorporate American values and teach students to put the society's needs above their individual desires. Elementary and secondary schools transmit the culture of the society and in so doing, promote national unity. Schools socialize new members into the society and transmit a common culture and code of ethics. But most of all, schools enable the society to train and select the best workers for various careers. They provide academic and career training and enhance social control.

The basic assumptions underlying the functional approach include the belief that society is stable and is composed of an ordered system of interrelated parts (structures). Additionally, functionalists assert that each structure in society has a function that contributes to the welfare and stability of the whole. Social institutions are the structures of society (the educational system, the family, religion, politics) and functionalists are interested in how these structures meet the needs of society. Because the functional perspective focuses on the issue of what schools are expected to accomplish for society, this approach seems to have dominated the literature during the past few decades.

Functionalists often equate society to a living body. Just as a living body must be healthy and work in harmony if the body is to survive, society, too, possesses functions which must be satisfied if it is to thrive. The Functional paradigm underscores the social benefits of education and schooling to society. To the functionalist, education is vital to the welfare and stability of the group.

The functional perspective is not the work of any one person. Its origins can be traced to the thinking of three early sociologists, Auguste Comte, Herbert Spencer and Emile Durkheim. Durkheim was perhaps the first to recommend its use in the study of education. His work clearly outlined its various functions and underscored the importance of education in building a communiy (Durkheim, 1956). Emile Durkheim saw in education the ability to transmit knowledge that was valued by the society. He believed that education *could arouse in the young, a number of mental states and images considered essential in all new members of that society* (Durkheim, 1956). He underscored the importance of education in creating values that could serve as a foundation for the society and above all, he believed that education was inseparable from the society of which it was a part. In fact, society and education mirrored each other. Education reflected the values of the society and any change in society was also reflected in the schools.

Contemporary sociologists concur with these beliefs and agree that the transmission of values represents the most important function of education. More recently, the approach has been delineated even further by Robert Merton. This modern American functionalist identified *manifest* and *latent* functions for the different social structures. Contemporary sociologists who employ a functional approach often distinguish between manifest and latent functions of the structures that they are examining.

Latent and Manifest Functions of Education

Another way that sociologists explore the purpose of education and schooling is to focus on the manifest and latent functions of education. Schools not only fulfill the manifest functions (intended) for which they were created but also execute latent functions (unintended) through many of their practices and policies. Latent functions are those which are unrecognized and *hidden*. They are consequences of an activity of which the participants are unaware. On the other hand, manifest functions are more open, explicit and intended. For example, coming to the same school each day, on time, and learning to raise your hand before you speak teaches children discipline, order and punctuality. These are important *latent* functions of education and they will also prove valuable character traits in later life. However, at the same time, the school is teaching the child to read and write. These *manifest (intended)* functions of education are likewise valuable. It is also important to note that since the needs and objectives of society fluctuate, a function that was manifest at one time may also become latent at another.

The core of the functional approach is clearly an explanation of why education is important to society. It stresses the numerous functions that education serves and how it contributes to the operation and stability of society. The following represents a list of generally accepted manifest functions of education.

Manifest Functions of Education

Socialization and Social Transmission. Because of increasing technology and complexity within societies, the family can no longer be counted on to transmit the unique culture, values and knowledge expected of new members. While families and peer groups remain important agents of socialization, schools, counselors, and teachers often assume responsibility for formal education. Contemporary schooling is a means of transmitting the knowledge and behaviors required to maintain order and stability in society. In elementary, middle and secondary schools, students are taught specific subject matter that will enable them to function in society. Clearly, it would be difficult for society to survive without an educated cohort of people.

Social Integration and Promotion of National Unity. Education provides for the integration and assimilation of newcomers into the society. It molds a diverse population into one society sharing common values, language and norms. School children are taught history, civics and social studies; they recite the pledge of allegiance and sing the Star Spangled Banner. In so doing, they solidify the nation and promote national unity and identity.

Social and Career Placement and Advancement. Functionalists underscore the role of education in sorting and selecting individuals for appropriate roles and career positions in society. Graduates are awarded the appropriate credentials in the form of diplomas or certifications that enable them to enter the workforce or professions. Education also provides an opportunity for social and economic advancement.

Change and Innovation.   Functionalists believe that schools act as agents of change. Usually at the college and university level, through the development of scientific research, schools create and produce new knowledge which acts as the basis for societal change.

Social Control/Order.   Schools teach values, discipline, punctuality and obedience. They stress the need for students to be law-abiding citizens and conscientious, hard-working Americans.

Latent Functions of Education

Education also transmits a number of latent functions (less obvious and often unintended consequences).

Schools as Babysitters.   Schools and their respective after-school centers provide a free form of baby sitting / child care service that keep children off the streets and enables parents to work and earn a living.

Schools as Havens for the Unemployed.   Schools also keep children occupied and out of the job market thus helping to keep the unemployment rate relatively low. Graduate schools also keep some students "employed" during recession and hard economic times thereby acting as havens for the unemployed.

Schools as Marriage Brokers.   Many American men and women usually choose marriage partners who are of a similar educational background. High schools and colleges serve as marriage markets and many colleges and graduate school students meet their partners while attending school.

Schools as Social Capital.   Very often significant social networks are developed at school. These social connections often provide important assistance in securing employment and other occupational opportunities later on in life.

Quite clearly, the functional paradigm of schooling rests on the assumptions that we are gradually moving toward a more democratic society where increasing levels of education contribute to higher levels of progress. It also subscribes to the belief in a meritocracy, in which educational credentials and occupational roles are achieved rather than ascribed. But not everyone is of the opinion that U.S. society is becoming more democratic, or that it is even now, meritocratic. Some argue that the vast expansion of schooling in America has not brought about many of the benefits claimed by functionalists. In fact, proponents of what has been termed the Conflict perspective, suggest that the expansion of schooling and the increased resources devoted to education have improved the lot of advantaged families often at the expense of those from economically disadvantaged homes. Proponents of this perspective also assert that the expansion has resulted in less favorable opportunities for the disadvantaged to secure a better quality of living including high-status positions.

The Conflict Perspective

While proponents of the Functionalist perspective underscore the ways that schools act to reduce social inequality, they rarely direct our attention to those who are most likely to fail in the educational system and why. Many also argue that they fail to focus on what it really means to be poor, Black or middle class in schools. On the other hand, the conflict perspective emphasizes the ways in which education and schooling perpetuate and even facilitate social inequality. This approach argues that students do not achieve in school because of ability alone. Rather, economically-privileged parents are able to negotiate the system by using money and knowledge to influence educational policy and practice, to assure a quality education for their children. They argue that schools often perpetuate inequalities related to class, race and gender as the advantaged attempt to maintain their positions of dominance in society. Proponents of this perspective are quick to point out how race and social class in contemporary society are related to income, education and even arrest rates. Because the Conflict approach is steeped in the intellectual tradition of mid-nineteenth century Europe, especially the work of Karl Marx, one dimension of it is also referred to as a Neo-Marxist approach. He and other more contemporary proponents of this view, such as Randy Collins, Sam Bowles and Herbert Gintis, underscore the ways in which tensions in the system rather than order and equilibrium characterize social organization. They also believe that these tensions are caused by clashes of power among various groups in the society. Rather than focus on the creation of order and equilibrium, this perspective concentrates on the sources and consequences of conflict and inequality in society.

As a proponent of Conflict perspective, Marx's interest in education centered on how it produced a disciplined supply of labor for industrial and military sectors which could be exploited by a dominant advantaged-class. Additionally, when access to certain occupations is controlled, access to different status and career positions is also controlled. Thus the school is capable of perpetuating the existing social class system. On the other hand, Weber considered the prime activity of schools to be the teaching of particular status cultures. Advantaged students have their status culture reinforced in schools while the poor are outsiders and face serious barriers to success in school (Scheurich and Imber, 1991). Schools train lower-class children to obey orders and respect authority—essential qualities for manual workers. By contrast, children of advantaged families are assigned college prep courses and those which place emphasis on decision making and critical thinking skills—qualities required of managers. Randy Collins, another proponent of this point of view, underscored the role of mass education in controlling admission to

higher levels required for certain types of employment or the role of credentialism in perpetuating inequality (Collins, 1979).

The conflict paradigm offers a very different interpretation of schooling in
America. Like the functional perspective, it sees a link between schools and
society but the link is caused by the demands and needs of an elite class. By
focusing on a meritocracy, one based on equal opportunity where status and
wealth depend on ability and effort rather than inherited privilege, functionalists do not call attention to who is more likely to fail in school. Neither do
they underscore the importance of class position in this process. In contrast,
proponents of the conflict perspective suggest that the educational system has
been designed by the ruling elite to maintain their dominance in the social order. Advantaged parents are able to buy a quality education for their children
and influence important policy decisions and practices in schools throughout
the nation. Schools, they assert, do not promote egalitarianism and equity.
They provide the illusion of opportunity but by means of a hidden curriculum, they teach docility and acceptance to children of the economically disadvantaged and prepare them to accept a life in the industrial working class.
On the other hand, children of the elite are provided with an enriched curriculum which stresses independent thought and creativity thus enabling them
to take their place as corporate leaders and CEOs. In time, the differential curricula and classroom treatment gradually erode the self-concept and efficacy
of working class children, which in turn impacts on their educational and career outcomes. An increasing body of research suggests that schooling causes
this inequality by a number of educational policies and practices that have
been permitted to develop unchecked. Some of these include the misuse of
testing, educational tracking and the hidden curriculum (Ansalone, 2001;
Wheelock, 1992).

Proponents of the conflict perspective also note the differential pattern of
access to education for the sexes. A contemporary manifestation of the Conflict perspective is Feminism and Feminist Theory.

The Feminist Perspective.   Closely related to conflict theory is the feminist perspective—the belief that men and women are equal, should be valued
equally, and have equal rights. Today, the study of feminist theory is perhaps
one of the most salient areas of sociology. On the educational front, this perspective examines in depth how access to opportunities in school and professional life are stratified by gender. Feminists are quick to assert that gender is
often a social category that is used to structure access to educational opportunities. Feminist theory attempts to identify exactly how norms, institutions
and expectations both control and limit a woman's behavior (Collins, 2004).
It underscores the point that inequalities of gender are not natural but are socially constructed.

Although Feminist theory is not one unified perspective but many, each of the various forms share common characteristics.

Liberal Feminism attempts to achieve equality in all areas of life and to transform traditional beliefs and attitudes about feminity and masculinity. It strives to transform the understanding of male and female roles in all sectors of society and insert choice rather than biology as the determining factor of what men and women do. In schooling, liberal feminism strives to remove traditional and sexist ideas of male and female roles from the formal and hidden curriculum.

Socialist Feminism suggests that gender equity can only be achieved if we transform the social system since gender oppression is a consequence of a patriarchal capitalistic system. Women are exploited by Capitalism in the work force and by patriarchy at home. Total gender equity is possible in schools if we eliminate the historically constructed patriarchy in today's schools (Kemp, 1994).

Radical Feminism traces the roots of patriarchy to the childrearing and childbearing duties that are performed by women. Rather than transform patriarchy, they advocate total separation from men and the development of a woman' culture. In order to accomplish this end, they encourage the development of single-sex schools (Hawthorne, 1991).

A Feminist perspective on education is useful in enabling us to understand the experiences of women in educational systems. For example, why do girls begin their school career scoring better than men but complete their schooling scoring behind them? In view of the limited rewards that women receive after completing an education why do they attain as much education as they do?

Feminists call attention to the fact that teachers in school generally hold differential expectations for the performance of boys and girls. Additionally, research finds that men are often treated differently than women. Research suggests that teachers pay less attention to girls in the classroom, interact with men more frequently and direct more questions to boys than to girls. Additionally, the wording of questions on standardized exams is often gender-typed (American Association of University Women, 1992). In the long run, this differential treatment may have significant consequences for women and impact on their academic and career outcomes (Sadker and Sadker, 1994).

Symbolic Interaction

The third major paradigm employed by sociologists is perhaps the most influential of the last decade. According to some educational sociologists, one of the major drawbacks of both the Functional and Conflict approaches is their macro-level orientation and the fact that they blur or provide little information about the thoughts, feelings and behavior of important players in the educational process, namely, teachers, students, and administrators. Neither do these approaches assess how these interactions impact on student outcomes. Symbolic Interactionism focuses attention on the daily interactions of students and teachers within the classroom. Sociologists who employ this approach are most interested in the meanings that people attach to behavior and how these meanings are created. The preferred methodological tools of this approach include ethnographies, participant observation, case studies and the interview. Research in this area enables us to understand and appreciate exactly how these interactions *create social reality.*

Symbolic interaction is part of an overall class of theories generally referred to as interpretive theories. Interpretists believe that as humans, men and women respond to each other on the basis of meanings assigned to people by the people themselves rather than on the basis of any objective meaning. Thus, our daily interactions with others are colored by three things: (1) our past experiences with those whom we are interacting—or what we know about the person from some stereotype or label, (2) our present encounters with the person, and (3) what we come to believe as our interactions with the person unfolds. Thus, the term—social *construction*, we socially construct our own meaning about the person. Additionally, they believe that reality, as we know it, is definitely not fixed, rather it is negotiated in the process of our daily encounters with others. This reality becomes the basis of our actions and behavior toward someone. Our very conception of truth is therefore based on our view of things as well as what we know about them, rather than any objective fact.

Functionalists examine education and explore how it may help to bring about an orderly and efficient society. They focus on the various socialization functions of schooling as well as the role of the official curriculum. Proponents of the conflict perspective examine how schooling may perpetuate social inequality. They are concerned with creeping credentialism, the prestige hierarchy of schools, and latent functions of education which might predispose some segments of our society to accept careers as workers in an industrialized economy. Both of these macro-*level* approaches provide interesting and important assessments of education. They provide us with an understanding of why some students fail or perform poorly in schools because of their position in the social structure—possibly because of race or as members of a minority or disadvantaged class. On the other hand, Interactionists are more concerned with the daily encounters that take place in a school setting and how the teachers' and students' social construction of reality influences student outcomes and academic achievement. Symbolic interactionists focus on communication patterns (linguistic gestures, words, facial expressions, and other body language) and practices within the classroom as well as educational structures in the school that may affect student self-concept and motivation.

The symbolic interactionist approach asserts that society is produced and reproduced through our actions with each other, utilizing language and gestures. Equally important is our interpretation of this language and the accompanying gestures. Through interaction with each other we create our reality. In doing so, we act toward things on the basis of the meaning we hold for them. These meanings are not fixed but are negotiated through time. For example, are students influenced by the expectations that teachers hold for them? Does their perception of these expectations influence their academic progress? Some of the more important issues studied by Interactionists include teacher expectations and the educational practice of tracking.

Teacher Expectations

Since the Interactionist perspective argues that our social world is constructed through interactions with others, a common focus of this approach is the daily encounters between teachers and students. Symbolic interactionists believe that students behave according to how they think others see them. They are especially interested in determining if and how teacher expectations for student academic achievement *can* actually affect student achievement. If teachers expect their students to do well, is it likely that their students will perform as expected? On the other hand, if teachers hold low expectations for their students' performance, might this expectation result in lower achievement?

Research suggests that students are capable of picking up cues from their teachers about their attitudes and expectations for their academic performance. This *cue taking* is accomplished by gestures, mannerisms and language. Research has revealed that teachers, who have high expectations for students, call on them more often and provide them with more praise and encouragement. They offer more support when these students respond to questions, and often wait longer in anticipation of a correct response. Research also suggests that teachers' expectations affect student behavior and achievement in very real ways. The cues that students pick up from their teachers are often internalized and become an important part of how students see themselves in the role of student. Educational sociologists refer to this as the Pygmalion Effect—the self-fulfilling prophesy (Chapter 6 will address this topic in detail).

Symbolic Interactionists are also very much interested in Tracking, the separation of students by ability and curriculum. This educational practice may also facilitate the development of negative or positive self-perceptions depending on the assigned track of students. When tracking is employed, teachers may prepare differently for a class or possibly even alter the curriculum.

Additionally, tracking may help create teacher expectations which can reinforce existing class, gender and ethnic inequalities (Sadker and Sadker, 1995).

Tracking

What teachers know about their students very often comes about from the students' track assignment. Tracks often place academically oriented labels on students (smart, dumb, gifted) and these labels are hard to lose. Interactionists are interested in the various interactions that take place each day within the various tracks. Specifically, they are interested in determining if track assignment is related to teacher expectations and if this negative or positive label associated with the track is related to academic outcomes. In general, teachers hold higher expectations for students assigned to upper tracks and lower expectations for those in lower tracks (Ansalone and Biafora, 2004; Wheelock, 1992). In light of this, track position may be strongly related to academic outcomes.

Tracking can create restricted learning environments for disadvantaged students since so many of them are assigned to lower tracks. It can also create a self-fulfilling prophesy of belief and acceptance on the part of students and teachers. It is likely that tracking may influence behavior outside of the classroom. Slow learners assigned to lower tracks may decide on careers that are less demanding intellectually. Thus because of their lower perception of themselves caused by years of tracking, they opt out of leadership positions and what they perceive to be challenging jobs that they might have attempted were it not for the tracking (Chapter 5 will address tracking in detail).

Contemporary schooling has developed into a major social institution in contemporary society. We now examine some contemporary explanations for its development and expansion in the United States.

THE DEVELOPMENT OF AMERICAN SCHOOLING

A Functionalist Interpretation

It was the Puritans of New England who brought to the colonies the idea of universal public education and probably contributed most to the development of schooling in America. These stoic and religious New Englanders were well educated themselves and maintained an enthusiastic attitude for education. They believed that education was necessary for good citizenship and an essential ingredient for eternal salvation. Their underlying religious belief and zeal, contributed to the passage of the Old Satan Deluder Act [1647], in the Massachusetts Bay Colony. This legislation mandated that every township with 100 or more families construct and operate a grammar school for the young children of that area. It was their hope that the availability of a school and some elementary education would enable men and women to read the Scriptures and elude the reach of Satan. At about the same time, New Englanders also addressed the need for an enlightened ministry and founded Harvard College to educate aspiring ministers. However, schooling and formal education were essentially limited to those who had the time and, above all, the finances to pursue it.

During the early development of the United States, when it was still predominantly an agricultural society, the lack of a formal school-based education was not considered a handicap for most Americans. Formal schooling was generally not available to most free men and was illegal for slaves. In some towns, Dame Schools, often operated by widows in the kitchens of their homes, were set up in New England towns to teach basic literacy to children of the poor. Girls were allowed to attend the Dame schools but the prevailing view of the time was that the appropriate education for girls consisted of only a little reading and spelling. Children in these schools used the Hornbook; a paddle-shaped book coated with a thin layer of sheath from a cow's horn to protect it from continued us. This book contained the alphabets, numbers and some relevant quotes from the Bible.

Grammar schools, with a curriculum modeled after the Latin schools of Europe, were available for the children of the well to do. The education offered in these schools was quite different and included Latin, Greek and other classical subjects necessary for admission to the University. Since students who entered the University during this period followed a classical curriculum similar to that offered in England, their Grammar school education facilitated their admission to this level of schooling.

Compulsory education or the concept that all students must have some elementary education did not begin to emerge until the nineteenth century. Immediately following the War of Independence the founding fathers of the new American republic proposed a universal system of schooling that would promote patriotism and create a uniform national culture for the new republic. Their steadfast belief in education as a necessity rather than a luxury helped to create the U.S. public school system. However by the early 1800s, the nation still lacked a national system of schools. In 1837, Horace Mann, an educator from Massachusetts, proposed the formation of "common schools" for his state, supported by tax dollars. In time, schooling became mandatory for all children who were sixteen or younger and Massachusetts became the first state to enact a compulsory education law. In time this idea would spread throughout most of the United States.

The idea of universal education was facilitated by the rise of industrialization and the influx of European immigrants into the United States. Both political and civic leaders recognized the need for an educated work force and some mechanisms to "Americanize" the newly arriving immigrants (Hellinger and Judd,

1991). During most of the nineteenth century many states did not have mandatory attendance regulations since education was still considered a luxury of the
upper classes. By the beginning of the twentieth century, however, the practice
of compulsory education was established in all but a few Southern states where
Black Americans were still denied formal education of any kind. As more
Americans entered the schools, curricula became more diversified and students
could select between academic and vocational tracks in order to prepare for
their future occupations.

During the next few decades, high school attendance for Whites grew
steadily. The percentage of Americans who earned a high school diploma
grew from less than 10 percent in 1910 to about 90 percent in 1997. Additionally, the passage of the GI Bill and the expansion of Community Colleges
contributed to the increase in college attendance. Regretfully, the number of
Blacks and Hispanics completing a high school diploma continued to lag behind that of White students. In 1990, only 53 percent of Hispanics and 75 percent of African-Americans completed high school.

Today, formal education is available to all and many Americans consider it
to be a vehicle for high status and career opportunity. Schools provide an en-
ergizing force in creating a cohesive society with a distinct sense of national
unity. From a functionalist perspective, schools are clearly related to the economic and reproductive needs of the society. They provide students with the
necessary tools for social functioning and represents the primary means by
which society transmits values and knowledge to its members. Above all, the
expansion of American schooling was a direct result of the emerging need for
increased cognitive skills in the workplace, the development of a moral consensus among all Americans and the efficient sorting and selection of talent
for new jobs and careers. This functional interpretation of the role of schooling in society underscores its purpose in training students for a new and increasingly technological society where new and complex jobs require more
and more specialized training. These skills, once transmitted from parent to
child or acquired on the job are now learned in schools. According to this interpretation, schooling provides the most efficient and equitable means of selecting and sorting individuals into various careers and their equivalent status
positions. In a democratic and meritocratic society, it also underscores the
value of effort and ability rather than family background and ancestry.

The Conflict/Neo-Marxist Interpretation

On the other hand, a substantial body of research has questioned the underlying principles and philosophy of this functionalist perspective especially the
assertions between jobs and education and the meritocratic nature of school-

ing (Bowles and Gintis 1976; Katz 1975). Rather than provide channels of upward mobility for the poor, compulsory schooling guaranteed factory owners an essential pool of workers for their factories. Proponents of this Conflict perspective also argue that rather than encourage literacy among the masses, it helped to promote the development of personality characteristics required for work in the factory. This Conflict interpretation also openly challenged the former belief that the increased resources devoted to the schools have resulted in increased opportunities for the underprivileged. In direct opposition to the functional perspective, the Conflict view assumes a basic struggle between forces within the society, the advantaged and the disadvantaged. Variations of this interpretation have developed from the writings of Karl Marx and I have referred to this perspective as the Conflict/NeoMarxist view. It argues that the primary purpose of the expansion of schooling in the United States has been the desire to maintain and train an effective workforce equipped with the appropriate personality characteristics of obedience, docility and punctuality.

Today, a contentious debate exists about the quality, purpose and future direction of education. Do schools exist to provide an opportunity for upward social and economic mobility or do they serve to reproduce consciousness and perpetuate the existing social class system. An increasingly large number of Americans argue that schooling lacks equity and excellence. It appears to be ineffective and often denies an equal educational experience to all students. Rather than teach, schools have a tendency to sort and certify that certain students are entitled to status positions while others are not. While many continue to debate the truth of each interpretation, there is some, but not overwhelming empirical evidence, to support the claims of the Conflict/NeoMarxist perspective. In all likelihood, each approach contains shades of truth. Their value rests in their ability to help us appreciate the socializing and stratifying ability of education and schooling.

DOES SCHOOLING REALLY MATTER?

Do schools have any impact on our lives? Is schooling related to career and social advancement? Does it lead to greater happiness and a better quality of life? For some, education is a great independent variable and has a significant impact on the lives of students. Repeatedly, research underscores the fact that those with more schooling are often wealthier, active in political matters, less likely to commit a crime and much more supportive of civil liberties (Kingston et al., 2003).

But what exactly is the relationship between education and life-course events? Recent research examining the connections between schooling and several different variables present some interesting findings. In one study (as determined by grade point average and self-reports of personal attitudes), was also related to the probability of committing a criminal act. Boys with below-normal verbal ability were more likely to be incarcerated than boys with higher verbal skills (Aarum and Beattie, 1999; Sampson and Laub 1993). Still another study uncovered that a school's institutional linkages to business also had important implications for student employment outcomes. Research by Rosenbaum and Binder (1997) uncovered that employers often afforded job candidates a significant edge based on the years of education completed and the fact that they have attended a favored school. This was true even for entry-level positions that did not require educational credentials. Still other research supports the correlation between greater educational attainment and financial rewards (Aarum & Hout, 1998). Clearly, it seems that education does matter and that no consistent factor including social origin explains the dynamic and seemingly ever present impact of the educational effect.

Education and Income

The adage that education *pays off* is generally supported by research. A moderately strong correlation exists between years of formal education and occupation. The higher a person's occupational status, the more formal education they are likely to have.

Christopher Jencks examined this relationship and uncovered that the correlation between actual years of formal education and occupation was .61. This represents a moderately strong association. However, the correlation between education and annual income was somewhat less, .33 (Jencks, 1993). So it seems that the impact of education is greater on occupation than on income. But the reality of the situation is that income brackets are consistently higher for those who have completed higher education. Additionally, the median annual income of men who earn a college degree is approximately 75 percent higher than that of men who have no degree. A degree from an elite school also substantially increases the earning power of graduates (U.S. Census Bureau, American Community Survey, 2006) (see Table 1.3).

The number of individuals with high school diplomas and college degrees has increased appreciably within the past 30 years. Because so many more people earn college degrees today, the overall value of the degree has declined slightly. This will make it particularly difficult for disadvantaged children who do not complete school. In all likelihood, they will earn less and have a more difficult time securing a job.

Gender also impacts on the relationship between education and income. The average income for women is generally lower than the average income

Table 1.3.   Median Earnings by Sex / Educational Attainment (25 Years and Older)

	Total	Males	Females
Less than high school graduate	18,641	22,151	13,255
High school graduate	26,123	31,715	20,650
Some college	31,936	40,217	26,300
Bachelors	45,221	55,446	36,875
Graduate or professional degree	59,804	73,991	49,164

Source: U.S. Census Bureau, 2006 American Community Survey.

for men at each educational level. In 2005, while a man with bachelor degree's earned $55,446 a year, women with comparable credentials earned only $36,875 (U.S. Census Bureau, American Community Survey, 2006).

Education and Quality of Life

In addition to additional income over the course of one's life, there are several advantages to obtaining a college degree. Advanced study often facilitates logical thinking, increases cognitive abilities and enhanced curiosity. It stimulates a thirst for knowledge and promotes interest and appreciation of the arts. What are some of the conventional characteristics that have been associated with increased educational levels?

Education and Civil Liberties. The more educated are more often supportive of Civil Liberties and are generally more tolerant of diversity (homosexuality and atheism) (Hyman and Wright, 1979).

Civics & Social Knowledge. The more educated are often more informed of current events, social developments and civic knowledge. They are more socially open and make more of a concerted effort to be informed about recent social and civic developments. They are also more concerned about the environment and subscribe to and read a daily newspaper (Kingston et al., 2003).

Gender Equity. The more educated are more supportive of gender equity. They support equality for women in politics and the workplace and other non-traditional roles for women (Harris and Firestone, 1998).

Social Capital. The more educated possess greater social capital—interpersonal connections that assist people to get ahead in school and career. They participate in more community and social organizations and may be characterized as being more 'socially connected' (Putnam, 2000).

Cultural Capital. The more educated demonstrate an appreciation of the arts and possess an elite cultural orientation. They like serious art and music and many believe this to be an advantage in their competition for economic status and social status (Peterson, 1992).

Education and Inequality

While many believe that education is key to social advancement and economic success, some also believe that it may foster and perpetuate social inequality. Clearly, educational achievement and attainment does enhance the
quality of one's life as we have already observed. But, the benefits of education do not necessarily accrue to all in equal measure.

American schools serve a number of important societal functions. They
transmit values and culture and teach us about success and achievement. But
they also socialize us to adhere to the rules of society and recognize our place
within the stratification system. Practices such as tracking, grading and testing help us to recognize our place within the larger society. In schools, children are labeled "gifted" or "slow" or "average" and learn to accept the consequences that come with each label. At each step in the educational system,
these labels impact on the quality and type of education that we receive. They
influence how we think about ourselves as students and the expectations that
others have for our success. In turn, these perceptions can modify or radically
change our career trajectory. Clearly education benefits all of us, but it does
not benefit all of us equally. In time we learn that achievement and attainment
is also as much about race, gender and class as it is innate ability and effort.

These inequalities are operationalized in interesting ways. Female students
are not called upon as frequently as their male counterparts. Handicapped students may be relegated to special education classes and because of this, begin
to think less of themselves. A disproportionate number of Blacks and Hispanics may be assigned to lower track classrooms where the curriculum is
"easier" and the teachers are more concerned with discipline than admission
to college. As time goes on, these macro-structural inequalities have an impact not only on the immediate educational experience of disadvantaged students but on how they perceive themselves as students and how much they
will achieve in life.

Time after time, sociological research has demonstrated that a person's social class and not education is a greater predictor of their occupation and income. Upper classes maintain their privileged position by sending their children to elite boarding schools. Here they are taught to be leaders and
managers. By contrast, working-class children are assigned to lower tracks,
which focus on discipline and the appropriate skills for an industrial economy. In sum, education can lead to a perpetuation of the social class system
and the reproduction of society (Persell, 1993; Jencks, 1993). Clearly, education affects our quality of life.

Part II

PREVIOUS EXPLANATIONS FOR UNEQUAL ACHIEVEMENT

Chapter Two

Explaining Unequal Achievement

Schools have rather modest effects on the degree of cognitive inequality among students.

Christopher Jencks

THE PROBLEM OF UNEQUAL ACHIEVEMENT

The unequal achievement of children in schools has been a persistent and troublesome problem in American education. In fact, few issues have sparked more controversy than the question of why students of different social origins differ so significantly in academic performance. Consistently, research has related a student's social class, race, and ethnicity to both educational attainment (years in school) and educational achievement (grades and test scores). Recently, new life has been infused into this discussion as studies continue to support the idea that academic outcomes are closely related to career trajectory, annual income and style of life (Davis et al., 2005). Additionally, since Americans believe that education is one of the most important vehicles for upward mobility and social advancement, the likelihood that children of disadvantaged families will not successfully complete school is a point of embarrassment for all those who subscribe to a meritocratic philosophy of education.

The Meaning of Underachievement

When we speak about unequal achievement we refer to the differential academic performance of children from different social origins. At the root of unequal achievement is underachievement. The term "underachievement" has been used in a number of different ways. Some define it in terms of a considerable discrepancy between one's measured intelligence (IQ) and general test scores. One problem with this definition is that it suggests, too strongly, that IQ is the one and only determinant of achievement. While IQ is always an important factor, achievement is also impacted by a number of other variables including self-perception, family, society and schooling.

Still others consider underachievers to be the academically low attainers when compared with other students (West and Pennell, 2003). This being said, when I use the term underachievers, I refer to students who demonstrate an inability measure up to their potential. They are low attainers or underachievers when compared with others. The concept of underachievement may also be used to describe the characteristics of particular groups and not just an individual. This usage is most often employed by educational sociologists when they use this term to describe the average performance of individuals from disadvantaged groups. If most children within a social group underachieve, the result will be unequal achievement for the group as a whole. In this work, I use these terms interchangeably as I look for a comprehensive explanation for this timely problem. Let us take a look at some of the consequences of unequal achievement.

The Consequences of Unequal Achievement

The evidence seems apparent. Some research has clearly linked social class, race, and ethnicity to academic outcomes. The relationship is consistent in terms of educational attainment (number of school years completed) as well as educational achievement (grades) (Jencks, 1972, 1998).

Consider the following:

Blacks and Hispanic are often less successful in school and educational attainment is lower among Hispanics than most other groups. Hispanic students are also more likely to drop out of school than most other groups (Headden, 2000).

Jewish and Asian-American students are generally more successful than the majority. Asian Americans have the highest educational attainment of any other group. They are also overrepresented at the top U.S. universities since they compose approximately 10 percent of the freshman classes while representing only about 3 percent of the U.S. college age population (NCES, 1992).

Children of low-income families do not do as well in school as children from more affluent homes. In fact, the influence of parental socio-economic status amounts to slightly more than two years in educational attainment. It is also interesting that these differences are cumulative over time.

Average test scores from the Scholastic Aptitude Test (SAT); the American College Testing Program (ACT) and average scores on IQ tests differ appreciably by ethnic and racial group, gender and socioeconomic status. The most recent research concludes that Whites score higher than minorities and children of higher SES groups score higher than those of economically disadvantaged classes. White Americans also score consistently higher than American Indians, African Americans and Latinos. As a group, Asian Americans score higher than White Americans on the quantitative portion of the SAT but lower than Whites on the verbal portion. In general, women of any ethnic or racial group score lower than men on the quantitative sections of the exam (The College Board, 2007).

Ethnic and racial diversity is usually negatively correlated with school retention rates. In areas where ethnic and racial diversity is higher, the retention rates of schools are lowest. Almost 50 percent of all Hispanic students dropped out of school before completing high school in the 1980s; while still high, this percentage dropped to 40 percent in 1997. In comparison, the rate for non-Hispanic students was 7 percent. Additionally, African-American and Latino students report feeling more alienated and experiencing a greater sense of powerlessness in school than white students. These feelings may be influential in any decision to drop out of school and, for the most part, dropouts are disproportionately male minorities from low-income families (National Center for Education Statistics, 1999).

Economically disadvantaged students start school with measurable but not huge differences in skills compared with white middle class students. Differences also exist by race and ethnicity in the average test scores of children even before they begin kindergarten. Scores are related to SES, and the average cognitive score of children in the highest SES groups are approximately 60 percent higher than average test scores of children in the lowest SES groups (Lee and Burkam, 2002). Ironically, following a few years of schooling, these academic differences grow significantly larger (The College Board, 2007).

Race and ethnicity are related to SES. Approximately 30 percent of all black and Hispanic children are in the lowest quartile of SES compared with only 9 percent of white children (Hurn, 1993).

How can we account for these troublesome statistics? Many Americans believe that this differential success rate is a function of student motivation, while others point to the poor quality of the schools available to disadvantaged children. In an attempt to shed light on the widely documented problem of underachievement, researchers have predictably relied on three different explanatory theories. For the most part, these macro level theories attempt to explain the underachievement of select portions of the society based on their low position within the social class structure. Essentially, they focus on broader issues including the larger societal structures of inequality.

EMPLOYING SOCIOLOGICAL THEORY
TO EXPLAIN UNEQUAL ACHIEVEMENT

Sociologists often use different frames of reference to explain what they see. Some of their descriptions and explanations are broader in scope and focus on complex patterns of social interaction. They provide us with an understanding of an *entire* issue—how it is organized and how it reacts to change. They often focus on societal forces and social structure including the economy and social class to explain the cause of certain problems. In many instances, they consider the relation of groups to one another and the type of power that one may have over another. Theoretical frames of reference that employ this approach are referred to as macrosociology. On the other hand, microsociological explanations employ a *narrower* view; they focus on a smaller and less complex part of the whole. Microsociology focuses on face-to-face interactions of individuals in society and is more concerned with describing intimate and less differentiated patterns of interaction. Both of these perspectives are essential if we are to arrive at a comprehensive understanding of underachievement. Neither of these approaches contradicts the other, rather, they work in harmony to provide an understanding of what is happening and why.

For the most part, educational sociologists have generally attempted to explain the perplexing disparity in achievement in terms of broad based macrotheory, which for the most part relates success or failure in school to the social class system. In employing this approach, key stakeholders in the education process, parents, teachers and students, must be viewed within the broader context of how these groups relate to each other and what position they hold in the social class system. This position often guides their behavior and directs their actions. For example, in the United States, education is closely related to social class. In general, the amount and quality of one's education increases as one ascends the social class ladder. Members of the middle and upper class place considerable emphasis on schooling since they consider it a prerequisite for social mobility. Additionally, their class position enables them to pay exorbitant tuitions for admission to elite schools and support their children's education with valuable learning resources and enriching cultural experiences. In sum, their social class position provides them with better schools, better culture and greater opportunity to learn (Beeghley, 2008; Rohwedder, 2007).

This chapter discusses three of the leading macro-theories that have been often called upon to explain underachievement in the schools. These sociological theories include the Quality of Schools argument, Cultural Deprivation and the Heritability Deficit theory.

THREE EXPLANATIONS OF UNEQUAL ACHIEVEMENT

For the last half century, researchers have attempted to explain the dramatic differences in educational achievement and attainment between students from different social origins. Most often, their research has predictably focused on three distinct theories: the quality of schools argument, the cultural deficit explanation and the IQ –heritability theory. Although each of these theories has been criticized extensively, each continues to hold some widespread, popular appeal.

The first of these explanations revolves about the inferior quality of schools provided to children of disadvantaged and minority parents. It underscores the role of deteriorated facilities, a watered-down curriculum and poor teaching in the creation of school failure. Proponents of this perspective argue that poor schools impact negatively on academic achievement. Much of the work in this area is a scathing indictment of the financial disparities between school districts resulting from differences in community wealth.

The Quality of Schools Argument

The Quality of Schools explanation for underachievement focuses on the striking difference in type and quality of schools attended by advantaged and disadvantaged students. It examines the imbalance in economic resources available to Black and minority school districts and the differential educational opportunity accorded to these students as a result of inadequate funding. Those who advance this argument underscore the gross differences in class size, teacher qualifications and technological resources as a contributing factor in underachievement.

In 1996, the National Center for Education Statistics Report concluded that the overall quality of schools in economically disadvantaged areas contributed to the academic failure of students from low-income families. Their reasoning was stimulated by the knowledge that schools in these areas suffered from deteriorated facilities, high enrollments and a high rate of teacher absenteeism. These schools were also plagued with truancy, discipline and safety concerns. The Report also cited high rates of teenage pregnancy, single-parent families and a high exposure to serious crime including murder.

According to the report, underachievement was the consequence of this social disorganization (National Center for Education Statistics, 1999).

It is likely that schools that lack the resources to properly motivate and educate students can have a detrimental impact on student learning and academic
achievement. This point is dramatically demonstrated by Jonathan Kozol, one
of the foremost proponents of this view. Kozol's *Savage Inequality* impres-
sively documents the disparity in funding between economically advantaged
and disadvantaged schools in over thirty American neighborhoods. He paints
a gloomy picture of garrison like schools in the crime ridden neighborhoods of
the south Bronx, East St. Louis and the east side of Chicago. His insightful
study provides vivid pictures of run-down buildings infested by toxic fumes
and sewer backups. By examining the disparity in school resources, teacher
qualifications and physical facilities in different socioeconomic areas, his
study describes in detail how these children are denied an education and a future. Above all, it presents a powerful argument for the underachievement of
Black and minority students over the past half century. Additionally, by underscoring that American public education is primarily funded by local property taxes, Kozol makes the reader painfully aware that children attending
schools in disadvantaged neighborhoods will probably continue to underachieve as long as this practice remains unchanged. This, combined with the
fact that children from lower socioeconomic homes are more likely to be assigned to the lower tracks of schools, suggests that American schools often become institutionalized mechanisms for perpetuating the class structure rather
than avenues of upward mobility (Kozol, 1992, Marger, 2002). Clearly, this research provides an interesting insight into the problem of inequality in American schooling. It offers an informative perspective on a disgraceful corner of
American education and remains the epicenter of what has been termed the
quality of schools argument.

For many, it seemed logical that unequal educational resources could result
in unequal achievement. And since most disadvantaged children attend
schools with questionable resources, it was no surprise that many were underachievers. But, Kozol's conclusions were not universally accepted. Some
suggested only a limited relationship between school resources and academic
achievement. Consequently, many questioned the extent to which school
quality and funding influenced academic outcomes. The research of James
Coleman was the first to provide an in-depth analysis of this relationship
(Coleman, 1966).

School Quality: The Coleman Study

Many Americans were of the opinion that school quality as measured by physical facilities and teacher credentials did make a difference in student achieve-

ment. Coleman's Equality of Educational Opportunity Study (EEO) was an early attempt to establish a credible link between these two variables. Quite simply, this federally sponsored research was an attempt to prove, beyond all reasonable doubt, that school funding was related to achievement and that by increasing funding for educational resources in economically disadvantaged areas, the academic outcomes of students could also be improved. The report surveyed over 570,000 students and 60,000 teachers in 4,000 U.S. public schools. As a result, Coleman expected to uncover appreciable differences in the quality of education offered to advantaged and disadvantaged students. For many, this study also represented an attempt to document the extent of segregation in American schooling in order to enable the federal government to finally enforce the 1954 *Brown v. Board of Education* decision.

The Findings

The Coleman study yielded surprising results! It uncovered little, if any, relationship between school quality (as measured by annual per pupil expenditure) and academic achievement (as measured by test scores). In fact, school facilities, curricula and teacher characteristics were found to be fairly similar between the schools and whatever differences did exist seemed to have little impact on student test performance. The study also revealed that the quality of teaching had a modest impact on achievement scores but greater per pupil expenditures and up-to-date buildings did not. In other words, the differences in school resources between districts were not large enough to explain the differences in student performance. Coleman and his researchers uncovered almost no relationship between measures of school quality and student achievement! In support of this finding, he found that differences in the academic achievement of students *within* schools were greater than differences in the academic achievement of students *between* schools. This later finding was a strong indication that school facilities did not play an important role in the development of academic achievement. Rather, the most important determinants of school success were family background and individual student attitude. Children's social environment including the attitudes and behaviors of family members and their willingness to participate in the education of their children figured much more significantly in how well the child achieved.

Coleman revealed another interesting finding. To the surprise of many, the gap in achievement (as measured by standardized examinations) between White and Black students was only one to two grade equivalents in the early grades. This gap typically increased to a three to four grade equivalent by high school. The study also uncovered that differences in test scores of advantaged and disadvantaged children increased with each additional year that the children remained in school. Thus, the longer that advantaged and disadvantaged children remained in school, the greater the achievement gap between the two. Schooling seemed to help middle-class children and work against the poor. Finally, while minority and middle-class children both considered schooling to be important, those minority children who attended school with middle-class children, rather than primarily only disadvantaged children, seemed to exhibit much higher levels of academic achievement. In other words, the report underscored the importance of peer aspirations to successful academic achievement.

Since the Coleman Report was able to uncover a relationship between the social environment of students and their academic achievement, it went a long way in recommending the racial and socioeconomic integration of students in schools. Essentially, the report revealed that the racial context of the school had a consistent positive impact on achievement. Blacks in desegregated schools did better than Blacks in segregated schools. As a result, many school districts adopted a program of busing students to achieve a better racial balance. In time, busing became one of the most widely used strategies to affect racial balance within various school districts. Interestingly, Coleman, himself, did not enthusiastically subscribe to busing and argued that it made more sense to focus on contextual factors that affected learning including reading and writing support programs and compensatory education (Coleman and Hoffer, 1987).

As can be imagined, many of the conclusions of the Coleman Report remain controversial to this day. The report contradicted the expectations and desires of many educators and policy makers. By suggesting that school resources and facilities had only a modest impact on achievement, it deflated the national debate surrounding increased funding for schools. It suggested that academic achievement was related to family background and the characteristics of one's fellow classmates seemed to be as important as where one studied.

The Coleman Report: Synopsis of Major Findings

Some of the major findings of Coleman's Equality of Educational Opportunity Report included the following:

1. Segregation was alive and well in the United States. Most Black and White students attended racially segregated schools. About 80 percent of Whites attended White schools while 65 percent of Black students attended predominantly Black schools.
2. A comparative analysis of physical facilities and teacher characteristics uncovered that both were surprisingly similar between schools. In some cases where differences did exist, they had little impact on the test scores of students.

3. The SES and racial context of the school had a consistent impact on student test scores.
4. More variation in the achievement of students was uncovered *within* rather than *between* different schools.
5. The academic achievement gap between Black and White students increased with each year in school.
6. Home background variables and student attitudes had the most significant affect on student achievement.
7. For the most part, *families* and not schools were responsible for much of the difference in academic achievement between students.

Understandably, the controversial nature of the Coleman findings eventually led to cries for a reanalysis of the data. In time, this task was assigned to Christopher Jencks. Utilizing a more sophisticated analysis, he eventually reaffirmed many of the Coleman conclusions. (Jencks, 1972).

School Quality: The Jencks Study

Several years after the release of the Coleman findings, Christopher Jencks (1972) reexamined the data collected by the Coleman researchers. The resulting reanalysis, *Inequality,* concluded that school resources remained a poor predictor of academic achievement. Rather, academic outcomes were influenced by poverty and social class rather than schools. Agreeing with Coleman, family background was identified as the most important variable in school success and failure. Middle and upper-class students had a natural edge on other students since their families could provide the cultural and social advantages which were generally unavailable to disadvantaged students. In fact, according to Jencks, if everyone's social environment could be equalized, test score inequality would decrease by 25 percent to 40 percent (Jencks, 1972, p. 109).

Quite surprisingly, this reanalysis of the Coleman data goes on to conclude that since schools can do little in affecting change, large scale redistribution of wealth in the United States is the only practical way to provide an equitable society. The Jencks interpretation also received considerable support from researchers studying the same question in foreign countries (Heyneman and Loxley, 1982). Regretfully, in the United States, Jencks's interpretation of the data was interpreted by many to suggest that schools have absolutely *no impact* in the quest for equality.

Criticism of Coleman and Jencks

Many considered the research conclusions of both Coleman and Jencks to be inconsistent with good common sense. Objections were raised due to the "crude" measures that were employed to assess input ($) and output (academic achievement). Still other researchers claimed that much of what is learned in schools cannot be measured accurately by standardized tests and objected to the discriminatory nature of these tests, especially their bias toward the middle class student. Additionally, many educators found it particularly difficult to understand how quality schools could not help underachievers and that better schools would not teach students *more* than deficient ones. In fact, several of these researchers argued that Coleman's findings simply implied that schools did make a slight difference in student learning while families made an even bigger one (Levine and Bane, 1975).

Perhaps one of the greatest results of the Coleman and Jencks research on school effects was that it paved the way for a new crisis in thought about inequality in American schools that persists to this day. Clearly, both reports seemed to transfer blame for poor academic achievement of Black and minority students from the school to the students themselves, their family background and their social origins. Another unanticipated consequence of the report was that it put an end to the liberal rhetoric for increased funding to schools attended by disadvantaged children.

Quality Schools Make a Difference

As might be expected, Coleman's conclusions were by no means accepted by all. Many rejected the conclusions of this report outright! In fact, more recent research suggests that schools do make a difference. Quality schools foster strong academic norms, encourage positive teacher expectation and encourage student self-efficacy. They provide a favorable physical learning environment and facilitate the teaching-learning process (Arnold, 1993; Hastings, 1995). Quality schools in more affluent districts are generally newer, better equipped, staffed with certified teachers and less crowded than deficient schools in lower socio-economic areas. Yet, they do make a difference wherever they are located.

The contention that schools promote strong academic achievement finds support in several studies. One cohort study of the Baltimore public school system found that minority students' test scores reflected less improvement over the summer months, when schools were not in session, than over any other three month period when schools were in session. The resulting "faucet theory" asserts that disadvantaged children stop learning when schools are not in session. These children do not enjoy the social, cultural and cognitive support of a middle class family which supplements their knowledge during the summer. In sum, this research strongly suggests that schools DO make a difference (Entwisle, 1997).

Research by Hedges (1994) provides additional support for the Quality of Schools argument. This researcher reveals that variations in academic achievement are related to variations in school expenditures. His study concludes that an average increase in $500 per student is associated with a 0.7 standard deviation increase in academic achievement. This gain is equivalent to a grade level increase of two years. In a more recent study, this same researcher arrives at similar conclusions. Both findings are remarkable and both obviously suggest that increasing school funding can have a positive impact on scholastic achievement (Hedge, 1996).

Certainly, funding impacts school resources and quality. Unlike most other nations, the primary source of school funding in the United States is the local property tax. Schools located in affluent neighborhoods will always receive significantly higher tax support than those in less affluent areas, thus denying poorer districts the opportunity to secure essential resources for teaching and learning. On average, expenditures for students in New York City schools amount to approximately one half of the amount spent in the surrounding suburban school districts, while faculty receive about 25-30 percent less pay. If school spending were on par with the suburbs of Long Island, in 1988, a class of thirty-six children would have been allocated an additional $200,000! This would be more than enough to hire two additional certified teachers, divide the class into two smaller sections of eighteen each, purchase new textbooks, and provide computers, air conditioners and new learning materials! Additionally, this amount would provide for the cost of extra counseling for those children who must cope with many of the problems encountered by less affluent families.

For the most part, the school quality research of the 1960s and 1970s led to the conclusion that school failure in Black and minority children was probably caused by the social environment—their families, their culture. Schools could do little to reduce the ever increasing gap between White and Black student achievement. In fact, schools might even reinforce and perpetuate inequality. Therefore, increasing school funding, hiring more teachers and improving the curricula were not likely to reduce unequal achievement in schools. Regretfully, the large-scale research on school effects of the 1960s and 1970s deflected attention away from the schools and on to the very students themselves as the cause for underachievement. In time, it set the stage for an elaborate set of student-centered explanations for underachievement in schools. One of these centered on the cultural limitations of disadvantaged populations. Could the differential achievement of students be caused by cultural deprivation of certain ethnic and racial groups? The most prominent of these theories placed the blame for unequal achievement on what many referred to as their deficient and different culture.

Cultural Deprivation and Underachievement

The Cultural Deprivation perspective explains differential success in school as a function of differences in students' cultural backgrounds, linguistic preferences, and childhood experiences. It argues that children of families in poverty are raised in an environment that lacks the intellectual stimulation and parental support required to nurture the development of intelligence.

This perspective gained momentum during the 1960s when educational sociologists began to turn their attention away from the school and to *the home* in order to explain underachievement. For many, identifying the family, its values and material resources as a prime cause in differential achievement was not a new idea.

At least three different models of cultural deprivation have been identified by the research: cultural deficiency (*the absence of culture*), cultural depravity (*a culture that is lacking*) and cultural difference (*a culture that is at odds with the dominant white, middle-class culture*). Cultural deprivation theory suggests that individual inequalities are not heritable but socio-cultural in origin. Accordingly, it argues that the cultural, linguistic and family backgrounds of disadvantaged children are so different or inferior that they cannot realistically be expected to learn and succeed in school.

The Cultural Deficiency Model

The *cultural deficiency model* suggests that some children and their families are so disadvantaged that they possess a deficit culture, that is, *no culture at all*. In the absence of an enriched home environment, the development of language and intelligence falls short. In the words of one researcher, these children are "stranded on an island of nothingness by misfortune and circumstance" (Stein, 1971, p. 182). The point is also brought home by Wax and Wax, who vividly recount the difficulties encountered by schools in teaching these children . . . "their homes have no books, radios or newspapers—they are empty . . . their experiences are less than meager . . . they come to school with an empty head and it is a triumph if they learn anything!" (Wax and Wax, 1971, p. 129). The deficit model represents one of the more extreme forms of cultural deprivation, a more common type is seen in cultural *depravity* as a cause of unequal achievement.

The Cultural Depravity Model

The second model of cultural deprivation—*cultural depravity* views the child as having some form of culture, but sees this culture as lacking—and the cause of serous problems. In turn, this cultural depravity is reflected in the low achievement of these children (Rainwater, 1970). This view is synonymous with the "culture of poverty" perspective which argues that some disadvantaged children do not succeed in school because of an inadequate home environment, poor childrearing practices and undeveloped language usage.

As early as 1932, Fraizer developed the idea of a dysfunctional and pathological lower-class culture that facilitated social disorganization. One obvious result of this pathology was failure in school. The thesis was further developed by Daniel Moynihan (1965) in his controversial and much debated government report "The Negro Family." Using the observations of Frazier, Moynihan argued that the black family was enmeshed in a "tangle of pathology and deterioration." The theory identified the value system of Blacks and other minority students as deficient and dysfunctional. It asserted that disadvantaged students were raised in a culture that was *lacking and inferior* and the prime cause of student underachievement. This culture of poverty explanation focused on the distinctive social environment of the economically disadvantaged and suggested that it facilitated underachievement by retarding intellectual growth, rejecting the concept of delayed gratification and the belief in schooling as a means to success. The thesis clearly identified differences in students' cultural backgrounds, childhood experiences and linguistic expressions as items contributing to school failure. By not providing children with enriching experiences so necessary for the development of language, their environment fell short of fostering cognitive development and ultimately, success in school.

According to Moynihan, a proponent of this view, the Black family was highly unstable and at the point of complete breakdown. Black males occupied an insignificant place in the American economy and because of this, often relinquished their roles as strong fathers and heads of households. Black children were raised in one-parent households dominated by women. Male children were rarely given the opportunity to develop a relationship with male significant others. Consequently, black children were immersed in a deficient environment which contributed to their lack of success in school and often facilitated their entrance into deviant activity. And so, Moynihan concluded by recommending massive federal programs to create jobs and special assistance programs for black families and their children.

Today, proponents of this perspective cite the meagerness of intellectual resources in economically disadvantaged homes as well as the indifference to literacy and the paucity of language as forms of intellectual starvation for children growing up in these homes (Brooks, 1966; Hunt, 1964). Those who ascribe to this explanation for unequal achievement believe that if these conditions were removed, most if not all of the academic disadvantages that Blacks and minorities experience in schools would be ameliorated.

In time, the research by Coleman and Jencks underscoring the importance of the family in school success was viewed as a strong confirmation of this theory. In many ways, by suggesting that schools had little independent effect on educational outcomes, the large-scale research of Coleman (1966) and Jencks (1972) gave further credence to the validity of this theory. In time, the work of Moynihan, Coleman and Jencks and the dozens of studies that followed painted a horrific picture of the deteriorating impact that disadvantaged families had on their children and the limits of schooling in ameliorating these negative effects.

The idea that cultural explanations could be utilized in explaining school success or failure was also promoted in the works of Pierre Bourdieu (1984). Bourdieu argued that children from high-status backgrounds with strong cultural capital started school with an advantage since they possessed a similar culture to those who managed the educational system in which they were competing. In turn, these students were assessed by teachers as being more capable since they possessed the requisite cultural capital. Cultural capital was also found to influence the time one spent in schools, college attendance and graduation (Di Maggio, 1982; Sullivan, 2001).

The theory of cultural deprivation found unconditional support among the liberal reformers of the 1960s who were quick to point out the dramatic disparities between the homes and schools of the rich and poor. This theory was also responsible for the introduction of many compensatory education programs including the numerous "Safe Harbor" and "Head Start" programs that were considered academic strategies to reverse the adverse effects of a deprived home environment.

The Cultural Difference Model

By the end of the 1960s, the theory of cultural depravity as an explanation for unequal achievement was beginning to come under heavy criticism. Critics suggested that it wrongly focused attention away from the real problems, the schools, their middle-class oriented curriculum and the culturally biased testing instruments. In fact, many argued that it wrongfully blamed and attacked the victims of poverty, rather than the cause. Since these children were able to function quite well within their own environment, it was soon suggested that they might be more correctly considered culturally *different rather than deprived.* The cultural difference model that developed contended that some disadvantaged children did in fact have a culture and that it was not pathological or lacking. They considered this culture to be a separate and distinct set of values and rules—a *different* culture valid in its own right and as legitimate as mainstream culture. Some proponents of the cultural difference model even argued that matricentrism family structures and even father absenteeism were not necessarily pathological but, rather, another cultural *difference* between poor black and middle class white families.

Neither was the language development of poor Black children inferior or inadequate. Rather, their language was a different, yet fully developed, form of communication and they were speaking correctly within a set of completely different rules (Valentine, 1968; Baratz and Baratz, 1970). Speaking this form of the language (non-standard English) was a distinct disadvantage for the Black student within the middle-class oriented classroom. Here rests the disadvantage, they insisted.

Some theorists also argued that considering these children as culturally deprived portrayed a racist and ethnocentric conception of black and minority families. Such a consideration reflected the biased preference of white-middle class society. Once again, proponents of cultural difference theory suggested that considering these groups as deprived and deficient was deliberately removing the blame for the disparity in achievement from the schools and the lack of culture to the poor victims of poverty, themselves.

The theory of cultural difference was ultimately accepted but considerably refined by Oscar Lewis. By falling back on his earlier research in the barrios of Mexico and Puerto Rico, Lewis considered these disadvantaged children to be culturally different. It was here that he first uncovered a distinct *culture of poverty* that was characterized by little control over aggressive impulses and a strong belief in fate and superstition as the prime determinants of one's future. Individuals believed that they had little control over their environments. They were haunted by low aspiration, a deep sense of hopelessness and loss of control. Lewis referred to this culture as distinct and not inferior. He believed it to be quite different from a lower-class culture and composed of cultural patterns that were at *variance* with the dominant white middle-class culture.

Proponents of cultural difference suggest that the possibility for school failure is increased when there is a marked difference between the culturally derived white-middle class patterns of communication of schools and those of the students' home culture. Adherents of this perspective explore discontinuities in communication patterns between the school and that of the student's home. They argue that interactional difficulty in school is clearly related to differences in styles of communication (Cazden, John and Hymes, 1974; Heath, 1983; Labov, 1972) and that academic achievement can be improved if teachers adapt and show greater respect for the culture of minority students. In so doing, students would become more at ease and show less resistance to school in general (Erickson, 1984). One prominent researcher of this period noted that African-American children who used dialect (non-Standard English) were more often corrected during the course of the school day and actually obtained lower scores on reading tests than did those children who were permitted to use BEV (Black English vernacular) without any corrections (Piestrup, 1973).

Critique of Cultural Deprivation Models

The cultural difference view insists that lower-class families are functional, adequate and able to foster intellectual development in their youth. While this may be correct, this author's greatest objection to this theory stems from the fact that it blatantly ignores the issue of significant differences in academic achievement between students from different social origins. By insisting that Black and minority children are not less intelligent than middle-class white children and that the cause of the differential school success rests totally in culturally biased tests and schools that reward only middle class behavior, this model fails to address the fact that disadvantaged children enter schools with fewer skills required for academic success. Rather than deny this problem, it is more important to understand why these children fail in school. In fact, the model diverts attention away from our understanding of this problem.

Critics of cultural deprivation argue that *all of the models* place blame for school failure on the children and their families. In so doing, these theories direct attention away from the school and the educational programs or even the everyday interactions of students and teachers (this will be addressed in Chapter 6). By accepting these theories, teachers and society begin to believe that certain students are not capable of learning and these assumptions likewise begin to insure that children will not learn. Ironically, the model is validated by the fact that teachers begin to develop certain expectations for some students which in turn solidifies the results.

Those critical of the Cultural Deprivation Model also assert that intergenerational poverty results from structural conditions within the society as well as outright discrimination. The low levels of self-efficacy, apathy and sense of control often cited in the culture of poverty thesis are actually situational responses within each generation to the economic and social discrimination. They insist that it is not the child that is broken but, rather, the school and a society that borders on racism.

Finally, if it were a deprived culture that produced low self-efficacy and self-esteem one would assume that the same level of these variables would be present in both young and older disadvantaged children. Yet, the opposite is true. Research has uncovered that the longer the children remain in school, the lower their self-esteem. Clearly, these findings suggest that something must be happening in the schools that facilitates a low self-esteem among Black and minority students.

If the absence or lack of a stimulating culture cannot account for under-achievement and if research has questioned the association between school resources and achievement, then some other variable must be at work. Some have suggested that the differential success rate may be attributed to a herita-ble difference.

Heritability Deficit Theory: The Intelligence Debate

The failure of large scale research to establish a credible link between school quality and achievement as well as the apparent problems with socio-cultural explanations led researchers to conclude that the major source of unequal achievement must rest in a heritable genetic factor. In other words, if schools and socio-cultural factors could not be blamed for the differential achieve-ment of students from different social origins, then perhaps biology could! The genetic thesis stands in direct opposition to the socio-cultural view and offers a much more pessimistic alternative—that the underlying cause of the differential achievement is rooted in innate biological differences among students of different social origins. The intense discussion that ensued from this perspective has been referred to as the intelligence debate. Since IQ cor-relations of siblings have been employed as a means of demonstrating the existence of a heritable factor, it has also been referred to as the IQ Deficit theory.

Few topics in the social sciences have generated more discussion than the relative impact of heredity and environment on human intelligence. Clearly, the debate has generated controversy because different views on the hered-itability of intelligence contribute to quite different social and political impli-cations. Proponents of a strict genetic component to personality suggest that every human is born with a fixed amount of intelligence and that there is lit-tle that anyone can do to enhance this level. Even remedial and compensatory education programs offer little if any value. In contrast, those who believe that intelligence is primarily a function of the social environment believe that supplemental education programs designed to enrich and compensate for the devastating effects of cultural deprivation can have a dramatic effect on in-telligence.

A Historical Perspective: Heredity as the Basis for Intelligence

The IQ deficit theory has been around for many years. It thrived in the racist climate of the late nineteenth and twentieth centuries and generated a consid-erable amount of research in support of a strong relationship between intelli-gence and heredity. Samuel George Morton, one of the earlier proponents of this view claimed that he could judge the intellectual ability of a race or ethnic group by the size of its cranial cavity (Morton, 1839). Since the cranial cavities of Africans and Native Americans were somewhat smaller than Europeans, he argued that they were intellectually inferior to Europeans. His primitive "scientific" approach, which employed measuring the amount of birdshot that could be held by the cranial areas of various races, was widely accepted as gospel truth and helped popularize the idea that intelligence was a heritable factor. Morton has been accused of exaggerating and altering the truth whenever his findings disagreed with his theory (Gould, 1981).

At about the same time, Francis Galton became the first to advance some experimental studies on individual differences among humans. His controversial and much debated research, *Hereditary Genius*, was the first to apply a statistical method to genetics in order to create a positive link between individual difference and heredity (Galton, 1914). Early public sentiment was also shaped by the educational psychologist, Sir Cyril Burt (1883–1971) who also argued that heredity and not environment determined one's ability. He advocated the idea that intelligence was innate and heritable and that the economically disadvantaged were less intelligent. We know now that much of this early research was based on fraud, omission, carelessness and misrepresentation of fact (Gould, 1981).

The point of view expressed by these early pioneers greatly influenced the work of Alfred Binet, a psychologist who expressed interest in measuring intelligence. Binet was primarily obsessed with the problems of reasoning and intelligence. In 1904, he accepted a commission offered by the French educational ministry, to differentiate between underachievers and the feebleminded children attending Parisian schools. His research led to the development of a test that he believed was capable of measuring intelligence and identifying mental defects in children. In time and with the help of Louis Stern, the test became the first IQ (intelligence quotient) examination. Interestingly, neither of these researchers believed that the intelligence quotient of an individual was fixed and unchangeable although, their work has been interpreted as demonstrating this relationship.

At about the same time that scientists were struggling with the issue of intelligence and testing, American educators were struggling with a massive influx of children into the public schools of their largest cities. The decades between 1890 and 1920 witnessed one of the most extensive migrations in our nation's history with the population of the United States increasing by over 40 million. Many of the new arrivals were from Western Europe but the great influx was also intensified by the increased flow of southern Blacks into the North. Clearly, the schools could not deal effectively with this new constituency and for whatever reason; the underachievement of these children presented the schools with a unique challenge. Accusations that most of the new children were social misfits and suffered from mental retardation were quite common. Administrators and politicians sought a new "unbiased" and scientific instrument that could admit these children to school but keep them separated (by their ability) from the others. Upon hearing about the development of a new IQ exam that could measure intellectual capability, many American researchers expressed interest in having it brought to America. In time, the exam was transported to the United States by Louis Terman.

It was no secret that Terman, a hard-core social Darwinist, considered poor blacks and newly arriving immigrants to be social misfits who impinged on the education of other children. While he believed that they were not capable of learning, he sought to provide them with some basic educational skills that would, at least, make them competent workers. He envisioned the newly developed intelligence test as a scientific means of sorting them into vocational tracks within the schools. The new IQ test was welcomed in most American schools and in a relatively short time became the final step in a tracking process that enabled schools to identify academic ability levels and sort students accordingly.

Recent Attempts to Link Intelligence and Heredity

The debate about the influence of heredity on intelligence continued for several decades. In the 1970s the crusade to link these two variables was led by the writings of Arthur Jensen, (1969), Richard Herrnstein (1973) and William Shockley (1973, 1992). Each advocated the belief that the intellect of African Americans was inferior to that of European-Americans.

Jensen believed that social scientist had grossly underestimated the total impact of biological factors in determining individual intelligence. He referred to studies of laboratory rats and argued that their ability to negotiate a maze quickly and efficiently (his index of intelligence) could be influenced by selective breeding and that the manner by which the rats responded to their surroundings was contingent upon their genetic makeup.

For humans, he concluded that 80 percent of the variation in intelligence was determined by heredity. His argument was based on existing studies of kinship IQ correlations: studies of identical twins raised apart; studies of similarities between identical and fraternal twins raised together and studies of adoptive children (Burt, 1966; Juel-Nielsen, 1965; Newman, Freeman and Holzinger, 1937; Shields, 1962). For example, the correlation between IQ scores of siblings reared apart was higher than that of children who were unrelated and raised together (within the same home). Additionally, since identical twins (monozygote) had similar genetic makeup, what differences occurred in intelligence was a function of the social environment. Accordingly, small differences in their IQs implied that heredity played an important role in determining IQ.

While few deny some heritable factor in the development of intelligence, Arthur Jensen's exaggerated statements and statistics were based on previous research that had been criticized for its verbal contradictions, arithmetical inconsistencies and lack of procedural details (Wade, 1976). After careful study of the four twin studies he employed in his research, one researcher, Leon Kamin concluded that the claim of racial differences to genetic factors is the "compounding of folly with malice." Ironically, Kamin's assessment of his research concludes that some of Jensen's data also makes a strong case for environment as a factor in intelligence (Kamin, 1974, p. 177).

Herrnstein and Murray

Another recent attempt to establish a link between heredity and IQ can be seen in the work of Herrnstein and Murray (1994). Their work, *The Bell Curve*, one of the most controversial books dealing with this subject, suggests that intelligence is distributed among the general population in the form of a bell curve. For these researchers, intelligence is one-dimensional, inherited and not appreciably influenced by the conditions of one's social and educational environment! The authors also believe that there is only one, rather than several, types of intelligence and this determines how well children do in school. Herrnstein and Murray also estimate that intelligence is approximately 70 percent heritable (the other 30 percent is determined by environment) and that African Americans are intellectually inferior to other races. The authors arrive at their conclusions using the existing studies of monozygote (identical) twins formerly utilized by Jensen. These twins, separated early in life and then raised apart, are practically duplicates of one another. They contend that any similar features that remain similar between them after separation must be the result of genetics. The similarity in intelligence between the twins is approximately 70 percent—therefore this must be the result of hereditable factors. Ironically, closer observation of their data, however, reveals that some of the twins were actually separated more than others and that the more separated they were, the more different they were in intelligence. Thus, reflecting the impact of the social environment on intelligence. Additionally, the similarity in intelligence between separated twins more likely ranges from 30–50 percent rather than the 70 percent statistic arrived at by Herrnstein and Murray (Bouchard and McGue, 2003; Taylor, 1996).

The Herrnstein and Murray thesis denies any negative impact that might have come about due to poverty! Essentially, it suggests the presence of inherited genetic differences and contends that the genetic deficiencies of Black and disadvantaged children account for their underachievement and disparate career trajectory. Since intelligence is largely determined by heredity, they argue, policies attempting to enrich the child's school environment are doomed to failure.

Most contemporary educators regard the striking differences between some racial and ethnic groups as purely the result of environmental factors, that is, differences in family, social class, and childhood socialization experiences. There is little of substance to suggest that these differences are the result of biological or genetic factors. It is possible that certain within-group differences may possibly reflect genetic differences among persons within the same racial/ethnic group, but still the effect of the social environment is considered to be greater than the genetic effect (Taylor, 1996). Additionally, the cultural bias inherent in many of the instruments used to measure intelligence casts serious doubts on the conclusions arising from this research. Clearly, much stronger evidence is required before we can accept this explanation. However, the notoriety that this book received provides us with a fairly good idea of how strongly the genetic bias remains embedded in our contemporary society.

A More Balanced View

So what is the upshot of the research on the heredity of intelligence? It seems that the existing evidence does make some argument for an association between the two, but exactly how much intelligence is inherited? Today, most researchers agree that heredity and environment have a mutual and interacting influence on intelligence. Most argue that heredity places limits on the possible range of intelligence; while the environment determines where, within these limits, the person's IQ will be. This seems reasonable. Despite this prevailing view, social researchers continue to have different opinions about exactly *how much* each of these variables contributes and how they interact. The truth is, we really don't know! We can assume that heredity and environment do interact. This being said, is it possible for the IQ differences between Black and White students to be caused by the genetic differences between races?

Some research provides support for a strong environmental impact on intelligence. It suggests that the longer disadvantaged Black children interact within a White middle class environment, the higher are their achievement scores (Coleman, 1966; Bronfenbrenner, 1972). Other researchers (Scarr-Salapatek and Weibberg, 1975) have also addressed this issue and arrived at similar conclusions. These researchers uncovered that, within just a few years following their adoption, the IQ scores of Black children adopted by White parents averaged approximately 105. By comparison, the scores of White children adopted by these same families averaged about 111, a difference of only 6 points rather than 15, which is the national average. Additionally, the black children lived with the white adoptive parents for fewer years than the white children. Here again, we note a strong case for the impact of environment over heritable factors on IQ.

Clearly, the heritability of intelligence thesis seems to rest on questionable ground. IQ seems to be the instrument of choice in assessing intelligence and it remains an extremely inappropriate means of assessing ability. This is especially true when the subjects are disadvantaged and minority children. The unexamined assumptions of IQ including the socio-cultural bias of this test make it especially inappropriate.

Like the cultural deprivation model, hereditability theory also places most of the blame for the underachievement of children directly on the children themselves thus diverting attention away from the policies and practices of schools and the possibility that a more realistic solution can be found. In time, it is also likely that these explanations for underachievement themselves may have contributed to the development of a self-fulfilling prophesy of academic failure. Accordingly, as children and their parents begin to internalize these negative assumptions about their ability to achieve, it begins to insure that they will not achieve. Thus, they become underachievers and also corroborate both of these models!

Today, intelligence is not considered to be one-dimensional (a master capacity that humans possess); rather, it represents a measure of a broad range of human abilities. Originally, Alfred Binet thought of intelligence as the exercise of many mental abilities. Regretfully, his colleague and successor, Charles Spearman attempted to identify *one* common factor that he believed was common to all mental facilities. He referred to this factor as general intelligence—the *g* factor. More recently, in 1990, the *g* factor conception was discredited and no longer dominates thinking on intelligence.

One of the most recent and widely accepted formulations of multidimensional theory is MI (multiple intelligences) theory, developed by Howard Gardner (1993, 1999). This approach suggests that cognitive abilities of one kind are not necessarily accompanied by cognitive abilities of another. Abilities are distinct and separate and ability in one does not necessarily accompany ability in another. Presently, our schools focus most of their attention on linguistic and mathematical ability. Students who have facility in these subjects are considered intelligent. However, Gardner argues that there are at least eight different forms of what we call intelligence and students who demonstrate strength in these areas should also be considered intelligent. The eight areas of intellectual ability include—linguistic (facility with language), musical, logical-mathematical (mathematically inclined), spatial (visualization skills), bodily-kinesthetic (athletic ability) interpersonal (interpersonal skills) intrapersonal (ability for self-introspection) and naturalistic (nature smart).

Recognizing the existence of several forms of intelligence has many advantages for teaching and learning. The approach suggests that teachers should present their lessons in a wide variety of formats addressing each of these potential strengths. Accordingly, students who do not necessarily have strong linguistic capabilities may achieve when the same material is presented in another format. One of the most significant features of Multiple Intelligence theory is that it presents eight different and exciting pathways for students to learn.

CONCLUSIONS

Most previous explanations for underachievement fail to present an acceptable theoretical explanation for this critical problem. For the most part, they assign blame to the students themselves or the schools they attend. In and of themselves, each theory is too simplistic and none really accounts for the many disadvantaged students who do succeed in school. Heritability deficit argues that biological deficiencies of Blacks and other minorities ultimately result in school failure. Theories of cultural deprivation suggest that the socio-cultural environment of underachieving students including their linguistic ability and motivational background is absent, deteriorated or different. This results in their inability to learn. Finally, school deficit theory argues that their schools lack the basic resources essential for learning. Each of these explanations has been considered; yet, each fails to explain a number of inconsistencies.

In the case of the first, Heritability Deficit, some degree of credibility is lost when attention is called to the likely socio-cultural bias of the instruments used in testing. Also questionable is the ability of these instruments to assess general intelligence. Additionally, more recent research has called into question the underlying premise that disadvantaged children are genetically inferior. Unquestionably, the available evidence strongly suggests that these children *are* capable of learning under the proper circumstances. Clearly, the Faucet Theory suggests that disadvantaged children are capable of learning and certainly do learn when the learning faucet is turned on. On the other hand, when schools are not in session, disadvantaged children begin to experience a lag, which places them at a disadvantage with middle-class children who continue to learn from their parents.

Additionally, research points out that Black children residing with white adoptive parents experience an increase in test scores. Thus, if achievement is related to economic or social factors, it is not heritable. Considerable research also suggests that socio-economic status is more significant for academic achievement than IQ. Neither is Heritability Deficit theory able to account for the academic success of so many Black and minority students. Clearly, some other factor must be at play.

The cultural deprivation argument likewise fails to explain a number of inconsistent findings. Interestingly, the argument does not appear in less industrialized nations and one might expect that if deprivation of culture were related to economically disadvantaged, we would also expect to find this in developing nations of the world (Persell, 1977). Additionally, if cultural deprivation were a valid explanation, the achievement gap between White and Black students would be expected to be greatest at the time they began school and then hopefully decrease over time. Ironically, the opposite is true! Further, the cultural deficit argument places blame on the students themselves and the truth is that if disadvantaged children suffer from cultural deprivation which impairs learning, they would never be able to learn anything. More recently, a reevaluation of the Head Start data also suggests that compensatory education actually works. Headstart children achieved better math achievement scores than those disadvantaged children who did not attend Head Start programs (up through grade 5). Additionally, fewer were assigned to special education classes and most reported having pride in their school experiences and accomplishments (Entwisle et al., 2000).

Neither can school deficit theory provide a comprehensive reason for underachievement. Certainly, it cannot explain the Coleman finding that academic differences between students are greater within the same school than between schools of different resources. If it is possible for some of the greatest academic differences between students to be found within the same schools, then the argument for deficit theory is substantially weakened.

Part III

THE ROLE OF FAMILY

Chapter Three

Explaining Unequal Achievement: The Family

The sources of inequality appear to lie first in the home itself and the cultural influences immediately surrounding it.

James Coleman 1966

THE IMPORTANCE OF FAMILY BACKGROUND

To claim that families have a dramatic influence on the lives of their children is an understatement. Increasingly, researchers have concluded that the family into which a child is born is often the best predictor of student achievement and attainment (Henderson, 1994). From the very beginning of life, families play a critical role in the socialization of their children and are essentially responsible for their evolving personality and identity. Families monitor behavior, transmit values and take an active part in the development of language. They provide affectionate and loving relationships and have a dramatic impact on aspirations, self-efficacy and motivation. By so doing, they provide the child with resiliency to adversity as well as the inner belief that one can achieve academically. Without the support of family, children may begin to doubt their ability to succeed or even fail to perceive education as a vehicle for advancement. Above all, the family provides its members with an ascribed status based on social class, race and ethnicity. As we shall see, each of these background variables affects students' educational opportunities and life-chances. In the past, much research has underscored the importance of one of these variables, socioeconomic status (social class), on academic achievement; but, this relationship is often complex and involved. Social class has also been related to a host of other factors that also impact learning. For example, economically advantaged parents read more and have more reading material available in their homes. They visit libraries and museums more often and generally interact on a more intellectual plane with their children than do poor families. Additionally, advantaged parents usually have more complex lives and careers and frequently share their experiences with their children, often leading to stimulating and resourceful discussions (Menaghan and Parcel, 1991). An abundance of research underscores the association between family background variables and academic achievement.

There is little doubt about the family's ability to contribute positively to the child's academic achievement. Coleman was among the first to underscore the importance of family and although his conclusions were received with skepticism, the sophisticated re-analysis by Christopher Jencks (Inequality, 1972), strengthened rather than modified much of his conclusions. Schools count, but the best indicator of school success is the home! As early as 1980, Whitfield's international analysis of research in eighteen countries revealed the importance of home background variables on the academic achievement of students (Whitfield, 1980). Similarly Paul Barton and Richard Coley (1992) examined a number of family controlled factors including the availability of reading material in the home, the number of hours spent reading or watching TV, the number of student absences from school and concluded that these variables accounted for over 90 percent of the difference in eight grade math test scores on the National Assessment of Educational Progress Exam.

Middle class families are also more involved in the education of their children and the differential impact of parental involvement in the education of their children continues to be the focus of considerable research. More and more studies reveal a positive association between this family variable and increased student academic achievement (Crosnoe, 2001; Drumond and Stipek, 2004; Hill and Tyler, 2004). More recently, research has also articulated exactly how some middle-class families are able to secure academic advantage for their children by manipulating the educational system in their districts (Brantlinger, 2003). Clearly, the family remains an important variable in accounting for much of the differences in average student academic achievement.

This chapter examines the influence of family on school achievement. Here we consider two vital currency resources dictated by home background variables which have often been associated with student academic outcomes. These resources, cultural and social capital, remain important to the child's educational and career trajectory (Bradley and Corwyn, 2002; Tardiff, 2002).

This chapter also explores the many ways that families behave, interact and provide advantage for their children. It focuses on the relationship between several ascribed background characteristics (social class, gender, race, religion) and achievement, and attempts to peel away the layers of this complex association. The role played by family configuration (structure), family size, and parental involvement as possible mediators of student achievement is also examined. During the course of this discussion we raise several interesting questions about the relationship between family and academic achievement.

How may social class, race, or religion impact school success?

Does family composition (size and structure) affect student achievement?

What is the relationship between parental aspirations, family values, parental involvement and academic achievement?

What do we mean by social and cultural capital and how might it influence student achievement and attainment?

There remains little doubt about the importance of the family to the academic achievements of its children. One thing remains certain, if we are to solve the riddle of underachievement, schools must do more than just educate children. They must be able to mediate the inequalities that some children bring with them as a result of their family background. In other words, for schools to be effective, they must free academic achievement from the restrictions of the home. If they cannot, we run the risk of increased student failure.

THE CONCEPT OF CULTURAL CAPITAL

The French sociologist, Pierre Bourdieu, first developed the term Cultural Capital in the early 1970s to explain differences in educational outcomes in France. For Bourdieu, cultural capital was a style of life that differentiated one social class from another. It included distinct ways of acting, speaking, dressing, and socializing that were ingrained in the child from birth by the family. Bourdieu believed that members of advantaged classes were taught to subscribe to certain values, competencies and consumption preferences. Beginning in early childhood, their socialization included an introduction to an elite culture which encompassed the arts, music, and literature as well as the ability to appreciate certain high-brow experiences like lectures and exhibits.

In his work, *Forms of Capital* (1986), Bourdieu identifies three types of Cultural Capital. The first, referred to as *Embodied Capital*, is composed of those socially learned traits of culture which are transmitted through the socialization process. The ability to use language masterfully and distinct ways of speaking are forms of embodied cultural capital. The second, *Objectified Capital*, refers to Cultural items or goods which are owned and can be transmitted physically including paintings and sculpture. Finally, *Institutionalized*

Capital is typified by some academic credentials which often guarantee a certain monetary value in recognition of a certain level of institutional achievement. Each of these forms of capital provides an advantage to those who possess them and a handicap to all who lack ownership of them (Bourdieu, 1977, 1986; DiMaggio, 1982). Without a doubt, cultural capital is passed on to children by the family and this valuable commodity contributes appreciably to the child's academic success.

Cultural capital is also often referred to as "currency" since the ability to demonstrate knowledge of these cultural resources provides a special type of social status or currency to all who possess this knowledge. In society, it identifies certain individuals and groups as worthy of high achievement. By interacting with one another, advantaged members of society create and articulate a shared culture which identifies them as privileged. For this reason, the concept of cultural capital is often employed to explain how social class impacts on life-chances and career trajectory. Without a doubt, the most valued cultural capital is possessed by the dominant culture and the prestige of individuals clearly depends on how much and what kind of cultural capital they possess (Bourdieu and Passeron, 1977).

DeGraff (2000) employs a more limited version of this concept when he defines cultural capital in terms of understanding and participating in a "highbrow culture" such as theatre, classical music and art. Others (Kingston, 2001) suggest that cultural capital is enjoyed only by the elite in society and that in order to succeed in education lower classes must somehow acquire it.

Cultural Capital and Academic Achievement

How is it possible for cultural capital to translate into positive academic outcomes? More recently, researchers have employed this concept to underscore how schooling plays a part in facilitating school success or failure. Cultural capital is passed on from parent to child and the quantity and quality of the capital differs according to social class. Cultural capital possessed by advantaged classes is the most highly valued and often comprises the basic elements of what has been referred to as the hidden curriculum (the subtle messages about race, gender and social class that are conveyed to students in classrooms). Hence, those children who possess this resource begin school with a unique positive advantage.

Bourdieu argues that children who are socialized to appreciate these upper-class cultural forms will eventually possess the highest forms of cultural capital. In schools, greater accumulations of this type of cultural capital are recognized and rewarded by teachers as being of higher value and merit. Differences in cultural capital thus result in differential treatment and academic outcomes.

Research has also uncovered a significant relationship between the cultural capital of a family and the academic achievement of its children. Children who lack capital are perceived as less competent and not capable of achievement. For example, if students do not use Standard English or fail to dress according to middle-class standards, it is likely that they will be perceived as less intellectually competent. The most valued cultural capital is that which is possessed by the dominant culture and school children are often evaluated on how closely their family's cultural capital resembles that of the dominant group.

Cultural capital provides an academic advantage to those who possess it in other ways as well. Parents provide their children with a Cultural capital that makes the school a familiar place in which they are comfortable and in which they can succeed. The positive impact of cultural capital will be especially important in the early elementary years when teachers are making initial assessments of all children. In turn, the same assessments may provide the basis for future teacher expectations for these children. Possession of more rather than less cultural capital will also trigger positive teacher expectations for the academic achievement of students. It is also likely that school personnel might identify children coming from families with high cultural capital and provide them with a greater amount of attention and consideration. Hence, those students lacking cultural capital may receive considerably less of a teacher's time and even be assigned to a less desirable class or track where the return for their education is significantly less. In this way, it is possible for economically advantaged families to translate this capital into higher grades for their children (Bourdieu, 1977; DiMaggio and Mohr, 1985; DiMaggio, 1982). In his critique of the remedial and compensatory programs introduced in disadvantaged areas, Bourdieu concluded that these programs were doomed to failure primarily because they could not be institutionalized substitutes for growing up in a middle-class family and having access to this valued cultural capital (Bourdieu and Passeron, 1977).

Cultural Capital and Inequality:
The Reproduction of Consciousness

In relation to the educational system, the concept of cultural capital is especially useful in examining educational inequality. Perhaps the greatest advantage provided by this concept rests in its ability to focus attention on how educational institutions play a part in creating inequality.

The concept of cultural capital was developed in order to demonstrate the function of schooling in the transmission of economic and cultural wealth. Rather than view schools as promoters of democracy and equity, the works of several researchers including Bourdieu (1977), Passeron (1977) and Illich (1979) suggest that schooling often reproduces the values and the ideologies of the dominant social groups. Schools often accomplish this by what theorists term *the reproduction of consciousness.*

The expectations that schools hold for students are taken directly from dominant middle-class culture. The body of knowledge they teach is also predicated on middle-class values and conveys a middle-class consciousness. In time, as students are immersed in the culture of the school, they begin to devalue their own culture and assume that the only acceptable and valuable knowledge is that which is contained in what they learn in school (Illich, 1979). At the same time, the curriculum supports the view that knowledge contained in the curriculum and valued by the dominant middle-class culture is the only important knowledge. In effect, the school reproduces a certain kind of consciousness that discredits popular culture and personal feelings.

Schools have always stressed the importance of classical music, art and the classics. They actively teach the superiority and importance of what has been termed "high culture." Students who cannot relate to this culture are considered misfits and unworthy of success. Accordingly, since middle-class families normally convey these values to their children they are also providing them with important prerequisites for success in school (Bourdieu and Passerow, 1977). In sum, schools teach that the educated elite hold the only acceptable culture and consciousness that is legitimate and valued.

In his writings, Bourdieu also makes mention of another type of capital-social capital, the power resulting from group (social) relationships and networks of influence. He argues that social capital is equally important as a family variable which is related to success. More recently, a number of researchers have expanded Bourdieu's concept of cultural capital. The work of Stanton-Salazar and Dornbusch (1995) examines exactly how some students are able to mediate cultural capital into a form of social capital with key personnel in schools enabling them to further their potential for success.

THE CONCEPT OF SOCIAL CAPITAL

Closely related to his concept of cultural capital is Bourdieu's idea of *social capital.* This concept is often employed to enable us to understand how the middle class negotiate success for their children. It explains how some students gain more success than others through their excellent connections with other people and underscores the importance of networks and networking.

Social capital is composed of the relationships between family members, close friends and their children. Simply stated, it stresses the belief that social networks have value and that these networks can increase the productivity of students. Putnam defines the concept of social capital as the collective value of all social networks and the inclinations that arise from these networks to do things for each other (Putnam, 2000). A high degree of social capital can often result in positive educational outcomes for children and poor families are often at a disadvantage in this respect. Coleman argues that social capital is a special type of currency that accrues from the relationships between and among actors that facilitates social outcomes. Thus, social capital refers to the time and care that parents spend interacting with their children, in supervising their activities and promoting their educational accomplishments (Coleman, 1990). It refers to the ability of a network of extended family and friends to invest attention, advice and support in their children. In sum, it refers to the bonds between parents, friends and children that are useful in promoting achievement. It represents yet another way in which the middle class family may negotiate success for their children.

We noted earlier that a child's family is a major determinant of his/her academic success. Since education is a major vehicle for status attainment in our society, it may be interesting to explore some of the family characteristics that affect educational attainment and achievement.

FAMILY CHARACTERISTICS AND ACADEMIC ACHIEVEMENT

Coleman was among the first to suggest that the cognitive inequalities of disadvantaged children were considerable from the very beginning of their school careers. These inequalities he attributed directly to the family. Additionally, one would normally expect schools to increase the academic achievement of all students, regardless of family background characteristics. But is it possible for schooling in America to eliminate many of the long pre-existing inequalities that accompany children when they enter schools?

Educational sociologists have always underscored the importance of family background in the determination of a student's school success. Here, we will be concerned with how access to education and educational opportunities are stratified along dimensions of family characteristics. Two categories of family characteristics that impact student academic outcomes are examined. Each affects academic achievement both directly and indirectly because of its impact and interaction on other variables related to achievement. The first of these categories, *ascribed characteristics*, represents those assigned to children by virtue of their family membership. This category includes social class (socio-economic status), gender, race/ethnicity and religion. Socioeconomic status is generally considered to be achieved. However, since young children take on the SES of the family, here, we consider it to be an ascribed variable. The second category examines *family composition* which includes family configuration (structure) and family size. Exactly how do these two factors influence academic outcomes?

Ascribed Characteristics

Socioeconomic Status (Social Class) and Academic Achievement

Socioeconomic status (SES) is the one background characteristic of the family that is most often associated with school success. In the United States, children from families of high socioeconomic status (middle-income, professional, college educated) are more than two and a half times more likely than low-SES children to continue their education beyond high school and six times more likely to attend college. Consistently, research has pointed out that the higher the socioeconomic status of the family, the higher the school attainment (school years completed) and achievement (grades) of the student. Interestingly, this relationship holds true in virtually every Western society regardless of the measure of SES employed. In short, student grades, achievement scores, dropout rates and educational attainment are all related to the SES of the family. Interestingly, this research has also revealed that disadvantaged students begin school with lower cognitive achievement skills than their middle-class counterparts and that this gap increases with each year of schooling.

The existence of a strong positive correlation between income and academic achievement should not be taken to mean that rich kids are born smarter than children of the poor. Rather, as we begin to peel away the complicated layers of this intricate relationship, we find that in more affluent families, children are more likely to be confronted with more interesting and stimulating experiences which, no doubt, foster intellectual development. It is also likely that the strategies employed by advantaged families to manage their children's education are quite different from those employed by economically disadvantaged families. The relationship between academic achievement and SES is truly complex.

In their study of forty families from various economic backgrounds Baker and Stevenson (1986), explore the relationships between family SES and children's academic achievement by focusing on the specific actions taken by the respective parents to manage their child's education. While all parents were aware of actions that could be employed to improve their child's performance in school (visits to the school, monitoring their child's course selection and homework, letter-writing, helping with homework) the high SES mothers in the study were more likely to use the strategies to influence their children's academic outcome. The researchers found that advantaged parents were eleven times more likely to have employed one of the suggested strategies to influence their child's academic progress. Clearly, in this and similar studies, high SES children do better in school because their parents have superior management skills and take a more active part in negotiating their child's success (Baker and Stevenson, 1986; Lily, W.F., 1990).

Using data from the High School and Beyond (HSB) national survey conducted by the National Center for Education Statistics, Eva Eagle (1989) explores whether or not each of the five different family characteristics that comprise SES (mother's / father's education, family income, father's occupation and major possessions) is related to student academic achievement. This researcher concludes that student achievement is related to each one of the indicators of the SES composite. However, when she examines the family characteristics that are most often associated with achievement in families of all class levels, she uncovers that families of good students more often stress the following things: reading together as a family, providing a quiet place for study and parental involvement in the educational experience of their children. Interestingly, all of these practices are common in middle and upper class homes. In her study, parental involvement was defined as talking to teachers regularly, monitoring children's homework and assisting in school activities. Hence, while family SES and educational level remain positively related to student achievement, these important variables are also related to other variables which, when introduced into the mix, may also improve the academic achievement of all students. Therefore, it is likely that parents from all SES levels can actively assist their students to achieve by becoming more involved in their education and following some of these practices.

Time after time, research supports the strong correlation between SES and student achievement. Students from economically-disadvantaged families have lower average scores on the Scholastic Assessment Tests (SAT) and the American College Testing (ACT) program. Additionally, as family income increases so does the average mean test score of students (College Board 1999). SES is also related to cognitive achievement scores of students even when such factors as race/ethnicity, family expectations and access to child care are held constant. In fact, some research reveals that the socioeconomic status of the family accounts for more of the variation in cognitive achievement scores than does any other variable (Lee and Burkam, 2002).

Utilizing data from the National Longitudinal Study on college graduation rates, Alexander et al. examined the impact of race, gender and SES on the educational attainment of students. His study revealed that "the average controlled effect of SES on educational attainment was .22 percentage points"—even after controlling for race and sex. Another way of looking at this data is that on average 22 percent more of the higher SES students completed college than did students from low SES homes (Alexander et al., 1982). A more recent meta-analysis by Sirin (2005) of seventy-four studies consisting of over 6,800 schools in 128 school districts also supports this conclusion and revealed a *medium to strong* association between academic achievement and family SES. The unusually strong correlation between SES and student achievement is supported by a number of other independent studies (Muijis, 1997; Lee, 2002; Lee and Burkam, 2002; Haveman and Wolf, 1994).

The strong relationship between family background and academic achievement begins early in the student's career. Some research has speculated about the impact of differential verbal ability on the future academic achievement of children. It is generally recognized that children from middle-class homes begin school with much higher verbal and math skills than do their counterparts from economically disadvantaged homes. Speculation for this differential ability includes the possibility that lower SES children are born into families which interact less frequently with them. A recent study associated the frequency (the number of mother-child interchange activities during the course of the day) and elaboration (the detail and complexity of the interchange) of mother's speech to the vocabulary development of her child. Researchers observed that the mother-child interactions were strongly related to social class and that early vocabulary development was strongly associated with later positive school performance (Hart and Risley, 1995). Similarly, utilizing one hour tape recordings of children aged ten months to three years, these same researchers examined the verbal exchanges between parents and children of forty-two professional, working class and welfare recipient families. This research concluded that by the age of three, children of professional parents had developed a vocabulary of over 1,100 words. In comparison, children of working class parents and those receiving welfare had developed a working vocabulary of 750 and 500 words respectively. It is likely that the opportunity for dialogue with adults in lower SES families is much more limited than it is in middle and upper class families since mothers and older siblings are more likely to be working and have less time to spend in conversation with these children (Alexander and Entwisle, 1996; Huston, 1994).

Another commonly offered explanation for the correlation between SES and children's cognitive growth revolves around the financial advantage that middle and high-income families have in providing more and better learning resources for their children. Research has uncovered that economically advantaged families spend a greater portion of their income on educational games and learning resource materials. The link between economic resources and learning is well documented. Entwisle (1997) found that children from disadvantaged families were less likely to have daily newspapers, magazines, or an encyclopedia in their homes. On the other hand, advantaged students in her study were twice as likely to attend summer camps or visit zoos, museums, and libraries on a regular basis. She argues that these activities enhance learning and facilitate cognitive development. Additionally, they provide stimulating and rich experiences, which not only help to enhance vocabulary but often provide these students with a competitive edge in the classroom.

In addition to spending more of their household income on enrichment activities and learning resources, research has uncovered that the activities of advantaged families also differ from those of poorer households in other ways. A recent study conducted by Lee and Burkam cites five family activities that have special relevance for learning. These include: weekly television viewing, purchasing children's books, the number of hours parents report reading to their children, visits to the local library and using a home computer. Each of these activities has also been associated with social class membership. On average, middle and upper SES children owned more than three times the number of books than children from economically disadvantaged families. SES was also related to the number of hours watching television. As one might expect, watching television declines as family SES increases. It was also uncovered that economically advantaged parents spend more time interacting with their children. Owning a computer was also related to family SES. Most middle and high income households (85 percent) reported ownership of at least one computer in their home. This was true in only 19 percent of the cases in low income families. Computer ownership and frequent use are likely to build confidence in students and provide the type of latent research skills that students will find valuable in their future school career. Finally, a much higher proportion of White children's parents (87 percent vs. 67 percent) report reading regularly to their children compared to parents of Black children. The relationship between SES and reading regularly also seems to be linear. This being said, it is likely that spending less time watching television and more time reading and using the computer impacts positively on their academic achievement. Certainly, poor families are at a considerable handicap in this respect (Lee and Burkam, 2002).

Finally, we cannot rule out the possibility that a stressful home environment resulting from a relatively low income may act as a factor in student achievement. In addition to the lack of resources needed to supplement the educational experiences of their children, economically disadvantaged families may have some degree of difficulty meeting expenses and providing adequate food, clothing, and medical care for their children (DuBois, 1994). The frustrations arising from a lack of ability to meet these expenses may lead to difficult situations within the family which may impact negatively on children and their school work.

The relationship between SES and academic achievement is complex and often confusing since SES is related to so many other variables which are also related to school success. But, the direct impact of economic factors should not be discounted. Children from lower income families may be eliminated from participation in school life and activities because they lack the economic resources to participate actively in the culture of the school. They may lack the money to purchase tickets to sports events, dances, or other weekly social activities. It may be difficult for them to obtain the necessary school supplies or purchase new clothes, which in turn may increase absenteeism. Additionally, many students cite the need to work in order to supplement their family income or make ends meet. Thus, limited income interferes with full participation in school, which may also have an impact on school achievement. In light of the strong association between SES and achievement, is it possible for schools to mediate this relationship?

Socioeconomic Status, Achievement, and Seasonal Learning

Because of the strong association between social class and student achievement, some researchers have speculated as to whether or not schools can have any impact on leveling the playing field. While many assume that the family into which a child is born is a determining factor in academic outcome, some research has underscored the importance of schools in reversing this trend.

Research suggests that the learning curve experienced by poor children might be more episodic or seasonal and confined to periods when these children actually attend school. The Faucet theory, as articulated by Entwisle (1997), suggests that when schools are not in session (the summer months), disadvantaged children stop learning! On the other hand, the curve for advantaged children may be more consistent and continue during these periods. Utilizing data from the Beginning School Study of the Baltimore Public Schools, Entwisle reveals that academic gains of children during the first five years of school are quite similar for both low and high income groups for winter and spring terms. However, the summer gains are appreciably different for low and high SES students. Poor students gain little if anything during the summer months! Interestingly, the Faucet theory underscores the importance of the family as well as the school in the overall academic development of the child. It is likely that the rich resources available to middle and upper class families act as a "faucet" of knowledge for their children even during the summer when schools are closed. Without a doubt, poverty may place limits on the learning activities that low income families may be able to provide their children, thus denying these children the enrichment they need for intellectual growth during this period.

There is little doubt that SES is correlated with student academic outcomes. But as we have seen, the overall relationship might be more complicated than previously expressed. Certainly, SES is related to other family characteristics which are also related to achievement and these variables may also influence a student's academic outcomes. Three other ascribed characteristics which may influence the academic achievement of students are gender, race, and religion.

Gender and Academic Achievement

Gender is often considered an important characteristic in determining student outcomes and the research literature focusing on this topic is considerable. On average, in the United States, girls start out ahead of boys academically and then begin to lag behind them during the high school years. In elementary school, girls achieve higher grades than boys especially in reading, writing and verbal ability. On the other hand, the grade point average of boys and girls is more comparable in high school; boys do better in math and science while girls excel in reading and writing (Alexander and Entwisle, 1988; Nowell and Hedges, 1998; Stumpf, 1995). For the most part, boys excel in the sciences and the attrition of females from the sciences begins in high school and continues through college (AAUW, 1992). It is also likely that the difference in quantitative ability between the sexes is related to the different courses in which they enroll. Girls may be less likely to register for math/science courses because of what they perceive to be the lack of opportunity in this field and the likelihood that they will pursue a career in these areas.

In spite of this, one cannot eliminate the possibility of bias. The Scholastic Aptitude Test sponsored by the Educational Testing Service provides a major index of academic achievement in the United States. Although the gap between men and women is narrowing, women more often score lower than men on both verbal and math portions of this exam. As a means of accounting for this gap, researchers have suggested a major bias in the exam in favor of males since the greater portion of the exam is composed of science and short answer questions. A new version of the exam has recently been developed which also reflects a narrowing of the achievement gap. It is also likely that this decreasing difference in scores between men and women may also be a function of the increasing number of women now seeking careers in math and science.

But the key question remains. Do inequalities persist in equity and access for females? Despite the progress made in educational attainment by women in U.S. schools, reports continue to document a growing concern regarding their treatment. Increasingly, critics argue that the educational and occupational aspirations of women are often lowered by our educational system. Researchers argue that women may not be afforded equal opportunity and equal access to education. They suggest that women receive unequal treatment in classrooms and that teachers often devalue the work of females relative to males. As a result, they assert that the self-confidence and esteem of women may be seriously damaged (American Association of University Women, 1998; Sadker and Sadker, 1994). But, how is this accomplished?

Some claim that the various implicit messages that are transmitted in the classroom often act against females. In the classroom, it is not unusual for males to dominate discussions. Research reveals that teachers usually pay less attention to girls and interact more frequently with boys. Until recently, the very organization of the school relied heavily on male supervision. Males outnumber females in positions of power, that is, in school managerial and administrative positions. They manage female teachers, dominate the various policy decisions and control the overall operation of the local school boards and district offices (deMarrais, 1999). Some research has also uncovered that many teachers often hold quite different expectations for males than for females and in so doing actually influence the academic performance of these students. Teachers, regardless of ethnic and class background, address more questions to male students. One researcher finds that for every three questions addressed to males, only one is addressed to a female. Additionally, this research points out that boys' more aggressive behavior is encouraged in the classroom since they more often "shout out" answers which are accepted by teachers while girls wait to be called (Sadker and Sadker 1994).

It is also likely that educational structures impact negatively on women. Tracking, the separation of students by ability and curriculum, is also related to gender. In high school, a larger proportion of men are enrolled in science and math tracks and it is not unusual to hear teachers commenting that boys are better in math and spatial skills.

A gender gap is also visible in after-school activities. In the area of extracurricular activities girls are encouraged to participate in sports as cheerleaders and reminded of the importance of being attractive. On the other hand, boys' athletic programs promote competition and achievement. The competitive nature of the classroom and the extracurricular culture are problematic for girls since they are taught to value relationships and collaboration

(Shakeshaft, 1986). In short, the competitive nature of the school offers an advantage to boys.

Gender Differences in Educational Attainment

In recent years, however, the tide seems to be turning and women have made considerable advances. Today, more than 50 percent of all undergraduates are women, although most still choose to restrict their studies to the liberal arts and education. Formerly the exclusive domain of men, women have increasingly entered the realm of business and presently one in every five business majors is now a woman. More women than men graduate from high school and more women receive college degrees. However, men, more than women, are enrolled in professional schools and Ph.D. programs. Additionally, men continue to dominate certain fields including engineering, mathematics, and biology. On the other hand, women have a strong presence in the social sciences and humanities. Some recent evidence suggests that these differences are becoming smaller (Mickelson, 2000).

The Current Status of Women

A comprehensive study undertaken by the American Association of University Women (1992) addresses the issue of how girls are faring in American schools. This report, *How Schools Shortchange Girls*, provides a review and analysis of over 1000 studies dealing with the education of girls in grades K-12. This watershed report documents disturbing inequities in the educational experience of girls in U.S. schools. In sum, it argues that girls are often ignored in the classroom and neglected in the curriculum.

More recently, the AAUP commissioned a second report to track the progress made in this area. *Gender Gaps: Where Schools Still Fail Our Children* provides a number of interesting findings in the area of schooling and gender. The report reveals some encouraging progress and finds that over the past six years there has been a "profound reshaping" of American education enabling girls to make considerable strides in areas formerly dominated by males. However, while the gender gap in math and science has become smaller, it still persists and other gaps are beginning to emerge.

Gender Gaps: Where Schools Still Fail Our Children

A summary of the basic findings of the report Gender Gaps follows:
Boys register for all three science courses available in high schools—biology, chemistry, and physics and are more likely to register for advanced math courses. A wide gender gap persists in physics, where girls' enrollment lags

behind boys'. The areas of biotechnology and environmental science are also likely to become areas with increasing gender gaps.

Girls are significantly more likely to register for computer *data-entry* classes, but constitute only a small percentage of students in computer science and computer design classes. Girls also come across fewer active role models in computer games and software and actually use computers less often outside of school. Clearly, computer science is becoming the new domain of men.

A greater percentage of boys than girls receive top scores on the National Assessment of Education Progress (NAEP) exam and the gender gap in achievement increases with age. The highest scores in math, science and geography are still earned by boys, while girls earn higher scores in writing and reading.

Scores on the Third International Math and Science Study (TIMSS), an achievement exam taken by boys and girls in forty-one countries, also suggests a gender gap in these areas which increases with age.

Finally, in the area of placement, School-to-Work programs provide women with little assistance in breaking into nontraditional fields of employment. One study listed in the report finds that of the fourteen work-to-school sites more than 90 percent of the women were clustered in five traditionally female occupations.

Race and Academic Achievement

The subject of race and academic achievement has been the focus of considerable research. Literally thousands of studies have attempted to explain the differential success of Black and White students and the degree to which these differences are a function of unequal opportunity and school resources. Studies have consistently revealed that Black, Latino, and Native American students have lower scores on standardized tests than White and Asian students. This difference in performance among races has been referred to as the *achievement gap* and evidence of this "gap" can be found in just about every indicator of academic achievement including grades, test scores, educational attainment and college completion.

The greatest manifestation of this achievement gap is that Black and Hispanic students enter Kindergarten behind White students in reading and math scores and continue to fall behind as they progress through elementary and secondary school. In fact, some researchers assert that children's race will ultimately predict how successful they are in school, whether or not they attend and complete college, and the size of their adult paycheck. Although some suggests a narrowing of this gap in recent years, it remains substantial, and at the current rate of change it may take decades to disappear completely (Hedges and Nowell, 1998). This being said, what do we know about the impact of race on academic achievement?

Coleman's Equality of Educational Opportunity report provides the most comprehensive information on this troublesome topic. His research surveys 5 percent of all public schools in the United States and reveals that average Black students' scores on standardized tests are distinctly lower than those of White students. In fact, Black scores are about one standard deviation below White scores in the first grade. Additionally, the difference in overall achievement becomes progressively lower for black students as they advance in grade level (Coleman, 1966). From this data, he concludes that schooling in America does little to remediate the initial deficiency with which Black and minority students enter the schools. Ironically, it seems to intensify the academic disparity between the races. How is it possible to account for this disturbing finding?

Coleman attempts to explain this finding by looking at the students themselves. His research examines their aspirations, motivations and attitudes about schools and education. For the most part, he finds that the attitudes of both Black and White students are quite similar. Both express about the same positive desire to remain in school, complete homework and continue their education. But interestingly, the report does uncover a distinct difference in how Black and White students operationalize their aspirations. Fewer black students report following through on their articulated plans. Only a few actually made calls to college admission offices, completed applications for admission or sent for and reviewed college bulletins. In short, fewer black students took active steps and had *definite plans* to attend college in the immediate future.

Ainsworth-Darnell and Downey (1998) also examine the aspirations and attitudes of Black and White students in their attempt to explain differential achievement. These researchers also conclude that both Black and White students have pro-school values and high regard for school achievement. However, these researchers attribute the overall lower academic performance of Black students to their general lack of resources. While many of these students value schools and understand the importance of an education, they lack the backup that magazines, books and computers in their homes can provide. Their findings are also supported by other researchers (Cook and Ludwig, 1997; Conley, 1999; Oliver and Shapiro, 1995; Orr, 2003).

In another interesting study, Amy Orr argues that wealth (the total of all assets owned by a family minus any debts) accounts for the disparity in academic outcomes between Black and White students. She believes that wealth is an indicator of both financial and human capital and that it has a direct impact on academic achievement. Wealth has a direct bearing on the current achievement gap between students of different races since it influences students' aspirations, educational expectations and self-esteem. Wealth can be converted to social and cultural capital by enabling parents to spend more time with their children and by providing them with knowledge and appreciation for the finer things in life (concerts, cultural performances, exhibitions, and a cultivated self-image). It can provide an abundance of educational assets in the form of computers, tutors, enrichment courses and elite private schools. In assessing the impact of wealth on academic outcomes Orr concludes that it is bound to expand the educational opportunities of advantaged children and have a positive impact on achievement. Since Blacks have less accumulated wealth than Whites, it may place them at an educational disadvantage even if their incomes are adequate.

Another interesting variable which has been explored to explain differential academic performance is students' sense of control. It has been suggested that students with a higher sense of control are more likely to have higher achievement test scores. In his study, Coleman uncovered that Black students, more often than White, expressed a lack of confidence in their ability to control the future direction of their lives. When responding to self-reports employed to measure sense of control, they more often reported that "good luck was more important than hard work" in getting ahead in life. Additionally, Black students more often agreed with the statement that "people like me don't have a chance to be successful". Interestingly, those black students who exhibited a higher "sense of control" score were able to achieve higher grades on achievement tests.

Notwithstanding the impact of attitude, motivation and sense of control on academic achievement, it is possible for race itself to have an effect on student achievement due to the systematic forms of discrimination which are often practiced against racial minorities. However, the impact of race on achievement is difficult to determine because race is related to so many other variables that influence achievement. It is likely that the interaction between two or more of these variables, for example, race and social class, may account for differential academic outcomes. A study by Hess, Shipman, and Jackson clearly reflects the intersection of race and class on student achievement (Hess, Shipman and Jackson, 1965).

Hess, Shipman and Jackson examined what they referred to as the socialization styles of 160 Black middle and working class mothers. The study is interesting because it allows us to examine whether the actions taken by these parents were uniform across racial lines or if they were in any way influenced by the social class of these mothers. Each of the mothers was closely observed by the researchers as they taught their four-year-old children a series of three tasks. While all of the mothers expressed about the same amount of affection to their children during the interaction, the observers noted that the middle-class parents appeared to be more skilled in communicating to their children exactly how to complete each task. The researchers concluded that this *clarity of instruction* provided the middle-class children with a competitive edge in accomplishing their task. Additionally, when the researchers asked how they would prepare their children for school, the responses of the working-class mothers indicated that they would teach their children to be more passive and docile in learning situations. They stressed following the instructions provided by the teacher and exhibiting good behavior. By contrast, the responses of the middle class mothers suggested that they encouraged their children to become active learners, to ask questions and seek out information from teachers (Hess et al., 1965). In this study, it was clear that the impact of race varied by the social class of the parent.

Our evidence suggests that the achievement gap may be more than racial. It is complicated by many layers of variables which are themselves also associated with achievement. Some of these include socio-cultural factors related to attitudes and behavior, child-rearing practices and family expectations. But some may also be attributed to the stark inequalities of attending an inner-city school. Poor children are more often educated in schools that are less than adequate. They provide fewer educational opportunities and are unresponsive to many of the basic needs of these children.

More recently researchers have noted how racially segregated, inner-city schools limit the educational opportunities of the Black students who attend them (Wells and Crain, 1997). Students often attend these schools because their parents lack the resources to explore different academic possibilities for their children. Additionally, these same poor children are so often from homes where daily survival drains so much energy that little is left to gather information on school choice. While they want the very best for their children, parents often permit them to attend these schools because they are the neighborhood school. Their choice in decision making is not to choose (Wells and Crain, 1997). In this case, the achievement gap is merely another dimension of the disparity in experience and life-chances for individuals of different racial groups. But how does the research explain the differential performance of students of color in what may be considered "better" schools or the less-than-good achievement of middle-class Black and Latino students?

While it is relatively easy for us to understand the underachievement of poor children in inadequate schools; it becomes more difficult to understand why some children of color fail to do better when they are assigned to better schools. Another interesting dimension of this issue arises when middle-class African-American and Latino students continue to lag behind Whites on many tests of achievement. This unique feature of the achievement gap underscores

the association between race and academic achievement and has provided the
basis for new and interesting research.

Petro Noguera a researcher at Harvard has explored academic outcomes of
Black and White students in fifteen racially integrated, affluent school districts in various American cities. Here, a disproportionate number of African-
American and Latino students continue to underachieve. He concludes that
students of color have always been perceived as disadvantaged regardless of
social class. Educational practices and policies continue to favor White students and a large body of research points out that Blacks and Latinos are more
often assigned to lower track classes and excluded from gifted and honors
courses. In many instances, he uncovers that even when these students meet
the criteria for admission to advanced classes, they are more often assigned
to remedial or special education classes on the recommendations of a counselor or teacher. Further, he notes that cultural factors including child rearing
practices differ by race and that students of color spend less time on homework and reading and that they study in less affective ways than do White
children. More importantly, Noguera's research suggests that schools play an
important part in shaping racial identity as well as what students believe they
can accomplish academically. Since these students see themselves relegated
to inferior and marginal classes within a White school, they also begin to believe that some courses are racially defined and off limits to them. Even in
schools where some minorities are admitted to advanced or honors courses,
they tend to decline or eventually drop out of them since acceptance to these
classes might isolate them from their peers. These courses are perceived to be
the domain of White students and in spite of their parents' encouragement to
do well, they are held back from doing so because the peer group with whom
they identify may have a stronger influence on them (Noguera and Akom,
2000).

Without a doubt, the research literature suggests an association between
race and achievement. But race is clearly not the only factor that may affect
achievement. Once again, the issue is that race is associated with so many
other variables that are also related to academic outcomes that it becomes difficult to assess how much of the influence on achievement is due to race and
how much is due to other factors (family background, attitudes, motivation,
SES). Clearly, as members of the larger social class system, the educational
opportunities and life-chances of students accrue according to their position
in the stratification system. Certain ascriptive characteristics including race,
class and gender, which help to define a person's exact location in the social
system, can impact educational opportunity and career trajectory. In turn,
early educational opportunities can have a significant impact on whether or
not they will be successful in school and later life. But even one's position in

the social structure cannot guarantee or always predict who will be an achiever or who will fail. Each year many disadvantaged students succeed in spite of their position in the social structure. What might be important for us to understand is how these students develop an image of who they are and what they are capable of accomplishing academically. In other words, what influences their self-concept?

One interesting factor that has only been considered marginally is the issue of perception and self-image and how school policies and practices impact on this important variable. Macro sociological research allows us to understand how some students may be placed at risk in the educational process because of race, gender and class. It describes the problems inherent in unequal funding, inadequate schools, and lack of social and cultural capital. But it fails to explain the vast number of students who overcome these handicaps and succeed. Clearly these risks do not always translate into academic failure.

A more comprehensive explanation is offered when we examine micro sociological analysis. Interactionist theory rests on the assumption that humans act and react to the subjective interpretation of how they view the world. It suggests that this interpretation is a never ending process which is constructed each day through our interactions with others. Students and teachers are no different than other human beings. They socially construct reality by their daily encounters and interactions with others. They, too, have preconceived notions of how "achievers" look and speak; how they dress and where they are located within the social structure. Acting on their intrepations of these cues, they treat and react differently to students via their body language, gestures and comments. In turn, students "pick up" these cues and begin to construct a self-concept of who they are as individuals and what they are capable of achieving as students. As time goes on, this self-concept is strengthened by the symbolic interaction occurring each day in the classroom and the expectations that teachers consciously or unconsciously communicate to them. Thus by examining the day-to-day interactions of teachers and students, we have a better appreciation of how social structure may affect academic achievement. We also begin to understand how educational processes like teacher expectations, testing, and classroom interactions can enhance or harm student self-concept and contribute to a self-fulfilling prophesy of success or failure. The process by which this social construction occurs is described in Chapter 6. Another family characteristic which may be related to a child's school success is religion.

Religion and Academic Achievement

Ever since the publication of Max Weber's *Protestant Ethic and the Spirit of Capitalism* (1930), sociologists have expressed interest in the influence of religion on achievement and motivation. More recently, a number of polls and surveys suggest that American teenagers are still fairly religious. Over 75 percent of adolescents between the ages of thirteen and seventeen report that they believe in a personal God; while 30 percent of all high school seniors indicate that religion is "very important" to them (Donahue and Benson, 1995). While it is true that polls alone cannot provide a clear picture of how involved they are in the practice of religion, it may be reasonable to believe that since religion plays a part in their lives that it may also influence their academic achievement.

An impressive array of studies attempts to explain the influence of religion on achievement and career trajectory. Weber's research was among the first to suggest that religious values have the ability to influence the believers' views of the world and the extent to which they are concerned with achieving economic success. The Weberian thesis stressed the value of hard work and supported the contention that prudence in this area would gain God's favor in the form of worldly success. Some years later, interest in the relationship between religion and achievement was once again heightened by the publication of Gerard Lenski's *Religious Factor* (1961). This controversial work faulted what it termed Roman Catholic authoritarianism and anti-intellectualism for the poor educational outcomes among Catholics. Obviously, the lag in achievement by Catholics has all but disappeared in the past few decades and some research has also highlighted the recent success of Catholic schools in promoting achievement among its students (Parcel and Dufur, 2001).

More recently, social researchers have speculated about the role religion plays in affecting motivation and worldly success especially among disadvantaged populations. Religious affiliation and involvement are prime socialization forces, second only to the family. Some suggest that religion, especially church attendance, constitutes a form of social integration that serves to support and maintain values that are conducive to goal-setting and achievement (Regnerus and Elder, 2003). This may be especially true for youth in high poverty areas since religion may provide a functional community and everyday direction in the midst of disorganization. Clearly, religion encourages support for family values, parental support networks and societal norms (Regnerus, 2000). Religion also shapes parenting behavior, thus, it begins to have an important impact at birth. It affects beliefs, behavior, and attitudes, all of which are closely related to educational achievement and attainment (Wallace and Williams, 1997). But the question remains, does religious affiliation (sect or denomination) and religious involvement (church attendance) have anything to do with achievement and attainment?

Some evidence for a positive relationship between religion and achievement exists and recent studies have uncovered that religious involvement generally affects education positively. In one study, regular church attendance has been credited as the second strongest influence on the decision to attend regular after-school study sessions among a group of Vietnamese adolescent students in a study conducted by Bankston and Zhou (1996). Controlling for competing variables, church attendance remained positively correlated with students' grades and the desire to attend college. These researchers also related church attendance at this ethnic church to more positive feelings about the future and increasing the sense of ethnic cohesion among immigrant members.

In another interesting study, Regnerus and Elder (2003) explored the overall impact of religion on educational achievement and concluded that participation in religious activities helped to develop higher educational expectations among disadvantaged tenth graders attending public schools. Students who identified themselves as "religious" also secured higher grades on standardized math and reading exams, even after other predictors of academic success were held constant. Here again, the researchers argued that religious involvement created a level of social control and strong motivation for education. Regnerus and Elder also explored the possibility that religious involvement assisted disadvantaged youth to remain in school. Utilizing data from the national longitudinal survey, the researchers were able to determine that church attendance contributed to achievement and school retention. As the neighborhood rates of unemployment, poverty and female-head of households increased, the relationship between youths' church attendance and academic progress became more beneficial. In fact, not only did Church affiliation stimulate the achievement of at-risk students, it also improved test scores among some of the brightest students as well (Regnerus and Elder, 2003).

A positive association between religion and achievement was also uncovered in a study by Muller and Ellison. Employing data from the National Longitudinal Study, Muller and Ellison found that religious involvement was a prime factor in positive academic achievement. These researchers employed attendance at church services and perception of oneself as "religious" or "non-religious" as measures of religious involvement. The research uncovered that religion became a form of social capital to students in the community which indirectly translated into improved academic achievement. Students attending church services regularly and considering themselves "religious" also reported greater parental expectations for their academic success. Additionally, they also held more positive expectations for their own academic success, more so, than students who did not attend church or consider themselves to be religious (Muller and Ellison, 2001).

Some research has also explored the impact of religious cultural orientation (denomination) on academic achievement and attainment. In his research, David McClelland finds that Protestant parents set earlier standards of independence for their children. In turn, he argues that having to make decisions at an earlier age contributes to the development of higher achievement motivation among children (McClelland et al., 1955). In another interesting study, Darnell and Sherkat also examined the role played by denomination on achievement and attainment. Using data from the Youth Parent Socialization Panel Study, the authors conclude that fundamentalist beliefs combined with conservative Protestant affiliation had a significant and substantial negative impact on educational achievement and attainment. Youth in the study who held these fundamentalist beliefs were less likely to have taken college-prep courses and reported lower educational aspirations for themselves. The authors also suggest that the fundamentalist (literal translation) tradition of their parents contributed to their rejection of college prep-courses. A similar association between fundamentalism and achievement was uncovered by Parcel and Geschwender (1995).

The impact of religion on achievement seems also to be supported in the research of Keysay and Kosmin (1995). These researchers studied educational attainment among American women in twelve different religious groups. Almost 75 percent of Jewish women and 25 percent of Protestant Pentecostals embarked on higher education. Baptists and Pentecostals fared worst in achieving a college education while Methodists, Episcopalians, and Jews fared the best.

It is possible that the cultural orientation of some religious denominations may actually conflict with the academic goals of society. Contingent on the degree to which participants in these religious denominations subscribe to their respective beliefs, many may approach education with disinterest and or distrust which may also explain their lower achievement or attainment rating.

Some research has also documented the indirect effects that religion may have on academic achievement. Students attending religious schools tend to demonstrate a higher level of achievement than their peers in public institutions. This is especially true in low SES areas (Neal, 1998). It is likely that the social capital that is derived from participating in a religious school where parents, teachers and administrators share similar values and may even participate in the same church services may enhance the achievement of children. It is likely that this bond and communication between parents, teachers and schools may enhance educational outcomes.

On the other hand, some suggest that strong family values and not just religion have a dramatic impact on student academic performance. Examining the experiences and attitudes of Indochinese families, some researchers conclude that previous studies may have overestimated the role that religion plays in encouraging values and attitudes that foster positive academic achievement. They suggest that strong values and positive attitudes of parents towards education also seem to improve the child's academic performance (Mitrsomwang, Suparvadee, & Hawley, 1993).

In addition to the ascribed family characteristics which we have already examined, family composition, that is, its configuration (structure) and size may also have a strong impact on academic achievement.

Family Composition

When we speak of family composition we refer to the configuration and size of the family. Several researchers have suggested a relationship between these variables and academic achievement.

Family Configuration (Structure)

During the past two decades, educational sociologists have increasingly turned their attention to the changing structure of the family and the effect of this change on student behavior and achievement (Jeynes, 2002, 2005; Raley, Frisco and Wildsmith, 2005; Wallerstein and Lewis, 1998). In the past, the traditional family consisted of father, mother and siblings with the father as head of household. For the most part, heterosexuality was assumed and a division of labor based on gender roles were taken for granted. The mother was entrusted with supervising the children and the father's attention was primarily focused on work and career. The contemporary U.S. family has recently undergone a vast transformation and researchers argue that this will eventually result in significant changes for children. The traditional family no longer exists and one of the most notable changes in family structure has been the increase in one-parent families.

Single or one-parent families are defined as those in which one adult, most often the mother, bears responsibility for raising the children. The number of one-parent homes in America has increased dramatically in the past three decades and approximately 27 percent of all U.S. households are now single-parent homes (Bianchi and Casper, 2001). The astounding reality is that 50 percent of all U.S. children live in a single-parent home before age eighteen. Research has also associated family structure with income, race and ethnicity. Fifty-four percent of Black and 27 percent of Hispanic children reside with only one parent as compared to 15 percent of White children (Lee and Burkam, 2002). A number of social and cultural trends have contributed to this fact of life including the increasing divorce rate and the greater number of births to unmarried women. The situation has also been compounded by the significant proportion of unmarried teens having and raising their children. Unlike past generations, these teens are much less likely to marry and regardless of race, unmarried teen mothers are the most economically vulnerable and educationally disadvantaged group in the nation.

Single Parent Households and Academic Achievement

Researchers have uncovered that coming from a single-parent household is associated with lower academic achievement even when race and SES are considered (Amato and Keith, 1991; Zill, 1996). Dozens of studies have concluded that children who grow up in single-parent households are much less likely to complete high school or attend college. Consequently, these children more often drop out of school, have criminal records and ultimately become divorced themselves (Menaghan, 1997). Hetherinton, Camara and Featherman (1983) found that children from one-parent households scored lower in achievement exams than did children from two-parent households and that the overall difference was about one school year. The research of Thompson, Alexander and Entwisle (1988) likewise concludes that children from one-parent families achieved lower scores on verbal and quantitative tests, and this was especially true among Black children.

Research employing the High School and Beyond data also reveals that students from one-parent households have significantly lower grades than students from two-parent families. One-parent household students have test scores that are .30 SD (standard deviations) lower, but this finding is explained by differentials of race and ethnicity as well as the educational level of the parents. When controls are applied for race and educational level of the parent, the effect of parental absence is reduced to .13SD (Mulkey, Crain and Harrington, 1992). While having a small but negative impact on academics, Mulkey et al. suggest that the impact on grades results less from the household's lack of resources than from the apparent problems arising in attempting to manage and control the children. But what is it about coming from a single-family home that almost always seems to deflate student achievement?

One interesting explanation, referred to as the Pathology of Matriarchy theory was first articulated by Patrick Moynihan (1965). This theory argued that father absence in a family was destructive to children, especially boys. Father absence relegates the family to economic hardships and a void in discipline and guidance that only a father can provide. While the Pathology of Matriarchy perspective has been considerably modified in recent years, research continues to reveal that single-mother families have lower achievement rates than children from two-parent families (McLanahan and Sandefur, 1994).

Other researchers have attempted to explain lower achievement on the part of children from single-family homes in different ways. Some research suggests that single-family homes lack a social environment which is conducive to the development of proper social development and an emotional stability required for academic success. The children emerging from these homes are harmed by psychological stress and a socialization process that is incomplete, even in affluent one-parent households. Students who are born into one-parent homes are disadvantaged on several counts. These children are late for school twice as often as those from homes with two parents and are more often classified by their teachers as possessing poor classroom conduct. By contrast, those from two-family homes are more often rated by their teachers as being cooperative, interested in the school and having a higher attention span (Thompson, 1988).

Evidence over the past few decades suggests that children raised in single-parent households generally have lower average levels of psychological well-being and socio-economic achievement than those raised when two parents are present. This research views the emerging difficulties in these homes as being more emotional and the function of managing behavior in one-parent households to be more difficult (Amato and Booth 1997; McLanahan and Sandafer, 1994). Several other researchers have concluded that children from one-parent households may have more behavioral problems than those raised in two-parent households (Deslandes et al. 1997; Sarcona-Navarra, 2007). Understandably, the absence of one parent may have a negative effect on the child's socialization and reduce the family's ability to provide optimal amounts of time, supervision, and direction. For one thing, two parent families can do significantly more parenting. They can exert more pressure, provide greater assistance, and monitor their children's activities more closely. Clearly, economic resources may also be more vulnerable in single-parent homes and family economic standing has been found to affect achievement gains of children in the early elementary years (Entwisle and Alexander, 1996).

Most researchers also agree that family structure has a controlling impact on school success because it almost always places restrictions on the amount of time that parents can spend with their children (Crane, 1996). Single-parents are often less likely to assist with homework and school projects. Children of parents who are more involved with the education of their children are more likely to achieve better grades for academic subjects and conduct. It is also likely that family structure helps to determine the nature and extent of parents' involvement with their children's education. It is not difficult to understand how two parents may have a greater impact on child development than one.

On the other hand, some suggest that it is unfair to categorize all one-parent homes as dysfunctional and before considering the impact on academic achievement, some clarification is required about the differences in one-parent households. For this purpose, we have divided single parent households into three categories: families headed by widowed mothers, mothers who have never been married and mothers who are divorced. At the beginning of the twentieth century, most single parent homes were headed by mothers who had experienced the death of a spouse. Beginning with the 1960s, divorced parents began to equal in number those of widowed families. Today, about half are divorced or separated while a second category consists of those who have never been married. Research has especially underscored the problems arising in homes where the mother has never been married.

One Parent Households: Mothers Who Have Never Married

For the most part, single-parent families consisting of mothers who have never been married are most often headed by women living in poverty. Their economic vulnerability takes an enormous toll on the resources that they can provide for their children. In fact, most of these women lack a formal education and few have any marketable skills. Without a doubt, children of mothers who have never been married are the most economically vulnerable. Their median family income ($14,800) is about two-thirds that of divorced families. These mothers are more likely to have given birth as teens when compared with mothers from divorced or separated families. Mothers in these families also have lower educational levels and it is likely that childbirth may have had an impact on their ability to attend school. They spend less time than divorced mothers interacting with their children (Entwisle, 1997) and it is likely that they are not able to provide a stimulating home environment which facilitates the academic development of their children. Children of mothers who have never been married are also the most educationally disadvantaged. They consistently receive lower grades in reading and math and are most often retained in the early elementary years of school. Teacher evaluations of these studens also suggest that they are regularly late or absent from class. Clearly, this suggests the absence of supervision on the part of the parent. Absences and lateness's often reflect a negative attitude towards school as well as ambivalence towards learning.

Widowed and Divorced: One Parent Households

Do single-parent families produced by divorce have more negative overtones for children than single-parent households resulting from death? Is it likely that widows with dependent children have more handicaps than divorced mothers?

Research suggests that divorced single-mothers participate more often in the paid workforce, hold lower occupational positions and report being financially stressed more often then their widowed counterparts. Accordingly, research also uncovers that children raised in single-family homes created by death have higher levels of education and occupational status when they reach adulthood. In fact, children emerging from single-family divorced homes have greater odds of never completing high school, less of a chance of graduating with a college degree and a lower average occupational status in adulthood (Biblarz and Gottainer 2000). Speculation surrounding this differential outcome is based on a marital conflict model. This model suggests that divorced parents are more likely to have had bitter conflicts prior to any separation which may have caused troubling short and long term consequences for children. In turn, this distress is often associated with a negative impact on self-esteem and educational attainment (Amato and Booth 1997). It is also likely that when parents move away from their families, children are left with bitter memories and a sense of abandonment. However, when separation is due to death, children more often develop warm feelings for their deceased parents and grow closer to the surviving parent. Still another family background characteristic that may have bearing on academic achievement is family size.

Family Size

As educational sociologists become increasingly aware of the role that family plays in the academic success of its children, some researchers have attempted to determine if family size is related to academic success. Specifically, efforts have been focused on uncovering a relationship between family size and student achievement.

There seems to be some agreement among some researchers that increasing the size of the family (sibship size) creates a negative impact on students' academic achievement, even when cultural and socioeconomic background variables are controlled. Those who adhere to this view suggest that smaller families produce a higher quality of student. They argue that there is no family size that is *too small* for the production of quality. In fact, they point to study after study of "only-children" who are usually classified as gifted. Some even go as far to suggest that the shrinking achievement gap between black and whites during the 1980s was a direct result of a smaller Black family.

What is the position of large scale research on this subject? Studies conducted in England, France, and Scotland conclude that, even when social class levels are held constant, an inverse relationship exists between sibship size (the number of children in the family) and several measures of ability as measured by test scores and educational attainment (Marjoribanks, 1974; Institut National d'Etudes Demographiques, 1973; The Scottish Council for Research in Education, 1949). A considerable number of smaller and more recent studies have also uncovered a negative statistical relationship between family size and a child's intellectual development. In other words, theories of family size-effect suggest that children from smaller families are generally more successful academically than students from larger families (Blake, 1989; Downey, 1995; Powell and Steelman, 1993). How is this relationship explained?

The Resource Dilution Model

In order to explain the relationship between family size and achievement, researchers have alluded to what they call a *Resource Dilution Model*. This model suggests that larger families will have less in the way of resources to devote to their children and as a result, the child's intellectual development will suffer. In other words, the more children in the family, the more the family resources will be diluted and hence, the lower the quality of the output. Family resources generally include material objects like books, newspapers, computers, music, etc., as well as the opportunity for parents and children to do things together.

But not all research supports this position. Some researchers conclude that while this inverse relationship exists, it may be more spurious than originally believed and when ethnicity and SES are controlled properly, the relationship is significantly moderated (Page and Grandon, 1979; Walberg and Marjoribanks, 1976). Additionally, Guo and VanWey (1999) found that coming from a smaller family had only a small impact on achievement. It had little impact on verbal ability and larger families may even have a positive effect on math skills. So what is the reader to conclude from these apparently contradictory findings? Is the Resource Dilution theory wrong?

Phillips (1999) suggests that additional children in larger families may dilute some of the resources that affect achievement—but that they may also enhance other resources that offset the possible negative consequences of a large family. Larger families have more people to turn to for social support, they may have older siblings that can assist with schoolwork, and children within these families may also be taught better time-management skills due to their increased responsibilities.

What we can conclude from the studies on sibship size is that its importance rests on how it affects other intervening variables—the child's ability, the child's perception of parental encouragement, and the cultural and physical advantages of the home environment. The intellectual environment and value system of the home also represent important factors. Parents who opt to bring fewer children into the world may have value systems which are quite different than couples who choose to have many offspring. It is also quite possible that parents who choose to have smaller families place a greater value on academic accomplishments. Since family size alone is not the only and actual cause of intellectual development, limiting family size may not necessarily result in a higher quality of children. To sum it up! It is likely that family size can have an impact on the academic development of children but clearly, this impact can be modified by other variables including family income and the degree of involvement parents have with their children. Recently, research has also focused on the role that parental involvement may play in the academic achievement of children.

PARENTAL INVOLVEMENT AND ACADEMIC ACHIEVEMENT

Parental involvement refers to the role parents play in the education of their children. The involvement may take on several forms: communicating frequently with teachers, attending school meetings, volunteering or merely assisting the child with homework. A growing body of research indicates that parental involvement impacts positively on student academic achievement (Epstein and Saunders, 2002; Hill and Taylor, 2004). At the elementary level, the results are quite conclusive. When families are involved in the education of their children, their children actually do better in school, regardless of the type of involvement that is expressed. At the same time, when parents are concerned and involved, the achievement and attainment level of their children increases and the schools they attend become better educational institutions.

During the past decade, researchers have examined the degree to which parents are involved with their children's education and how this involvement may affect academic outcomes. As organized efforts of school districts to engage parents in the education of their children has increased dramatically, so has the body of research attempting to document the impact of this involvement. For the most part, the research has concluded that involvement by parents has a positive effect on academic achievement and some learning variables associated with high achievement including self-esteem, behavior, attitude towards school, and attendance (Epstein et al., 1997; Ford and Amaral, 2006; Miedel and Reynolds, 1999; Jeynes, 2005). Research has also concluded that parental involvement is associated with higher levels of student academic achievement regardless of family income, the grade level or the location of the school (Phillips et al., 1985).

When parents become involved in the education of their children it is likely that they, too, begin to develop more positive attitudes about schools, administrators and teachers. It is also likely that the increased involvement enables parents to develop a greater sense of self-confidence and participate more actively in community affairs. Additionally, research points out that involved parents become more satisfied with schools and hold teachers in higher regard. These parents also report an increased desire to assist their children with home assignments (Dauber and Epstein, 1993).

Hara (1998) concludes that increasing the amount of parental involvement is the most important factor in improving achievement. In fact, it appears that the more schools assume a partnership with families, the more successful the school becomes in raising the overall achievement of all of its students (Carey, Lewis, Farris, 1998). Involvement facilitates positive academic experiences for children and also has a positive impact on parenting-skills. However, the relationship between involvement and achievement may not always be a direct one. Ford and Amaral (2006) conclude that parental involvement significantly contributes to other variables which are also highly correlated with strong academic outcomes like better student attendance, lower withdrawal rates and improved student attitudes.

Increasing family involvement has become an item of importance in most school districts throughout the United States. A comprehensive study undertaken by the Southwest Educational Development Laboratory (2002) concludes that students with parents who are involved in their education are more likely to earn higher grades, attend school regularly, have better social skills, enroll in more advanced classes, graduate, and eventually enter post-secondary education. Studies suggest that families from all social classes are involved with the education of their children to some extent. However, white middle-class families are often more involved at school and better informed about specific ways to assist their children. Since involvement benefits all children, encouraging more parental involvement from low income families may be an important strategy for addressing the achievement gap. To this end, a major position paper, Turning Points: Preparing American Youth for the 21st Century underscored the importance of involvement by suggesting the reengagement of families in the education of their children and, more recently, No Child Left Behind (NCLB) has made greater parental involvement a national imperative (NCLB, 2001). Clearly, there is a consensus among researchers that we must increase parents' involvement in the education of their children if we are to improve achievement and attainment levels (Baker and Sodden, 1997). But what types of involvement seem to produce the most positive results?

Types of Parental Involvement

Ballantine (1999) suggests that the term parental involvement is vague and that it denotes many different types of behavior. As research in this area continues to increase, researchers have attempted to operationalize this term in a

number of different ways. Some view involvement as holding positive expectations for a child's academic progress or supervising homework assignments. Others believe that involvement refers to parental participation in
school activities (volunteering) or communicating with teachers. Some have
even attempted to construct a composite of two or more of these factors in order to develop an index of involvement while others have employed a single
measure (Griffith, 1996). The overall value of these studies has been to underscore the merits to achievement when parents are involved. While each of
these activities has been associated with positive academic outcomes, it
would be advantageous to determine what specific type of involvement has
the greatest impact on school achievement. Clearly, it may not be unreasonable to suggest that certain types of parental involvement especially those in-
volving positive expectations and ongoing contact with teachers may have a
more positive impact on the academic outcomes of students.

As researchers continue to highlight the positive impact of parental involvement on student achievement, school districts throughout the country
have attempted to develop new relationships between students, parents and
teachers. In fact, one Collier County School District in Florida allows its parents to follow their children into the classroom via one of a number of web-
based programs. Power-book, Parent Connect and Power School permit parents to gain instant and unprecedented access to their children's assignments,
grades, lateness, and discipline records. Armed with a computer and a pass-
word, parents have the ability to monitor their child's grades and behavior
anytime during the day or night. These programs are presently available for
students in grades 6 through 12. While some see this new technology as an
advantage, others argue that it may be perceived as an intrusive form of surveillance. High school students, especially, should begin to assume responsibility for their own performance.

While many single parents are involved in the education of their children, time constraints may make it difficult for them to offer the same
availability to schools that may be offered by two-parent families. If certain types of involvement were proven to be more effective than others,
this knowledge might be used effectively by them in improving the
achievement of their children. For example, holding high expectations for
their children's success and verbalizing this expectation to them might produce more significant gains than attending every PTA meeting or school
function. However, for the present, research uncovers that all types of involvement, direct and indirect, have some positive impact on school
achievement. In sum, parental involvement encourages students' attendance (Cotton and Wikelund, 2001), improves achievement (Epstein and
Sheldon 2001), promotes positive behavior on the part of students (Cotton

and Wikelund, 2001; Brooks, Bruno and Burns, 1997) enhances reading (Jeynes, 2005) and mathematics scores (Muller, 1998). Additionally, the impact of parental involvement is so pervasive that it holds across all levels of parental education and ethnicity (Villas-Boas, 1998).

The bottom line is that almost any type of involvement facilitates academic success. It is likely that this positive outcome is derived from the increased social control it exerts on children as well as the overall increase in general awareness that it provides parents. Parental involvement increases social control over children's behavior and conduct in school. Parents who are involved with the school are able to work with teachers in determining the appropriate behavior for their children in school. More importantly, they are also better able to communicate this behavior to their children. This consensus often eliminates the possibility of classroom problems. Secondly, it is also likely that parental involvement increases parents' skills and information about the school. It helps them to learn about school policies and expectations. When parents are involved with the school, they become more aware of the daily problems that teachers and students face and how to find appropriate solutions to these problems. This information is often communicated to their children, which may provide them with a competitive edge in the classroom. It is also likely that teachers think more highly of parents who take an active part in the education of their children. They respect parents who are willing to volunteer in school, tutor students, serve on committees and maintain contact with the school administration. Conversely, teachers begin to develop higher expectations for students whose families are involved and collaborate with them. Finally, parental involvement in schooling is equally powerful whether the involvement takes place at home or within the school. It is likely that many potential problems fade when students recognize an alliance between their parents and the school. A positive connection between parents and the school provides a signal to the student that both have similar expectations and hopes for his/her academic achievement.

Putting the Pieces Together: The Impact of Family on Achievement

A major theme of this chapter has been that families make a critical contribution to the development of student academic achievement. This contribution begins at birth and extends well into the college years. The family is also the most accurate predictor of a child's future success in school and when families support the efforts of schools, appreciable strides in achievement and attainment are possible. While social class is often associated with achievement, research reveals that families providing a nurturing home environment filled with experiences that encourage and stimulate intellectual development provide a sound base for learning. The family can also encourage intellectual development by holding and expressing high expectations for their children's success. Additionally, attempts to increase academic achievement or attainment are significantly enhanced when the family is involved in the education of its children.

Understanding the total impact of family characteristics on intellectual development is a complicated puzzle. This chapter has attempted to fill in some of the pieces. The existing research suggests that the social characteristics of the child's family may have a significant impact on school success. Children of parents who are outside the social and cultural mainstream, those who are poor or belong to a racial minority, and have difficulty "passing on" social and cultural capital may have greater difficulty in achieving success. Without a doubt, socioeconomic status, race and ethnicity have the greatest impact on achievement and career trajectory. But as we have seen, the relationship between each of these variables, especially socioeconomic status and academic achievement, is quite complex. Additionally, more research is needed to identify those features of the family environment which enable socioeconomic status to have an impact on cognitive development and achievement in school. It is likely that several variables that are often also related to income come to play in this relationship. Our estimation is that some of these definitely include the articulated expectations of parents for the academic success of their children, the quantity and quality of verbal interactions between parents and children at an early age, discipline and social control strategies employed by the family and finally, the amount of parental involvement in the education of their children.

The contemporary research also cites the importance of family structure on school success and underscores how children raised in two-parent homes are generally better equipped to meet the demands and challenges of the classroom. In all fairness, we must also concede that there are many types of single-family homes and that some may be better than others in facilitating school success. Research has especially underscored the difficulties emerging in one parent homes where the parent has never been married.

However, simply put, two parents are usually better than one. Several studies also attribute academic deficit to lower economic resources, lower expectations and less involvement by parents in the academic life of their children (Alexander and Entwisle, 1996).

The presence of religion may also have a mediating effect on achievement. If the religion does not view education as threatening, its presence may support parental and societal values thereby having an indirect but positive impact on academic achievement. Religion may also provide a certain type of social capital to students thereby increasing the bond between members of a community which can likely affect social control and achievement in a positive manner.

Finally, we must also think about the impact of teacher and parental expectations on academic achievement. Is it likely that middle-class teachers hold more negative views of students coming from single-family homes? Are their expectations for these students different from students of widowed or broken homes? Clearly, we need additional research in this area. The power of teachers' perceptions can be relatively salient. On the other hand, do the expectations of parents from each of these family configurations differ and is it, in fact, the parental expectations that mediate academic success or failure? Parents who expect their children to do well in school may be more likely to engage in certain activities that indirectly affect achievement like buying more books and reading more to their children. They may be more attentive to their everyday questions and invest more time in their education. Each of these practices is itself associated with increased achievement. These types of activities are certainly available to parents of both low and high income but here the mediating factor becomes the parental expectations for academic success. But the family is only one component of the achievement puzzle. In the next chapter, we consider the impact of the school, its educational structures and policies, in facilitating student success or failure.

Part IV

THE ROLE OF THE SCHOOL

Chapter Four

Exploring Unequal Achievement: Differences Between Schools

Humanly speaking, schools make the difference between men.

Ralph Waldo Emerson

While some researchers have focused on the role of families in the development of student achievement; others have examined the function of schools in this process. In fact, the issue of "school effects" both *between* and *within* schools remains significant in educational sociology. School characteristics have always been a favorite discussion point for researchers exploring unequal achievement and most Americans continue to associate student achievement with school quality.

This chapter focuses on differences *between* schools and how these differences contribute to unequal achievement. I begin by discussing America's fundamental belief in schooling and consider some of the contemporary challenges to this belief. Next, I explore the issue of school funding and the relative impact of attending a private or public school. I also examine some contextual issues (those characteristics that give meaning to the school and contribute to its uniqueness) including the relative size, racial and social class composition of the school. Finally, I explore the impact of single-gender schools on achievement. The overriding assumption is that schools *do* make a difference and that differences between schools may be related to educational outcomes.

THE FUNDAMENTAL BELIEF IN AMERICAN SCHOOLING

Schooling in America has often been extolled and identified as an avenue of upward mobility. For Americans, schools embody the meritocratic society. They are places where social inequalities are equalized. Free access and excellence in education has been supported not only by our historic belief that education is valuable in and of itself but also by our commitment since the nineteenth century to education as the surest path to economic and social equality. For many Americans, the degree of equity and access to education is viewed as the nation's commitment to equal opportunity and social mobility. For decades educational sociologists have focused on the extent to which these variables are available to the most disadvantaged groups in the society. Limited access to education is viewed as a means of maintaining a caste-like system of stratification and a mechanism by which the rich maintain their privileged position. Karl Marx was among the first to call for universal and free public education. He believed that free universal education could break the strangle-hold that the advantaged held over the masses (Marx and Engels, 1844). Yet, it was not until the industrial revolution and the beginnings of urbanization in the United States, that schooling for the general population became a reality. Today, all Americans support the ideals of equity, excellence and access to education and most believe that school quality contributes to student academic achievement. But the unspoken reality is that unequal access to *quality* schooling remains pervasive and that *"savage inequalities"* between schools facilitate academic success for some and failure for others.

THE CHALLENGE TO EXCELLENCE AND ACCESS

The hushed assumption that American education was neither equal nor excellent gained momentum on April 26, 1983, with the publication of a Presidential report, *A Nation at Risk*. The report warned of a rising tide of mediocrity in American education (National Commission on Excellence in Education, 1983). In support of its bleak outlook for the future of education in the United States, the report cited falling test scores, the poor performance of American students on international exams and the fact that over 90 million Americans lacked functional literacy—the ability to read, write or do very basic math. Almost twenty years later, a study conducted by the United States Department of Education, The Condition of Education, 2001, reaffirmed the findings of this national commission and underscored disturbing gaps in educational access among different racial and socioeconomic groups in the United States (U.S. Department of Education, 2001). In short, many Americans were not receiving a quality education. Again in 2003, the Koret Task Force Report, formulated by Stanford University's Hoover Institute, reaffirmed these findings and pointed to the serious lack of progress in the area of educational reform especially among the disadvantaged (Koret Task Force, 2003).

What is most troubling about these reports is that they challenged the American belief in equity and access to quality education. While access to some form of educational experience is available to most Americans, educational outcomes vary dramatically for students attending different schools. The challenge to equity and access rests in providing a quality education to *all* students; one which ensures equality of outcomes.

Why Does This Disparity Exist?

Schools in America generally serve their surrounding neighborhoods and are supported by a system of *ad valorem property taxes*. American neighborhoods are relatively homogeneous with regard to race and class and homes are taxed according to their assessed valuation. Lower class areas with lower property values have significantly less tax revenues to spend on schools, teachers and programs. Accordingly, the end result is a form of *de facto segregation* which often results in a less-than-excellent educational experience for disadvantaged children attending schools in poor neighborhoods.

As a result of this disturbing reality, the most successful students are either White or Asian; while African-American and Hispanics lag behind (Tedin and Weiher, 2004). In 2004, almost 85 percent of European Americans over the age of twenty-five graduated from high school compared to 76 percent of African Americans. The 57 percent graduation rate of Hispanic Americans and the 50 percent of Mexican Americans in 2002 mirrors a much less successful attempt at education for these groups (U.S. Bureau of the Census, 2004). Research suggests that the continuing failure of Hispanics in this area is explained by their overall lower class status as well as the significantly different cultural background they bring to school (Jasinski, 2000).

Beyond the elementary and secondary school level, unequal access to higher education is a disturbing fact of life. Research reveals that first generation students who do not excel in high school are less likely to complete or even attempt a college degree. On the other hand, students from more advantaged social classes who have at least one parent with a college degree are most likely to pursue college admission (United States Department of Education, 2001). In spite of the many incentive programs, parental education and family income continue to be significant variables in predicting access to college (Duncan et al., 1998; Rouse, 2004).

Since the early part of the twentieth century, American schools have also served as sorting mechanism for the best careers and status positions within society. Those who live in prestige neighborhoods and attend the *best* public schools or those who can afford the tuition of private elite schools often gain the most preferred jobs. In so doing, schooling plays an important role in perpetuating social inequality (Persell, 1992). By awarding educational credentials in the form of diplomas and college degrees, schools validate the American commitment to educational opportunity for all without assuring *equal outcomes or results*. It is also true that a number of veiled criteria remain in place, whether intended or not, that serve to eventually limit equity and access. These also sort the advantaged from the disadvantaged for positions of unequal status in society. One such mechanism to equity and access, embedded in the culture and socialization process of each school, is the hidden curriculum. This unofficial curriculum sanctions the success of the advantaged and "cools out" the ambitious desires of the less-well-to-do.

The Hidden Curriculum

In addition to the overt curriculum which defines the educational experience of all students in a school, sociologists agree on the presence of a curriculum that consists of a set of unwritten rules and behavior patterns that are learned indirectly but are an implicit part of each student's socialization in school. These unwritten rules include such things as conformity to the cultural norms and expectations of dominant groups in society. This *hidden curriculum* consists of the implicit messages that are communicated informally from teachers to students, about the acceptable behavior and differential power structure within the school. It includes the relative worth of each student and represents a body of values that cannot be found in textbooks. Yet, these rules help to define and create the behavior and attitude of students attending these different schools.

The implicit lessons of this curriculum teach children that their role in life is to "know their place." The hidden curriculum stresses the unquestioning acceptance of the existing social order and teaches latent functions of discipline, sobriety, and respect for authority. Embedded in the culture of the school itself, the values and work habits it suggests to students vary with their social class. Students attending schools in lower socio-economic areas are taught to be loyal and to support the business elite. Within these schools, street language is permitted and not often corrected. On the other hand, advantaged students attending middle-class schools are encouraged to assume leadership roles. Teachers in these schools place great importance on speech, correct grammar and Standard English since the perception about these children is that they will one day be expected to run the nation's corporations.

Conflict theorists assert that the hidden curriculum legitimates inequality, justifies unequal spending and provides a rationale for segments of society to accept low-paying careers. They argue that it is concerned not only with social class but may be sexist and Eurocentric. The hidden curriculum perpetuates gender roles through a male dominated curriculum that utilizes sexist texts which reinforce sexual inequality. Proponents of this view also argue that, until recently, the conspicuous absence of formal curriculum relating to the role of women or minorities in American history presents students with a clear picture of what society considers important. By highlighting the contributions of Americans of European descent and promoting Eurocentrism, the curriculum presents students with an implicit message about what events are valued. Very obviously, children who study the history and accomplishments of white European males begin to assume for themselves who and what is important in this society. The gender component of the hidden curriculum is likewise asserted through everyday interaction in the schools. While boys are requested to help with the heavy work; girls are often asked to clean or decorate the room. Similar in principle to the hidden curriculum is the concept of the Correspondence Principle, which also poses a challenge to Equity and Access in American education.

The Correspondence Principle

The term, *Correspondence Principle*, is employed by Samuel Bowles and Herbert Gintis (1976), two avid proponents of the Conflict/Neo-Marxist perspective, to refer to the various ways that schooling corresponds to the social structure of society. A central thesis in their work underscores a correspondence between personality traits that are required in different forms of employment and the personality traits that are taught to different social classes in schools. Different schools mirror the societal expectations of dominant groups for the students within those schools and thereby perpetuate inequality. Thus, according to proponents of the conflict perspective, American schooling promotes capitalism, encourages competition, and extols the values of the dominant class. Its primary function is to create workers who will follow the system, pay attention to rules and perform their respective jobs in a capitalistic system. The school's organizational structure teaches children that the world of work is hierarchal. Disadvantaged students in poor schools are taught to accept authority, cope with evaluation and do a good day's work. Advantaged students are taught to be creative, engage in independent study and take a leadership role (Bourdieu, 1993; Falconer and Byrnes, 2003; Gracey, 1972).

Let us now turn our attention to specific differences between schools and how they may contribute to student achievement.

DIFFERENCES BETWEEN SCHOOLS
AND ACADEMIC ACHIEVEMENT

All Schools are not created equal. They may have quite different characteristics based on whether or not they are endowed abundantly, public or private, segregated or integrated. For the most part, schools serving economically disadvantaged students have fewer resources, face greater challenges in attracting qualified teachers and receive less support from parents. In spite of these challenges, their unique characteristics are important to student outcomes since they help to shape the quality of the learning experience and structure educational opportunity. But, is it possible for these articulated differences between schools to account for quite different learning outcomes?

Clearly, education in America is not monolithic, not all students receive the same type of education. Between-schools research explores the academic impact on students that results from attending different schools. It considers inequality resulting from the unequal distribution of school funding. It explores the academic outcomes of attending a private or public school and focuses on issues of school context—characteristics including school and class size, racial and SES level, gender, and how each may be related to academic achievement. On the other hand, the next chapter discusses within-school differences and is concerned with structures and policies within the *same* school and how these differences may mediate student academic success or failure. One variable that is primarily responsible for many of the differences between schools is funding. Let us begin our discussion of between-school differences with an examination of school funding practices and outcomes.

School Funding

For many Americans, differential school funding is at the very heart of unequal achievement. Consequently, the issue of school funding has remained a constant source of debate and contention for many years. In order to resolve this issue, as early as 1964, the US Congress commissioned a liberally funded study to demonstrate, once and for all, that the embarrassing problem of unequal achievement by students of different social origins was essentially the result of differential funding of the schools. The presumption was that disadvantaged students attended schools that lacked basic learning resources and were taught by less qualified teachers in an atmosphere that lacked academic rigor. In short, the quality of the schools attended by advantaged and disadvantaged students was to blame for the achievement gap between these two social groups. To this end, James Coleman was selected to lead the research effort that would gather "evidence" from over 4000 American schools. His research was expected to create a strong case for the equalization of school resources.

The resulting Equality of Educational Opportunity (EEO) study collected data on a wide range of achievement tests, reading levels and mathematical skills for more than a half-million students. The report uncovered many known but undocumented facts: American students attended schools that were essentially segregated, Black from White. White and Asian students performed better on achievement tests than did Black and Hispanic children. African-American schools and those in disadvantaged neighborhoods had appreciably larger classes and fewer resources (textbooks, playgrounds, computers, audio-visual aids, etc.). Surprisingly, Coleman and his team of researchers concluded that while important, these differences did not significantly explain the problem of differential achievement. Instead, Coleman suggested that the inequalities imposed on these children by their home environment and family background seemed to be the deciding factors.

For many educators and politicians, the surprising conclusions reached by this study ran counter to common-sense beliefs about schools and funding. Eventually, the academic community called upon another sociologist, Christopher Jencks, for a reanalysis of the Coleman data. To the surprise of many, the resulting study *Inequality*, reaffirmed the role of the family in academic achievement and suggested that any reforms in education could only affect a modest impact on social inequality. These controversial conclusions continued to trouble educators for some time and many researchers, to this day, continue to study the effects of school resources on students' academic achievement. Many refused to accept the idea that better equipped schools would not necessarily teach students more than inferior ones.

One of the most passionate rebuttals of Coleman's findings was offered by Jonathan Kozol (1992, 2005), a journalist who studied schools in about thirty American neighborhoods. Kozol was struck by the segregation and gross inequalities he uncovered in American education. His ethnographic research, based on direct observation as a teacher and extensive conversations with teachers and administrators, uncovered a shameful side of American schooling.

The work of Jonathan Kozol demonstrates how social problems within urban cities, combined with differential funding, influence the daily operations of schools. His *Savage Inequality* describes the deteriorated and crime-ridden areas of cities where many low income schools are located. His research paints a depressing picture of the residents who live in these areas, most survive on welfare and struggle for very basic needs. In great detail, he recounts the frustrations of teachers who teach without chalk, textbooks or lab equipment. His research reveals a disparity in funding *between* American schools which permits economically advantaged districts to spend twice as much as poorer districts in art, music, and language programs. He notes that high-income districts have 50 percent more librarians, guidance counselors and psychologists available to their students. On the other hand, schools attended by minority children are often so financially strapped that they lack the ability to maintain a regular teaching staff. Instead, administrators in these schools often resorted to low-paid substitute teachers or replace instruction with study halls. In sharp contrast, he transports his readers to the advantaged schools of Westchester and Nassau County where most students enjoy the advantage of computers, advanced placement courses and the opportunity to study a language of choice. His work questions the absence of a relationship between school funding and educational inequality and provokes both outrage and pity. Clearly, it provides an indictment of the financial disparities that exist between American schools (Kozol, 1992).

The debate over the impact of school funding and academic excellence is far from resolved. More recently, data from the National Assessment of Educational Progress concluded that school spending is at least indirectly related to academic achievement. The availability of more economic resources permits schools to have smaller classes, more experienced teachers and more positive school environments, all of which contribute to overall higher achievement (Wenglinsky, 1997).

The existence of a strong relationship between funding and achievement is also supported by proponents of the Conflict perspective who argue that unequal and inadequate funding seriously hampers minority and economically disadvantaged populations. As noted by Coleman, American schools located in disadvantaged neighborhoods are relatively homogeneous with regard to race, ethnicity, and social class. This veiled type of segregation combined with the current mode of tax assessment contributes to a culture of underachievement in these schools. On the other hand, it enables middle class communities to obtain more experienced teachers, purchase up-to-date equipment and provide a number of culturally enriching subjects to their students, all of which translates to positive academic outcomes. Additionally, the extra advantages which are provided in middle and upper class schools enable students to be better prepared for high schools and "status" colleges. Recently, the vast funding discrepancies between school districts have prompted legal action in several states and calls for a more equitable way to fund schools. To date, the dispute remains unresolved. School vouchers and calls for increased federal aid have been suggested as ways to alleviate this discrepancy. Nonetheless, the question of school effects remains a controversial topic. But if some public schools are so ineffective, are private schools any better? Is there any ground for the contention that private schools facilitate achievement in cognitive skills?

Public vs. Private Schooling

Public Schooling

Today, approximately 90,000 public schools educate about 85 percent of the nation's elementary and secondary school children. The remaining 15 percent are enrolled in private schools, most of which are sponsored by religious organizations including the Roman Catholic Church (U.S. Bureau of the Census, 2004).

Modern public education began to take shape in the United States from 1830 to 1865. This period, commonly referred to as the Age of the Common School, witnessed the establishment of state systems of education funded by direct taxation to support the new schools. The Common School movement was the result of several social and economic factors. During this period, the nation's size increased by over one and one-quarter million square miles of territory and the population increased from 13 to 32 million, 4 million coming from European immigration. Most of the newly arriving immigrants took up residence in the cities. This great influx was also accompanied by the migration of many Americans from farms to cities in order to take advantage of the employment opportunities created by the new factories. As might be expected, this influx put great pressure on existing schools and many called for an overhaul of the educational process to accommodate the masses entering the already crowded city schools.

The cry for universal free education became even more pressing following the Industrial Revolution. Ironically, the growing industrial centers of the East created an increased need for the education of all Americans as well as a decreased opportunity for many to attend school. Very often, entire families were employed in factories and reformers hoped to use education as a remedy for the social problems accelerated by industrialization. Some believed that schools could Americanize the new immigrants by providing them with a common language and the tools necessary to earn a decent living. The working class, too, viewed the new Common school as an avenue of upward mobility for the newly arriving masses, most of whom could not afford private education. Within the corporate world, too, leaders welcomed the abundant supply of literate workers that the schools could create for their mills and factories.

Revisionist critics likewise argued that the expansion of schooling in the United States was directly related to the factory mode of production and the need for an industrial and compliant workforce. They underscored the fact that schools expanded in towns and cities where a large segment of the labor force was engaged in manufacturing (Bowles and Gintis, 1976). They argued that schools enabled members of the dominant class to impose their beliefs, language and values on the non-English speaking masses. Without a doubt, public support for mandatory public education increased in the hope that all of these goals could be realized in the form of the public school.

Support for the public schools was also advanced by many articulate social activists. Concerned social thinkers and politicians like Horace Mann and Henry Barnard became activists for the common school movement. Mann asserted that education was the right of every child and worked diligently to increase public support for education. His tenth Annual Report as secretary of the Massachusetts State Board of Education was instrumental in the adoption by the state of Massachusetts of the nation's first compulsory attendance law (1852). His efforts on behalf of free public education influenced the entire nation. Like Mann, Henry Barnard labored to establish a State Board of Education for Connecticut. His philosophy, that schools should be good enough for the best students and cheap enough for the poorest, is remembered to this day (Pulliam and Van Patten, 2003).

But, the idea of a universal common school movement would only be effective if funds could be found to finance the system and make it affordable for both rich and poor. Beginning in the early part of the nineteenth century, several states began to provide funds for these public schools from revenues derived from direct taxation and the sale of land. By 1865, more than 50 percent of the nation's children were attending a public school in a system that now spanned most of the United States (Gutek, 2001).

The Evolution of Private Schooling

The private school option has been available as an alternative to public schooling for as far back as the colonial period. The majority of the private schools were created for a variety of reasons including religious instruction, military training or preparation for high school and college. The largest network of private schools in the United States is owned and operated by the Roman Catholic Church. During the mid-nineties, this educational system included over 8,000 schools serving approximately 2.5 million students. Of the three types of Catholic schools, parochial (sponsored and operated by local parishes), diocesan (sponsored and operated by the local diocese) and private (sponsored and operated by specific religious orders), the parochial schools account for about 60 percent of all Catholic schools and about one-fifth of the 26,000 private schools in the country. These schools serve approximately 1.5

Table 4.1. Catholic School Distribution in the United States by Region

	1996–2007		2006–2007	
	#	*Percent*	#	*Percent*
New England	554	6.7	501	6.7
Mideast	2,238	27.2	1,906	25.4
Great Lakes	2,068	25.1	1,789	23.9
Plains	955	11.6	882	11.8
Southeast	977	11.9	969	12.9
West/Far West	1,439	17.5	1,451	19.4
United States	8,293	100	7,498	100

Source: United States Catholic Elementary and Secondary schools—The Annual Statistical Report on Schools 2008, Enrollment and Staffing. National Catholic Education Association, Washington, D.C.

million students in grades K-12 and employ more than 77,000 teachers (U.S. Department of Education, National Center for Education Statistics, 1993–4).

The Roman Catholic School system developed during the nineteenth century as a reaction to the existing secular public school system. The speed and enthusiasm by which it was developed are often attributed to the great influx of European Catholics which began at that time and continued well into the next century. As an increasing number of immigrants poured into America, the cities of the Northeast became a melting pot for the different cultures and religions of Europe. The network of Catholic schools also developed as a response against any other educational system in which the religious tenets of the Catholic faith did not permeate the curriculum. The fear that Catholics might lose their faith was clearly expressed in a canon of the first Provincial Council of Baltimore held in 1829: "we judge it necessary to establish such schools in light of the loss of faith or corruption of morals to the young children of poor Catholic parent . . . and for the young to be taught their faith. . . ." (Rothman, 1963) (see Table 4.1).

Deprived of public funds, the only alternative available to Catholics was the development of their own system of schools supported by private donations and modest tuitions. Slowly, this concern materialized into the development of a number of private Catholic schools whose function it was to maintain the particular religious and cultural beliefs of the newly arriving Catholic immigrants. This trend was accelerated by the great influx of Irish immigrants during the early nineteenth century. By the mid-nineteenth century, Catholics had established over 75 parochial schools in the Northeast and the Baltimore diocese became the first to require that all parishes establish Catholic schools for their youth.

The private school movement was also assisted by the actions of the Lutheran church during this period which can be credited with founding the largest number of non-Catholic schools. The Quakers and Jews soon followed with schools of their own (Pulliam & Van Patten, 2003).

Today, most parochial school principals report that the most important function of their school is religious and moral development. Although Catholic parochial schools account for the greatest number of private schools in the United States, their recent financial difficulties and loss of students has led to numerous school closings. The recent tax credits and subsidies to parents of children in these schools have lessened the student drain from these schools. Projections suggest that the number of students attending private schools in the United States will remain about the same for the next few years. However, if a federally sponsored Voucher system is put in place then the percentage of students attending these schools may increase dramatically. However, the likelihood of this seems slim in light of the general opposition of private citizens to use public funds to support attendance at private schools (Rose and Gallup, 2004).

Today's contemporary private schools are considerably smaller than public institutions and have smaller academic and support staffs. For the most part, Catholic schools are located in urban areas; they constitute a large, relatively homogeneous sector of the private school market. The National Catholic Educational Association provides a directory containing locations and enrollments of Catholic School in the United States and several studies provide detailed information relative to student achievement and various measures of student outcomes (Evans and Schwab, 1995; Sanders, 1999; Sanders and Krautman, 1995).

The Debate over Private and Public Schooling

The recent No Child Left Behind legislation as well as earlier national reports questioning the effectiveness of American schooling have initiated a national debate over the quality and effectiveness of public schooling in the United States. Of major interest in this on-going debate has been whether or not private schools produce higher achieving students than public schools. For the most part, the resulting research has attempted to compare the academic performance of students in both public and private (Catholic) schools in an effort to shed light on this question. Proponents of public schooling argue that private/Catholic schooling results in the separation of racial and social groups since only economically advantaged groups can afford a private school education. They believe that this social separation can only result in divisiveness and enhanced social inequality. On the other hand, advocates for private education point to the possibility of better moral development of our youth as well as enhanced cognitive achievement. In this section, we address the research addressing this issue.

The Research Evidence

In 1980, Coleman was once again invited, this time by the National Center on Education Statistics, to conduct a study on the effectiveness of public and private schooling in the United States. His report, *Public and Private Schools,*

(Coleman et al., 1981) initiated another heated controversy. This time the debate focused on the effect of public and private schooling. The new study considered the differential impact of public and private schooling on academic achievement and considered whether or not Catholic school students performed better than their public school counterparts. The study also examined the impact of Catholic schooling on minority achievement.

In order to eliminate the possibility of a selection bias, it was essential for the Coleman researchers to look at achievement test scores while controlling for family SES. Fortunately, The High School and Beyond data employed by Coleman made this possible since it compiled a composite test score for math, reading, and vocabulary during the senior year for each of the students in the study. When controls for family SES were not applied, students in Catholic schools were 18 percent more likely to score higher on this composite score than were students in public schools. Therefore the uncontrolled effect of school type on test composite was 18 percent. When controls for family SES were applied, the overall percentage decreased. Nevertheless, Catholic school students from high SES were still *12 percent* more likely to score higher on the composite index than their counterparts in public schools. Interestingly, Catholic school students from low SES backgrounds (black and Hispanics) were *20 percent* more likely to score higher on the composite index than were students from public schools. Controlling for family background, Coleman revealed that students in private schools achieved at a higher academic level than students in public schools. Students in private and Catholic schools performed approximately one grade level higher on standardized tests of verbal and math achievement than comparable counterparts in the public education system. Additionally, Catholic private schools seemed to produce more positive effects on verbal and math achievement scores from grade 10 to 12; an advantage of one-half to one year over other students in public schools. This positive effect was especially noticed among students from black and Hispanic economically disadvantaged families (especially for those with less-well educated parents) (see Table 4.2).

Table 4.2.   The Effect of Catholic and Public School Type on Senior Year Composite Test Scores

Applying Controls for SES	
Catholic School	12%
Public School	20%
Applying Controls for Race	
Catholic School	17%
Public School	31%

Source: Crosstab results from High School and Beyond data, Coleman et al.

One interesting fact that emerged from the study was that Catholic schools seemed to increase achievement scores for all students but were especially helpful in boosting test scores for economically disadvantaged students. Similar results were revealed when results were controlled for student race. Subsequent research by Coleman likewise concludes that for high school sophomores and seniors, test scores in math and science were between 15 to 20 percentage points higher for parochial school students (Coleman and Hoffer, 1987). Hence, Coleman, who contributed so much to the overall belief that schools could do little to promote student achievement, now assumed a lead position in suggesting that Catholic Schools were more effective than public schools. How were these positive gains explained?

As a way of explaining these findings, the Coleman researchers noted that private schools had stricter discipline and higher educational standards for their students. On the average, Catholic schools assigned about 1.17 more hours of homework than the public schools. Smaller classes and greater student involvement were also more characteristic of private schools. In turn, both Catholic and other private school students were absent less frequently and experienced lower rates of withdrawal from school. The schools appeared to be more orderly and teachers expected students to complete more homework each evening. The report also noted that the Catholic schools provided safe environments for their students and seemed to have school climates that were more conducive to study than public schools. Finally, the study suggested that Catholic schoolteachers held higher expectations for their students' success and were more successful in encouraging students to take more challenging advance placement courses. But according to many, the most important finding of this study was that Catholic schools seemed to have their most positive effect on the achievement scores of economically disadvantaged children (Coleman et al., 1982).

Coleman's conclusion that Catholic schools were especially helpful in raising the achievement levels of minority students became the subject of considerable debate. The report purported to reveal that Catholic schools produced higher academic achievement in Black and Hispanic students. Yet others (Keith and Page, 1985) criticized the study and argued that the Coleman research, which controlled for SES, contained no controls for prior student academic ability and that this omission could lead to serious flaws in the conclusions. However, when the High School and beyond (HSB) data was reanalyzed adding controls for ability and SES, the overall difference between public and private student achievement remained but was significantly reduced. Other research, at this time (Greeley, 1982) also suggested a significant positive impact on minority achievement. In his analysis employing the HSB data, Greeley employed controls for student and family background characteristics (parental education, family resources, and student ability) and arrived at similar conclusions underscoring the considerable effect of Catholic over public schooling on minority achievement.

Another criticisms directed against the Coleman research was that it lacked longitudinal data and that the schools were not much different than the local public institutions but rather, they attracted a different type of student. Once again, Coleman addressed these criticisms by engaging in a second comprehensive analysis of public and private schools. The resulting study included over 15,000 students over a three year period and enabled him to compare the net achievement gains for the students over the length of the study while holding constant their initial level of knowledge. Findings support his earlier conclusions relative to the advantage of attending Catholic schools. Catholic school sophomores gained one full grade equivalent in verbal and mathematical ability over the three-year study compared to students in public schools. Little or no difference was found in the areas of science and civics. Once again, Coleman argued that the overall effectiveness of the Catholic school was due to its ability to provide a strong curriculum which contained little or no tracking or differentiation of students (tracking will be fully addressed in the next chapter), while making greater academic demands on their students. Hence, all students were provided with difficult material and expected to do well. Students were also provided with more intensive interaction with their teachers. Additionally, the educational environment seemed to be more orderly and disciplined which, for the most part, was possible because parents, teachers and students in these schools worked as a "functional" community of concerned individuals in assisting the learning process (Coleman & Hoffer, 1987). In sum, this continuation of their earlier study affirmed that Catholic schools perform better than public schools because of the relationship they build with parents and the degree to which they get them involved in the overall education of their children.

Other researchers have also reported a special advantage for students attending Catholic Schools. More recently, this advantage has been referred to as *The Catholic School Effect*. MacFarlane found that parents of Catholic school students were more involved in the education of their children and with the school itself. In all likelihood, this greater involvement of parents contributed to their increased awareness of the behavior and standards expected by the school. In turn, this awareness was communicated to their children, which resulted in less discipline problems. The report also uncovered less gang related activity and disciplinary problems in private schools (MacFarlane, 1994).

Two other researchers, Lee and Byrk, conclude that Catholic schools are more effective than public institutions. What is interesting about this research is that these researchers attribute the improved achievement in the Catholic Schools to less differentiation (tracking) of the curriculum. Catholic schools are generally smaller than neighborhood public schools. They depend upon tuition revenues for their operation and are less likely to provide the expansive amount of tracking that is often available at the local public school. Most students therefore register for the same rigorous academic courses and are usually assigned to one academic track. Lee and Byrak attribute the more disciplined and academically oriented education students receive in a Catholic school to a more intensive academic program (Lee and Bryak, 1988).

Chubb and Moe (1990) also underscore the positive impact of private schools and assert that there are clear cut differences in student learning and achievement between different public and private schools. Their research calculated an objective measure (index of school social organization) based on organizational characteristics of the school including the degree to which a school stressed academic excellence, the degree of teacher professionalism, fairness of disciplinary procedures, and dedication to a high priority of academic goals. Students attending schools with high ratings on this index learned appreciably more than students in schools with low ratings. Obviously, they found that public schools have a more ineffective organization than private schools because they are more rigidly controlled by sometimes ineffective school boards. Since schools do contribute to a difference in outcomes, these researchers conclude that public funding should be more equitably dispersed over *all* schools within a district and parents should be empowered to choose between any public or private school. These highly controversial conclusions continue to supply fuel for the continuing debate on private and public education.

Researchers continue to suggest that Catholic schools do, in fact, have an important, albeit smaller effect on student achievement and a real influence on the academic achievement of minority students (Keith and Page, 1985; Neal, 1997). It is also likely that the benefit to Black and Hispanic students may be realized because of the curricular differences, stricter discipline and increased workload demands of the Catholic schools. On the other hand, it is also possible that minority students, who select to attend Catholic schools, or their parents, may have higher educational aspirations than their public school counterparts and the increased achievement may be a product of higher level aspirations.

Notwithstanding the existing research, many continue to attribute the academic success of students in private schools to what may be termed a "selection bias"—the idea that students who attend these schools originate from higher SES families. Because of the higher tuition required in these schools, students and families are essentially economically screened, thereby fewer lower socio-economic children attend the schools. Additionally, both students and their parents *choose* to be there. Therefore students who attend Catholic or private schools do better because they hail from middle and upper class families and it is the family (as suggested by Coleman's EEO report) and not the school that contributes to this success. In addition, it is not unrealistic to suggest that parents of private school children opt for the expense of sending their children to private schools because they are more concerned about the nature and quality of their children's educational experience. These parents may also be much more determined that their children succeed in school and work harder to motivate and support their children, than the typical parents who send their children to public schools. Being more concerned, they may also be more "hands-on" and become more involved with their education and the school. This being the case, it is parental involvement rather than school effect that seems to account for the improved achievement.

In their ethnography of elite private boarding schools, Peter Cookson and Caroline Persell (1985) provide an interesting perspective on how advantaged students who attend these private schools are further advantaged by mixing with other economically privileged students. The researchers underscore the benefit to social capital (50 percent of the parents of the children attending these schools are doctors while 40 percent are high level managers) as well as the strong connections these schools maintain with prestigious colleges and universities. Public school students simply do not have this unique opportunity to accumulate this valuable social capital.

For the most part, the research suggests that private/Catholic schools produce slightly higher achievement in most students and are particularly effective for minority students. Further, it suggests that this is accomplished by providing a strong academic curriculum requiring more advanced coursework and presumably more student effort. Additionally, Private/Catholic schools view the school as an agent of the family and make a greater effort to involve the family in the education of their children.

CONTEXTUAL ISSUES

Is it possible that contextual differences between the schools themselves can account for much or at least some of the variation in academic achievement between schools? Some have suggested that one or a small set of variables that describe and define the school may also influence student behavior and outcomes. These variables include school and class size, race, socio-economic status, and gender.

For the most part, people usually act according to the norms of their membership groups and so, the validity of the contextual effects research is based on the belief that students are influenced by school culture, expected behavior patterns, and performance standards typified in the school. Although this assumption is challenged by those who relate academic performance to family background characteristics and not characteristics of the schools, the contextual research continues to spark debate on the causes of educational achievement and the role played by schools. This belief has contributed to the number of studies examining characteristics of the school and how they may influence student academic achievement.

How is it possible for school characteristics to play a role in student achievement? Does the registration of more middle class Whites in a minority school automatically improve achievement? Does attending a same gender school improve the academic productivity of girls? If so, how can a contextual variable impact learning? First, let us take a look at one interesting contextual variable-school size.

School Size

In an effort to improve the academic achievement of students, policy makers have continued to debate the question of school size. For the most part, the research examining the effect of school size on academic achievement is mixed. While some earlier studies associate larger size schools with more positive academic achievement, many contemporary studies suggest that smaller schools facilitate achievement.

In their study of what makes an exemplary school, Wilson and Corcoran (1988) uncovered that most, but not all, of the almost 600 U.S. schools that they listed as exemplary, had significantly larger enrollments than other secondary schools in the nation. Conant's early research on school size (1959, 1967) likewise uncovered a positive relationship between school size and academic achievement and concluded that larger schools were more capable of providing greater opportunities for their students than schools with smaller enrollments. Some of the advantages of attending a larger school included the availability of more diverse programs and a greater number of advanced placement and foreign language courses. Coleman et al. also argued that most small and rural schools had lower achievement than larger schools, but the largest and most urban schools did not have higher achievement than those of middle size (Coleman et al., 1966, p. 313).

To further complicate matters, some research suggests a link between small schools, student involvement in activities and increased academic achievement. Lindsey noted that students who attend small schools are more likely to participate in extra-curricular activities and school projects and inferred from the research that increased participation in activities enhanced academic achievement (Lindsay, 1984; Morgan and Alwin, 1980). Turner (1989) is also of the opinion that smaller schools enhance achievement and the school satisfaction rate of students. His research uncovers that students who attend smaller schools have lower dropout rates and participate more actively in student activities. He concludes that smaller schools can more easily provide personalized instruction and strong personal ties with students' families. Small schools also enable teachers and administrators to develop lasting relationships with their students. It is also likely that when teachers know their students that they can build lasting relationships and respond to their academic and social needs more quickly.

In his classic work, *A Place Called School*, John Goodlad (1984) finds that one of the most significant benefits of attending a small school is its ability to neutralize the negative impact of the youth culture. In this comprehensive study of thirty-eight schools, he argues that it is generally more difficult for radical and extreme elements within the student body to gain control in a small school setting. This sentiment is echoed in a study by McDill, Natriello and Pallas (1986) when the researchers claim that small schools of 300 to 400 have less social disorganization, fewer disorders, more student satisfaction and higher academic achievement rates than larger ones. Borland and Howse likewise conclude that an elementary school size of approximately 800 is optimum for achieving overall academic achievement among all of its students (Borland and Howse, 2003). Their study includes a measure of student ability as an explanatory variable in the student-achievement equation.

Fowler (1992) studied the impact of school size on academic achievement and found that the control and management of the school increased as school size decreased. Students in smaller schools reported being more satisfied, more responsible and less likely to withdraw from school. They were also less likely to use drugs and more likely to participate in extracurricular activities. Educational attainment and achievement, especially among minority students, was also higher among students attending smaller schools. In response to accusations that smaller schools were more likely to be found in higher socioeconomic areas, Fowler revealed that the positive effect of school size uncovered in his study remained even after social class was controlled.

For the most part, research on school size effect seems to be in agreement with general organizational theory, which asserts that larger organizations are generally less efficient at achieving quality outcomes. As the size of a school increases, so does bureaucracy, the budget and the number of personnel at the school. As a result, larger schools may be able to provide more resources to students and an enhanced physical plant. But then, as the size of the school increases, students feel less of a connection to the school and often complain of being alienated. This negative effect often outweighs the positive effects of a larger budget. Additionally, it is also likely that smaller schools may do a better job at enhancing interpersonal relations, especially between teachers and students. Smaller schools are also more likely to encourage student extracurricular participation and provide more opportunities to develop student leadership. They have greater control over student behavior; have more effective discipline and lower dropout rates and an overall better student climate (Irmischer, 1997). If school size can affect student outcomes, it is likely that class size may also be an important variable. Some research suggests that the relative size of classes is likewise important to student outcomes.

Class Size

More recently class size has been the subject of considerable research. While many consider it an important factor in student achievement; others are interested in class size since it has direct implications for school budgets. For the most part, teachers and parents agree that smaller is almost always better for academic achievement. However, motivated by the desire to contain the cost of education, administrators argue that class size is only one factor in quality and larger classes would result in substantial savings to districts which could be used to provide additional resources for all students. From the perspective of the teacher, smaller classes are obviously more convenient and easier to teach than larger ones. Fewer students permit teachers to devote more time to each student, spend less time grading exams and have greater control over the class. Smaller classes may also decrease disciplinary problems and provide more time for personal involvement with students. In spite of this assumption, a heated debate has developed over the size of classes.

To date, the empirical research that examines the relationship between class size and student achievement has produced inconsistent results. Research summaries suggest that a sizeable class reduction (one third) in the elementary grades may have a positive impact on academic achievement, albeit not a large one. Some theorists argue that the increased funds required to employ additional teachers might be better used in other areas. Essentially, the discussion centers upon the benefit to students vs. the overall cost effectiveness. Clearly, the question of how to allocate economic resources to maximize achievement for all students and further decrease the achievement gap remains a critical issue for educators.

The Empirical Findings

One of the earliest and still most often quoted studies on class size-effect was conducted by the Educational Research Service (1978). The report, a review of forty-one studies, concludes that reducing class size alone would not necessarily increase student achievement. Rather, it suggests that class size is related to achievement in a complex manner that varies with other factors including teacher characteristics, student ability and educational resources. Each of these factors has an equal impact on achievement and reducing class size alone may not improve achievement in all instances. Interestingly, the study did uncover some support for the belief that smaller classes (under twenty) at the primary level would benefit disadvantaged students, especially in reading and math.

In contrast, a meta-analysis employing almost eighty studies, conducted by Glass and Smith (1979) concluded that average student achievement increases as class size decreases. Their analysis uncovered a positive impact on student achievement when class size approached twenty and significant improvements in achievement as class size approached fifteen. The study also revealed that the mean achievement of students in groups of fifteen or less was several percentile ranks above that of students in classes of twenty-five to thirty students.

Several other widely publicized studies also suggest that reducing class size might be an academically profitable intervention. One point of consistency in the research is that gains are primarily achieved on the primary grade level and seem to be greatest for minority and economically disadvantaged students (Molnar et al., 1999; Robinson, 1990; Robinson and Wittebols, 1986; Yang, 2000). There is also some evidence to suggest that class size effects are most noticed on the very youngest children in school and at the first years of entry into the school (Mortimore et al., 1994). This was also the conclusion of Yang's meta-analysis which concluded that class size effect was related to age and grade. Smaller class size effects were revealed as the age and grade of the student increased. Slavin's analysis of class-size effects likewise suggests some modest gains in achievement when classes are reduced in size (Slavin, 1989).

An apparent flaw of much of the research investigating the effect of class size on achievement has been its relatively small scale and the fact that it has only explored achievement over a relatively short period of time. The Tennessee Class Size Experiment, commonly referred to as Project Star (Student Teacher Achievement Ratio), avoids both of these limitations. A four year, large scale randomized experiment, Project Star, is perhaps the largest and arguably the most important study dealing with class size. The study eliminates many of the methodological problems experienced by earlier research; it is large scale and measures the impact of small classes over a four year period. In so doing, it avoids many of the "effects" generally associated with short range "new experimental programs." The study also includes a broad range of schools in rather economically diverse communities, which provides the unique advantage of gauging the impact of smaller classes on different social classes.

Conducted in the State of Tennessee, this 12 million dollar experiment was commissioned by the Tennessee State Legislature and supervised by the State Education Department. The sample included 329 classrooms in 79 elementary schools in 42 school districts of the State. Approximately 12,000 students were evaluated over the course of the four-year study. The research randomly assigned Kindergarten students to one of three classes: (1) small classes with 13–17 students, (2) large classes with 22–26 students, or (3) large classes of 22 to 26 students which also had the advantage of a teacher's aide. The idea of creating a large class assisted by a teacher's aide enabled researchers to determine if reducing the teacher-pupil ratio would have the same impact on achievement as reducing the class size. In general, the study revealed consistent and statistically significant effects of small classes (about 15) on student achievement and supports the conclusion of earlier research that small class size, especially in the early grades, results in higher academic achievement (Word et al. 1990).

A summary of the results follows:

1. Statistically significant differences in class size effect were uncovered among the three class types on all measures of achievement and in all subject areas. No significant differences were found between large classes with or without the teacher aides.
2. The positive benefits were substantially greater for economically disadvantaged students and minorities in each year of the study (see Table 4.3). In reading, these students experience small class effects that are about 54-86 percent larger than those recorded for white students. These differential effects are 30–46 percent as large as the social class adjusted reading achievement gap between minority and white students in these data. In math, the differential effects of small classes for minority and disadvantaged students are smaller—14-26 percent as large as the small class effect for white students and 8-13 percent as large as the minority-white achievement gap. Clearly, the results imply that small classes could reduce the current minority-white achievement gap in reading by about one third to one half and achieve a more modest reduction in the math achievement gap.
3. Certain behavioral benefits seemed to persist into the fourth grade. Students who had been assigned to smaller classes were reported to spend

more time in learning activities, took more initiatives and rarely engaged in inattentive or disruptive behavior.

The academic achievement results from Star have been confirmed by several other analyses including Wisconsin's Student Achievement Guarantee in Education Program (Maier, Molnar, Percy, Smith and Zahorik, 1997) and the Burke County, North Carolina Program (Achilles, Egelson and Harman, 1995).

Table 4.3 indicates that the small class advantage for minority students is considerably larger than for white students. When considering the effect on mathematics achievement, the small class advantage for minorities is only slightly larger in Kindergarten classes but increases to 50 percent larger in first grade and again increases to nearly twice as large in second and third grades. The small class advantage for minorities in reading is about 50 percent in Kindergarten classes and increases to twice as large in grades 1, 2, and 3.

Project Star remains one of the key studies supporting the belief that smaller classes, especially at the early grade level, enhance achievement. Certainly, the behavioral benefits evolving from assignment to a small class may help us to understand exactly why some at-risk students succeed in this type of environment.

The available research suggests that students assigned to small classes are more likely to initiate contacts with teachers to ask questions or seek clarification of subjects (Finn and Achilles, 1999). Small classes also seem to be most beneficial for disadvantaged students who often become disengaged in the learning process, since they are more likely to enhance interaction between students and teachers (Finn and Rock, 1997). Perhaps, one of the greatest benefits of being assigned to a small class, especially for minority and inner city children, may be the increased student engagement that is experienced by these students. The personal relationship that is likely to develop between students and teacher, the name recognition and the fact that

Table 4.3. Small Class Advantage* (Effect Size) for White and Minority Students Project Star

Class Comparison	Math Effect Size		Reading Effect Size	
(Sm. vs. reg. classes)*	*White*	*Minority*	*White*	*Minority*
Kindergarten	.15	.17	.15	.21
First Grade	.23	.32	.16	.31
Second Grade	.12	.23	.14	.25
Third Grade	.11	.21	.15	.27

Source: Project Star: Tennessee small vs. regular class size comparisons, Tennessee State Education Department.
* Each small class advantage is shown as the difference between the mean achievement in small classes and that in regular classes divided by the overall SD of test scores at that grade in that subject.

every student is on the firing line when it comes to answering questions may encourage students to participate more actively and become more integrated into the academic life of the class.

In addition to school and class size, two additional contextual variables, racial and social class composition of the school are often examined for their possible impact on student academic achievement.

Racial and Social Class Context of the School

For those who look closely, Coleman's EEO report contains some salient data on the impact of school segregation on student academic achievement. After reviewing a host of school variables, Coleman finds that the peer composition of the school is the only school characteristic that most consistently affects test performance.

The Coleman Study examined peer composition (the racial and social class context of the school) and how it might impinge on student learning by measuring the proportions of variance in student achievement that could be connected to five school factors: school facilities, teacher quality, teacher attitudes, curriculum and characteristics of the student body. The study uncovered that the racial and income characteristics of the student body were responsible for about 5 percent of the variance in achievement. While not as important as family background variables and student attitudes (which account for approximately 30 percent of the variance), school contextual issues remained important in assessing why some students succeed while others fail (Coleman, 1966, p. 312).

Coleman was also among the first to suggest a positive effect of integrated schools on the achievement of minority students. His findings revealed that the racial context of the school had a consistent impact on achievement. As the White population of a class increased so did the academic performance of Black students, more so than they would have achieved in a segregated school. The Coleman data also attributed higher achievement for all students, both high and low-income students, to a higher average SES student body. Initially, this finding figured significantly in Coleman's support for racial and socioeconomic integration of the schools and ultimately what led him to favor school busing.

The impact of school contextual characteristics (SES) on student achievement is supported by subsequent research. In his reanalysis of the Coleman data, Christopher Jencks (1972) reaffirms the original EEO finding that affluent peers boost the academic performance of poor Blacks. More recently, this positive impact on achievement has been noted by Grissmer, Flanagan, and Williamson (1998), who suggest that desegregation in the South was initially responsible for an improvement in Black achievement and a decline in the Black-White achievement gap.

The differential impact of school contextual characteristics on academic outcomes has also been supported by Geoffrey Borman (2005, 2007). This researcher concludes from his recent reassessment of the Coleman data that school factors, including race and SES of the school, matter in determining how students fare. In fact, Borman suggests that such factors may actually account for up to 40 percent of the variation in achievement differences between students and that *who* students attend school with is more important than their skin color (Borman, 2005). The research continues to suggest that attending racially segregated schools or schools attended by economically disadvantaged students, impacts on student achievement significantly more than an individual's economic level or minority status. Without a doubt, it has the ability to mediate African-American students' ability to achieve academically on par with their White middle class peers. This research offers a dramatic alternative to the conclusions of the Coleman data in that it significantly modifies the effects of family background.

What accounts for this dramatic impact? How can contextual variables like class and race have such a powerful impact on student achievement? Some researchers (Boocock, 1980; Wilson, 1959) have suggested that as members of the student body, students respond to the culture and norms of the individual school or to other students who serve as role models. Thus, reference group theory enables us to understand how some students behave according to the unofficial norms of the school. In short, the social class and racial context of the school may have an independent effect on student aspirations. Formerly, it was believed that student aspirations were associated only with family background but it may be possible that they are also related to school characteristics. As early as 1959, Wilson asserted that children of manual workers might be more likely to adhere to middle class values and exhibit high educational aspirations if they attend a predominantly middle class school. By the same token, middle class children may be more likely to exhibit more modest aspirations if they attend predominately working-class schools (Wilson, 1959, p. 873).

Finally, the research on contextual effects has not always been consistent. Increasing the number of White and high-income students in a school might raise aspirations, but it may also produce lower academic performance among some minorities who are now confronted with appreciably higher academic standards (Jencks, 1972). Some research has also revealed that the benefits of integrated schooling are greater for younger rather than older children (Alexander, Entwisle and Dauber, 1994). Jencks (1985) has also suggested that the potential for academic growth among younger children is about ten times greater; suggesting that research on young may lead to quite different conclusions.

A final contextual issue that may have some bearing on student achievement is school gender.

Single-Gender Schools

In recent years, a great deal of attention has been focused on the contextual variable of gender and how it may affect academic achievement. Most public schools in the United States are coeducational but they employ this organizational strategy not necessarily because Americans believe that coeducation offers an academic advantage over single-gender schools. Rather, they remain unwilling to fund a dual track system for boys and girls requiring the duplication of scarce resources and personnel. Although coeducational public education has enjoyed great popularity in America, questions continue to surface about alternative organizational systems including the possibility of single-gender schools. Some researchers actually believe that these schools might improve the achievement of all students and eliminate some of the problems and accusations of differential treatment of boys and girls.

Researchers who advocate the use of single-gender schools argue that they enable teachers to modify their teaching style and course material to accommodate the individual learning styles of boys and girls (Warrington and Younger, 2001). Since current research has underscored the different learning style preferences of boys and girls, same sex schools may be an effective strategy to accommodate this difference and improve the achievement scores of all students (Dunn and Dunn, 1993). In spite of this research, some Americans remain doubtful and fear that single-gender schools may erode the equity gains achieved by women in recent years. Feminists, in particular, view a single-gender option as a form of foolish separatism that will eventually impact negatively on women.

As a result of this renewed interest, an emerging dialogue has developed which underscores a number of critical issues. Some doubt the ability of single-gender schools to provide adequate opportunities for cross-sex socialization and suggest that this will result in negative implications for adolescent social development (Marsh and Rowe, 1996). Others fear that the increase in all girl schools will result in more private and expensive institutions, further restricting access and opportunity to children of economically disadvantaged homes.

But what does the research evidence suggest? Recent research exploring the benefits associated with single-gender schools has resulted in mixed findings. Most studies have shown little if any benefit for boys in all male schools

(Singh, Vaught and Mitchell, 1998; Kelly, 1996) while, others have found a modest advantage for boys in coeducational schools (Dale, 1974). Using data from the National Educational Longitudinal Study (NELS), LePore and Warren (1997) found no special advantages to academic or social psychological outcomes from attending single-gender and coeducational Catholic schools. When specific subjects were examined, single-gender schools improved the physics achievement of all students but the achievement gap between coeducational and single-gender school students diminished after controlling for student family characteristics (income) (Young and Fraser, 1992).

Most studies exploring the impact of single-gender schools on achievement have focused attention on the advantage it may have for girls. Here, we have some consensus that they are better for girls than coeducational institutions. Girls grow in confidence; achieve higher test scores, and above all, their interest and participation in typical male dominated subjects like math and science improves in all girl schools (Brutsaert, 1999; Warrington & Younger, 2001). The research of Lee and Bryk (1986) concludes that attending a single-gender school is especially beneficial to girls since it increases their academic achievement, educational aspirations and self-esteem. Generally, more favorable results have been reported for girls attending single-gender schools.

Single-gender schools are believed to provide a better school climate due to the fact that students have fewer distractions and are more able to focus on learning tasks. Disciplinary problems are also much less in same-gender schools. It is also likely that single-gender schools provide less of an opportunity for discrimination against girls. Research has underscored the fact that boys usually dominate the classroom in coeducational settings, that is, they speak out more often and monopolize interactions with teachers (Francis, 1999; Younger et al, 1999). Whatever the specific benefits of single-gender schools, the advantages seem slanted in favor of girls.

Proponents of single-gender schools suggest that coeducation creates an educational environment with distractions that impedes learning and foster a youth culture opposed to academic achievement. Additionally, they argue that not all students in coeducational schools receive the full attention of the teacher, neither are all students encouraged to participate actively. They assert that when boys and girls are heterogeneously mixed in classes, girls are usually shortchanged. Girls are given less opportunity to participate in discussions; neither are they provided with full attention from their teachers (Riordan, 1990). In this regard, a study commissioned by the American Association of University Women underscores the presence of bias against women in the classroom and argues that much of this bias is eliminated in single-gender classrooms. Several other studies substantiate these claims (Lee and Bryk, 1986; Heffernan, 1996; Daly, 1995; Cipriani-Sklar, 1996).

Single-Gender Classes

Since the development of a single gender school is often a complex matter requiring a strong popular mandate, some school districts have opted for the creation of some same sex classes. This trend is especially popular in core subject areas like math and English. However, the movement to create same sex classes is proceeding faster than the evidence to support it. Marsh and Rowe (1996) investigated the impact of same and mixed gender classes on math achievement scores within a coeducational institution. Only modest support for same gender classes was uncovered by these researchers. Similar results were reported by Jackson and Smith when they explored the impact of same sex and mixed classes on English and math achievement (Jackson & Smith, 2000). In all likelihood, single-gender classes may impact more favorably on girls than on boys especially in some male dominated classes like physics and mathematics. It seems that there is modest evidence to support the existence of single-gender classes for girls but the evidence to support single-gender male classes is seriously lacking. Clearly, more longitudinal and larger studies are needed in order to shed light on this interesting subject.

Chapter Five

Explaining Unequal Achievement: Within-School Differences

There is far more variation in educational attainment between different students within the same school than between the average student in one school and the average student in another.

Christopher Jencks

Tracking and classroom assignment practices typically segregate students within schools and define an academic hierarchy through which rewards may be allocated.

Barbara Heynes

THE SIGNIFICANCE OF WITHIN-SCHOOL DIFFERENCES

The degree to which educational structures and practices operating within schools affect student academic outcomes has been the subject of intense research. Chapter 4 has already examined differences *between* schools and how these differences may influence the achievement of students. But sociologists also agree that schooling in the United States is stratified and that assignment to different classes *within* the same school may influence the content and quality of a student's educational experience. In fact, some even suggest that differences *within* the same school can have an effect on academic outcomes that is greater than the difference produced by inequality *between* schools. Our attention now turns to *within-school differences* and how they may become a source of differential achievement.

James Coleman was among the first to identify some of the practices and structures operating within schools that help to facilitate failure in some children and excellence in others. His research found that only 20 percent of the variation in student achievement rests *between* schools, while the remaining 80 percent occurs *within* schools (Coleman, 1966). Surprisingly, there are greater differences in achievement within schools than between schools. Additionally, children from disadvantaged homes begin school with small but measurable differences in academic skills compared with children from middle-class homes but this difference increases significantly with every successive year in school. Clearly, the family is responsible for the initial achievement gap; but schools must also bear some responsibility for the increasing cognitive difference that emerges over the years. In order to explain this disturbing finding, several researchers have argued the need to examine, more carefully, practices within-schools that may contribute to this disturbing deficit. Some have even suggested that examining within-school differences is more appropriate than exploring differences between schools in understanding how and why students learn (Carbonaro, 2005; Gamoran, Secada and Marrett, 2000). One such practice, tracking, is the focus of this chapter.

Tracking involves the separation of students into different classes based on their perceived academic ability. For the most part, many researchers find this practice to be inherently inequitable. They argue that tracking is undemocratic and that it perpetuates the separation of youth along racial and socio-economic lines. They contend that tracking fails to improve the achievement of all but the brightest students and that low track classes soon become the dumping ground for poor and disruptive children. More recently, the debate has focused on the distribution of learning opportunities. Opponents of tracking suggest that it restricts a student's opportunity to learn by limiting the quantity and quality of course material provided to lower track students. Tracking, they believe, allocates the most valuable school resources including a high currency curriculum, positive teacher expectations and more effective instruction to students who already possess the greatest social and economic advantage (Oakes, 1990, 2005; Yair, 2000). On the other hand, they contend that instruction in lower tracks is often fragmented; it stresses isolated pieces of information and often employs the use of secondary sources. Students in lower tracks also more often register for basic courses which fail to prepare them for college. Since they are unprepared for college many of them enter the labor market at an early age. Finally, since each of these variables is related to student learning, it is understandable how upper track students receive a higher caliber educational experience which assists them to succeed in school and later life.

This chapter examines the educational practice of tracking, one of the most socially contentious issues in education. First, we consider its popularity and examine its history and development. Next, we focus on the various arguments that are offered for and against its use. Finally, we take a close look at the various types of tracking that are employed in American schooling and offer an assessment of their impact on cognitive achievement. Some implications for educational policy are also included. No exploration of the causes of under-achievement in schools would be complete without a consideration of this educational practice. To many, it is the epitome of how differential opportunities for learning within the same school can lead to quite different academic outcomes and career trajectories.

TRACKING: A PRIME FACTOR IN UNEQUAL ACHIEVEMENT

Tracking, or grouping by ability and curriculum, has become a common management strategy for organizing learning in the schools of many industrialized nations. For some, the practice begins as early as the first grade. A study undertaken by the Educational Testing service reveals that about 70 percent of all classes in England, Germany, Japan, Taiwan, and Israel are tracked. Today, tracking is a reality of the American educational system and is practiced in approximately 60 percent of all elementary schools (Strum, 1993). McEwin, Dickinson and Jenkins (2003) found that 78 percent of all American middle schools employed some form of tracking. This percentage was up from 68 percent in 1993. Today, tracking in the United States is accomplished by individual course subjects or by an overarching program leading to vocational or academic training. Regardless, the fundamental element of tracking, the differentiated curricular, remains the same. The practice of tracking has enjoyed a long and controversial history in the United States.

Tracking: A Historical Perspective

Grouping of students according to ability and curriculum is one of the oldest and probably the most controversial practice in American education. The practice dates back to the middle of the nineteenth century, when the first form of flexible grading based on ability, the Harris Plan, replaced age-grading in the public schools of St Louis, Missouri (Pulliam and Van Patten, 1999).

The earliest tracking systems emerged within the urban centers of the North in an attempt to Americanize and socialize the newly arriving immigrant groups and the increasing number of poor Blacks arriving from the South. For the first time in our history as a nation, a highly diverse student population was entering the schools and most of these newcomers would not attend college or enter the professions. Studies undertaken at that time also revealed that the highest failure rates were concentrated among these children. Additionally, the traditional classical curriculum in place at that time seemed inappropriate for them.

As scores of new immigrants made America their home, a more efficient technique was needed to handle their influx into the schools and provide them with a suitable education. In time, the urban school with its common curriculum was soon replaced by factory-like structures where differentiated schooling could appropriately socialize the various groups of students into work roles appropriate to their class standing (Chapman, 1988). At about the same time, school administrators were discovering that many of these new children could not make it through the system. Claims of "retardation" became common and one researcher claimed that about a third of the new school population was seriously retarded (Ayres, 1909). The pressure for reform confirmed the need for a plan, which *sorted* children into classes for those perceived to be *slow*, *bright* or *deficient*. While noble in concept, the new plan, based on tracking by *perceived* ability, was complicated by the need for an instrument to efficiently and scientifically allocate the students into different groups. This need was soon filled by the discovery of intelligence in Europe and America.

In 1904, the Frenchman, Alfred Binet developed a scale which he believed was capable of measuring the intelligence of elementary school children in the schools of Paris. His goal was to identify the subnormal and segregate them into separate classes. Lewis Terman, a hard-fast social Darwinist, quickly transported the test to the United Sates. Terman considered the poor blacks and immigrant children who composed the new school population, to be social *misfits* who impinged on the achievement of other children. While they were incapable of learning, he sought to make them efficient *workers* and envisioned the new intelligence test as a scientific instrument that could sort them into vocational tracks (Chapman, 1988). A common curriculum would not be suitable for all students but providing each ability level with different knowledge suited to their future employment was considered an equitable outcome of schooling. Some would be taught to work with their hands while others would use their minds. In time, the new IQ test became the final step in a tracking process, which enabled schools to *scientifically* identify ability levels and sort students accordingly.

As tracking increased in popularity, the common curriculum was soon replaced with a multi-layered or parallel system. The specifics of each plan differed by city. In Cambridge, the superintendent of schools developed a two-track plan and students were divided into average and gifted groups (Chapman, 1988). These plans often provided a classical track for the gifted in order to prepare these students for professional careers corresponding to their position in the social structure and a vocational track which taught some trade or skill to average students. However, the frankness by which students were sorted into curriculum tracks based on race, class and ethnicity often raised concerns about the openness of the American educational system (Bowles and Gintis, 1976). The idea of selecting children for different tracks according to *ability* soon became institutionalized in America and the IQ test provided the first step in an elaborate tracking system that systematically denied some children equal access to knowledge.

The practice of tracking declined appreciably during the war years when immigration from Europe declined. The practice became popular, once again, following the major desegregation orders of the 50s and 60s as well as the enactment of the 1964 Civil Rights Act and the 1965 Elementary and Secondary Education Act (Losen and Welner, 2002). More recently, tracking has gained increased popularity and many view it as an insidious but seemingly benign tactic for avoiding racial integration. Today, tracking continues to be extremely controversial and has generated more research studies than almost any other educational practice (George & Alexander, 2003). Proponents and opponents continue to debate its strengths and weaknesses.

The Tracking Debate: Theoretical Perspectives

The arguments for and against tracking appear in several forms. Essentially, the literature contains several studies that favor its use especially for high ability students (Kulik, 1982), and many that consider it relatively ineffective (Slavin, 1990). Some also conclude that it perpetuates the current social class structure while denying access to knowledge and an equal educational opportunity to disadvantaged students (Oakes, 1993). For the most part, there is some consensus that tracking favors those placed in upper-tracks.

Supporters of tracking emphasize its capacity to enhance self-development, while critics underscore its negative consequences. In theory, tracking has the potential of increasing student achievement by reducing the wide disparity in student ability which often makes it easier for teachers to reach the whole class. Additionally, when classes are separated by ability, teachers are free to increase the pace of instruction for some classes or provide more individual attention to others. On the other hand, tracking often creates restricted learning environments which deny lower track students the stimulation and example provided by higher achieving students. Labeling students according to perceived academic ability also has the potential for creating an academic elite as well as a self-fulfilling prophesy of achievement which often works against students in lower tracks.

The Efficiency Perspective

The Efficiency perspective looks upon tracking as a means of increasing societal efficiency by contributing to the proper selection and channeling of national human resources. Schools are entrusted with the responsibility of channeling students into specific levels in the labor market. Vital to this approach is the use of IQ testing, early identification of student ability, tracking and the practice of vocational training and guidance. Proponents of this approach also claim that tracking enables instructors to adapt their individual teaching styles to the particular classroom group rather than attempt to teach those students who have been labeled "average" and miss those who have been labeled "slow" and "gifted." They also strongly assert that it would be unrealistic to expect all students to master the same curriculum as would be presented in one mixed-ability class. Those who favor this approach view tracking as an educational tool that ensures the best and most efficient use of human resources.

As exemplified in the writings of Rosenbaum (1976), and Young (1971), the school is viewed as a social sorting mechanism designed to guide, counsel, and provide select curricula for students of different abilities. Viewing school resources as limited, tracking is seen as the most efficient means of increasing the cognitive achievement of students whatever their abilities. Assumptions underlying this approach include the belief that early selection is accurate, tracking is efficient and that tracking improves academic achievement. Yet another view, the self-development perspective, envisions tracking as a pedagogical device which improves student affective development.

The Self-Development Perspective

From another perspective, tracking is viewed as an educational structure, which improves self-concept and self-development in the overall learning experience. Through tracking, students are allowed to advance at an appropriate pace with students of similar ability. By not having to make invidious comparisons with more able peers, students develop a more positive self-concept and motivation. Positive self-concept, in turn, facilitates academic achievement (Abadiz, 1985; Ansalone, 2003). According to the Self-Development perspective, the most significant contribution of tracking becomes the improved self-concept and affective development that results from this educational practice. However, not everyone views the educational structure of tracking in such a favorable manner. Conflict theorists argue that this structure blatantly denies equality of educational opportunity to many students. It channels minority and economically disadvantaged students to low tracks where they are presented with a lower quality curriculum which is presented in an unimaginative manner. In turn this leads to a widening of the achievement gap.

The Conflict Perspective

The practice of tracking is not without its opponents. Neo-Marxists view tracking as an attempt to perpetuate the stratification system and reinforce the separation of youth along ethnic or socio-economic lines [Bowles and Gintis, 1976; Hallinan, 1996]. Schooling is viewed as an attempt to instill in workers those attitudes essential to a capitalistic workforce, namely: order, docility, discipline, sobriety and humility. Proponents of this perspective agree that schooling in the United States is associated with the extension of the wage labor system and view the repressive nature of the schooling process [grading and discipline] as an attempt to develop in students, traits corresponding to those required on the job.

According to the Conflict perspective, stratification developed within the schools as a reaction to the influx of working class and immigrant children. As a result of this influx, the older ideology of the common school was replaced by a multi-tracked curriculum. The upper track or academic curriculum, with its emphasis on the humanities and critical thinking skills was reserved for the children of the rich, who would more than likely utilize these skills in college. The poor were relegated to a lower track, which focused on vocational skills since this would be most advantageous in their efforts to secure employment. The personality traits encouraged in students also varied with their anticipated position in the work hierarchy. For those marginal students expected to find employment in the lower sector of the workforce, obedience and submission were stressed, while decision making and independent thought were emphasized for students of "better" families. In sum, Neo-Marxists view the attempt to tailor education to the needs of all children as the desire to establish class-related curricula culminating in a highly stratified track system. Thus tracking becomes a major means of maintaining the stratification system in the American society.

Still other research employing the Conflict perspective concludes that tracking affects teacher expectations of student performance and may even impact on misconduct and demeanor [Goodlad, 1984; Reed, 1995]. In sum, supporters of tracking emphasize its efficiency and its capacity to enhance self-development, while critics of this educational structure underscore the negative consequences of stratification, separation, and misconduct. The tracking debate is fueled, in part, by the manner in which students are assigned to tracks and the likelihood that specific types of tracking structures have a potential to label students as underachievers.

GETTING ON TRACK: IS ACHIEVEMENT RELATED TO SPECIFIC TRACK STRUCTURE?

Loveless (1999) attempts to uncover the reasons why schools choose to track their students. His research suggests a curricular motivation as well as a desire to manage diversity in ability. Of the several hundred schools in California and

Massachusetts which are included in his study, those with large enrollments as well as those with a high degree of heterogeneity in achievement are more likely to track. On the other hand, others have concluded that tracking is not necessarily done for academic reasons but rather as a means of separating students of different races and classes. They assert that it represents a veiled attempt at implementing separate but equal education in schools (Ansalone, 2006; Vanderhart 2006).

Regardless of the reasons for its implementation, the experience of tracking is not necessarily the same for all students. Track assignments usually depend on the schools that students attend since procedures and practices employed in assigning students to a specific track vary according to school. Most schools take into account several academic factors including past grades and achievement test scores. However, it is not unusual to learn that students may be tracked based on the recommendations of a teacher or counselor. Mobility within tracks also varies by school. Some schools permit assignment to an advanced class for one subject and a remedial class for another. This process, known as Setting, is gaining popularity in many schools. The subject nature of tracks is also changing.

Traditionally, students were assigned to academic, vocational or business tracks. Now, it is likely that students will be placed in a basic, honors or college program. Research has also uncovered that even when social class, race and ethnicity are controlled, a greater proportion of minority and economically disadvantaged students are assigned to lower tracks. Higher social standing is almost always associated with higher track placement. Classification in terms of track assignment is a most powerful force in determining how students see themselves. Tracks can create a self-fulfilling prophesy of behavior and belief which can create and define the type of student that children believe themselves to be. It is likely that student self-perception will be affected by a student's track assignment.

Although tracking usually refers to the separation of students by ability and curriculum, the term is also associated with a number of different organizational arrangements within and between classes with the overall aim of facilitating instruction and promoting academic achievement (Slavin, 1987). Some researchers argue that certain types of tracking structures may create more inequality between tracks than others. At the same time, certain structures may be more academically advantageous than others (Gamoran, 1992; Slavin, 1986). Gamoran suggests that the overall impact of tracking on students is directly related to the specific structural characteristics of a particular tracking system. The research goes on to suggest that schools with less mobility between tracks produce greater inequality and lower academic achievement. An inflexible tracking structure is likely to produce greater inequality, especially in math and verbal scores, with overall lower math scores for all groups (Gamoran, 1992). In the next paragraphs, I explore structural characteristics and academic outcomes of various types of tracking structures that are used in tracking students in the schools. Between-class grouping (tracking) is one type that is commonly employed in American schooling.

Between-Class Grouping

The practice of Between-class grouping refers to a relatively common type of grouping plan, which entails assigning students to one self-contained class on the basis of perceived ability (Slavin, 1987). Many public school systems within large city systems continue to organize their students for instruction based on this organizational idea in spite of the literature, which refutes the claim that classes organized in this manner lead to greater cognitive gains (Oakes, 1985; Page, 1991). It is presumed that this form of tracking enables teachers to manage more easily wide-ranging ability among students. Opponents of tracking are critical of this method and suggest that it has the greatest potential to set in motion a labeling process, which can facilitate a teacher's ability to identify students as slow or bright based on their assigned track (Oakes, 1997). They also suggest that this form of tracking encourages teachers to modify the content of their courses as well as their approach to teaching based on their perception of the intellectual level of the class (Loveless, 1999). For the most part, the current research suggests that this form of stratification encourages a differential presentation of curricula with lower-tracked students receiving a limited portion of the curricula and presented in a less imaginative manner (Entwisle et al., 1997; Oakes, 1985, 1994; Riordan, 1997). Clearly, tracking significantly influences academic achievement when assignment to an upper level track permits students to learn more than if they are assigned to a lower level track.

Setting-Regrouping for Selected Subjects

Setting, another form of tracking, assigns students to "homerooms" of diverse ability for a portion of a school day and then reassigns them to two or three subjects areas which are tracked according to presumed ability (Slavin, 1987). The most commonly *Set* subjects are math, science, reading or English. As students spend most of their scheduled school period within the same "homeroom", this re-grouping *minimizes* the stigma and labeling impact that is often associated with tracking (Provus, 1960; Morris, 1969). One of the prime advantages of this tracking structure is that it permits the same student to be *set* in an advanced group for one subject and possibly even a slower-leveled group for another. Assigning students to grouped classes is usually on the basis of actual performance in a specific subject rather than on IQ as is usually the case for ability grouping (Slavin, 1987). Employing this type of structure makes it less likely for a student to be labeled as either *slow* or *gifted.* While additional contemporary research is needed, several earlier studies conclude that students learn more in *Set* classes than in heterogeneous groups especially when the re-grouping is for math classes (Provus, 1960; Moses, 1966).

The Joplin Plan

When re-grouping is conducted exclusively for the purpose of reading instruction, it is referred to as the *Joplin Plan*. This plan was first developed in 1954 and assigns students across grade levels to reading groups of similar ability. For example, a typical fourth grade reading group may include some fourth-graders, high-achieving third-graders and a number of low achieving fifth-graders. A properly administered *Joplin Plan* reviews students' assignments often, and re-assigns them as progress is achieved. Like *setting*, it is highly possible that this plan minimizes the negative impact of stigma, which may develop from exclusive assignment of students to a low achieving class (Oakes, 2005). This plan reduces this possibility since classes are composed of students from several different classes. Meta-analysis of research on tracking reveals that reading classes employing the *Joplin Plan* achieved more than controlled classes in eleven of fourteen research studies, and the remaining three classes found no difference in overall achievement between the plans utilized (Slavin, 1987).

Within-Class Groupings

Very often teachers employ some sort of within-class grouping in which students are assigned to one of a number of ability-level groups in the same class. Groupings of this nature are more informal and usually established at the discretion of the teacher. One modification of this method allows teachers to present a lesson to an entire class and then divide the class into two or three groups based on perceived ability. At this point, the instructor has the option of presenting remedial instruction to one group, and enriched instruction to another. Research favors this type of organizational idea over between-class grouping (Slavin and Karweit, 1985). Within-class groupings eliminate some of the potential for negative social and psychological effects usually associated with separating students into entirely different, permanent and identifiable tracks.

But what are the consequences of participating in a lower or higher track? Is academic achievement increased or impaired? Does tracking impact on students' self-confidence and self-esteem? We now direct our attention to the various tracking outcomes examined in the research.

TRACKING OUTCOMES

Tracking is practiced in most large, racially and economically diverse school systems in the United States and has become a common management strategy for organizing the learning experience of students. An examination of tracking outcomes can help us to understand how this practice affects students' learning experiences. We now turn our attention to some of the outcomes and processes that have been associated with tracking including its impact on academic achievement, a differentiated curriculum, opportunity to learn, friendship patterns, separation of social classes, affective development, misconduct, and teacher expectations. Perhaps the most important academic outcome of tracking is its ability to influence academic achievement.

Academic Achievement

One might assume that the most obvious reason to employ tracking is to promote the academic achievement of all students. Regretfully, our research fails to uncover evidence in support of this assumption. Some early studies of tracking do reveal limited gains for students grouped homogeneously, especially average and superior students. It is likely that as tracking gained favor in American schools, the academic community attempted to justify its use by conducting research that would underscore its effectiveness. In this context, it is important to note that the decades between 1890 and 1930 experienced one of the most extensive migrations in U.S. history. Thousands of immigrant children entered the schools and Americans searched for a strategy to effectively deal with the number and diversity of the new school-age population. Tracking emerged as an efficient technique that could provide a separate and equal school experience. In sum, the political tenor of the period, combined with the lack of strict methodological procedures, might have figured significantly in the early research findings.

As early as 1924, Cook observed ninth and tenth grade students ranked into two ability levels and found significant gains for superior students enrolled in history and for slower students in math. Additionally, this researcher reported few if any problems associated with the practice of grouping by ability. At about the same time, Moyer [1924] observed ninth grade students grouped by ability for mathematics and language. After a period of one semester, the study revealed gains for the superior group in language. On the other hand, the lower ability group performed better in both math and language. Jones and McCall's 1926 analysis of sixty-seven matched pairs of grammar school students also revealed a slight advantage for ability grouped superior students. Similar positive conclusions were reported by several other studies during this early period [Barthelmess and Boyer, 1932; Cook, 1924; Jones and McCall, 1926; Moyer, 1924; Wyndham, 1934].

While most early research reveals some academic gains by at least one if not all of the ability groups observed, more recent research finds that ability grouping has no significant positive effect on the average scholastic achievement of students [Betts and Shkolnic, 2000; Figlio and Page, 2001; Gamoran and Weinstein, 1998; Goodlad, 1984; Oakes, 2005]. In fact, this research suggests that ability grouping improves only the cognitive achievement of high ability groups and sometimes at the expense of average and slow groups [Gamoran and Marc, 1989; Vang, 2005]. It would appear that students in low ability groups suffer from the loss of intellectual stimulation generally associated with students possessing more social and cultural capital. On the contrary, it does not appear that upper track students suffer when left with low ability students. Some research also suggests that the achievement of lower track students does not suffer when placed in heterogeneous groupings [Esposito, 1973; Nolan, 1985; Dar and Resh, 1986]. It is also likely that the benefit to higher-track students may be the direct result of subtle processes occurring within the tracks rather than the tracking itself. Some of these processes include a differentiated curricula and style of presentation, restricted friendship patterns, class and race bias, differential impact on student self-concept, misconduct and teacher expectations. Foremost among these is the possibility of a differentiated curricula with students in upper tracks receiving an enriched program of study. We now turn our attention to the possibility that tracking results in a differentiated curricular.

Differentiated Curricula and Instruction

Most researchers agree that the course content and the manner by which it is presented vary considerably between tracks. Additionally, the quality of instruction is not just different in higher tracks it is much better! Classroom presentations conducted in lower tracks often lack the comprehensiveness and enthusiasm of those made in higher tracks. Under normal circumstances, one might assume that all students within the same grade level are taught a uniform body of information. However, the research literature confirms that ability grouping sets in motion a process of differentiated curricula with variations in both the content and method of instruction. In turn, this policy of differentiated curricula affects what has been referred to as Opportunity to Learn (the amount of potential curriculum content that is made available to students). OTL is measured by the percentage of the *intended* curricula, which is made available to students, and contemporary research indicates that it has a direct bearing on academic achievement. Certainly, students cannot learn unless they are provided with the opportunity to learn!

In her review of tracking procedures in twenty-five of our nation's schools, Jeannie Oakes found that the educational content and the manner of presenting it have consistently varied by track. In one instance she reported, "While upper track students were learning Shakespeare, lower tracks were calculating sales tax" [Oakes, 2005, p. 98]. This researcher also uncovered that instruction in lower tracks was splintered; it stressed isolated bits and pieces of information rather than a comprehensive inquiry. On the other hand, the instruction presented to upper track students was more coherent. Teachers usually taught across the curriculum and frequently related subject matter in an attempt to build upon previous learning.

Goodlad's analysis of over 300 schools likewise revealed differentiated curriculum by track. At one point, he observed that the classics, literary genre and critical thinking exercises were common in upper tracks. By contrast, students in lower tracks spent more class time completing worksheets and reading textbooks and secondary sources [Goodlad, 1984].

Similar variations in content and pace of instruction were reported by other researchers. Some found that instructors interacted more frequently and offered more praise and support to upper track students [Allington, 1983; Grant and Rothenberg, 1986]. Others noted that faculty provided appreciably more instructional time to upper track students than to those in lower tracks. Higher track students were also given greater opportunity to work independently and assignments that necessitated the use of higher order thinking skills. Likewise, research found that lower tracks were more often provided with remedial books and secondary sources. Finally, more off-task behavior was observed in low-track classes; teachers spent considerably more time on matters of discipline and less time on actual instruction (deMarrais, 1999; Dreeban and Bar, 1988; Firestone and Rosenblum, 1988; Hallinan, 2003; Lucas, 1999; Riordan, 1997; Pallas, 1994).

As a result of a differentiated curriculum, it is likely that high track students are provided with knowledge which is more highly valued in our society, while low track students are not. Students assigned to high ability tracks also learn more and at a faster pace. It is not difficult to understand how this educational edge can lead to achievement differences between different tracks and in time; contribute to a widening of the achievement gap. In turn, this differential treatment can place lower track students at a considerable disadvantage when they apply to college because they are not always presented with the knowledge and skills that are required for admission. Accordingly, the differentiated curriculum may also impact on career and future life choices.

It is also possible that the educational structure of tracking, with its high level of selectiveness, may give rise to a separate and distinct set of friendship patterns. This pattern may very well act to deny economically advantaged students, who are disproportionately assigned to upper tracks, the opportunity to mix with students of color and low income students who generally compose the lower tracks. The reverse is also equally important, in that less advantaged students are not given the opportunity to mix with economically advantaged students and the possibility of acquiring essential social and cultural capital. What restraints, if any, does tracking place on the friendship patterns of students?

Friendship Patterns

Several studies suggest that tracking may have an influence on who students select as friends. The terms social and cultural capital are often employed in the sociology of education to assist us in understanding exactly how social class impacts on life chances and outcomes. While social capital refers to the capacity for family and friends to invest attention and support in others, cultural capital is concerned with the knowledge base of individuals as well as the capacity to participate in high status cultural experiences. It refers to the way individuals speak, dress and act. If track assignment is related to friendship patterns, it may also influence the type of social and cultural capital an individual possesses and therefore have some bearing on future life chances.

Friendship patterns and the manner in which they impinge on a student's school plans and academic development have been the subject of considerable research [Gamoran, 1992; Heynes, 1974; Khmelkov and Hallinan, 2000; Persell, 1992]. Heynes finds that one advantage of participating in an upper track may be the opportunity to associate with economically advantaged and academically oriented peers. Alexander and McDill [1976] reveal that enrollment in an upper track appreciably increases the possibility of befriending economically advantaged students. Gamoran also reveals that students are more likely to select friends from within their respective tracks and that little interaction takes place between lower and upper track students.

In almost all cases, current research indicates that tracking is responsible for the development of a relatively separate and distinct informal pattern of friendships. In fact, only one early study Deidrich (1964) reveals no appreciable difference in the selection of friends between the tracked groups. The one significant difference in the Diedrich study, however, is that all students are members of the middle class. Hence, tracking may not necessarily influence friendship patterns when lower and upper track students have the same or similar socio-economic backgrounds. Considerable research is available which documents the fact that tracking also serves to separate students along racial and class lines.

Class and Race Bias and Tracking

Although the practice of tracking claims to sort students by academic ability in order to adjust instruction according to student needs, in practice, it often separates children into tracks according to race and socio-economic status. While students of all social origins have been identified as low or average in ability, economically disadvantaged Blacks and Hispanics are disproportionately assigned to low track classrooms (Ansalone, 2001, 2003; Bratlinger, 2003; Kershaw 1992; Rosenbaum, 1980). Ironically, contrary to the efforts of tracking proponents to explain the overrepresentation of Black and disadvantaged populations in the lower tracks by poverty, research has revealed that controlling for these variables does not explain all of the disparity (Losen and Welner, 2002). It is likely that the negative effects of segregation of students based on presumed ability might be similar to the negative effects of schooling based on social class and race. It is also likely that tracking creates a process of segregation that promotes and seemingly justifies racial and socio-economic inequality.

Considerable research suggests that tracking results in the separation of students along racial, socio-economic, and ethnic lines. In light of this research, tracking is viewed as an educational structure which limits the potential range and experiences available to students, seriously impacting on their social and cultural capital.

As early as 1961, Maurice Eash found that ability grouping at an early age seemed to favor the placement of children of high socio-economic groups in upper tracks. From his analysis, this researcher also concluded that grouping practices separating students on the basis of ability also reduced the possibility that students would be exposed to a broader range of ethnic and cultural differences. Another researcher, Douglas also found that upper class students were disproportionately represented in higher ability groups while students from lower classes were found primarily in the low-ability classes. This English study, *The Home and the School*, revealed that streaming (the English term for tracking) by ability reinforced the process of social selection since middle-class children were more often assigned to upper streams (tracks), more than their ability justified. Heathers likewise revealed that low ability groups in grammar schools had a disproportionate number of children from lower class and minority origin and concluded that tracking served as an agency for maintaining class and caste stratification in American society (Heathers, 1969).

Current researchers also underscore the disproportionate number of minority and poor children who are assigned to lower tracks (Ansalone, 2001; Darling-Hammond and Green, 1990; Loveless 1999; Hallinan, 1991; Oakes, 1987; Oakes and Lipton, 1994; Persell, 1992; VanderHart, 2006). Jeanne Oakes reveals that track placement is most often determined by student characteristics which include prior ability, race and socioeconomic status. Another researcher, Loveless, finds that tracking consistently relegates poor and minority students to lower tracks and by doing so, dooms most of these students to an impoverished education. In their comprehensive review of the extensive tracking literature, Linda Darling-Hammond and Joslyn Green find a disproportionate number of poor blacks and minority students assigned to lower tracks. Their data suggest that those children who are in greatest need of a strong curricula and sensitive teaching are less likely to receive it. Rather, they are assigned to schools or tracks where teacher shortages are acute and under qualified teachers are most numerous. The research is clear! Tracking perpetuates the existing culture of inequality as poor and minority students are more often assigned to lower tracks. Here they are unlikely to receive a high quality education, which in turn hampers their ability to attend college and secure a good paying job.

Students may not be intentionally sorted into tracks on the basis of class and race, but some research permits us to understand exactly how this may be accomplished. Decisions about track placements are made by schools and often based on nonrelevant ascriptive factors strongly influenced by class and race. Kindergarten reading groups may be arranged prior to the end of the first week of school and primarily based on class-related characteristics, including style of dress and parental occupation. It is also not unusual for students to be sorted on the basis of cultural norms, language, and disciplinary records (Ansalone, 2000). Linguistic expressions and cultural experiences conveyed by family members and students were prime determinants in college acceptance for students studied by Bourdieu and Passeron (1979). Additional research reveals that teachers often judge and sort children into tracks by the quality of their clothes and the manners displayed during the first few days of school (Page 1991; Rist, 1970).

Whether intentional or not, it has become increasingly clear that disadvantaged students are systematically harmed by an educational practice that has become pervasive in American schooling.

Student Self-Concept and Tracking

For the most part, researchers report negative consequences for the self-concept of students who are perceived to be slow and assigned to lower track classes. Interestingly, these students do not suffer a loss of esteem when placed in middle range tracks (Hallinan, 1996; Oakes, 2005; Page, 1987). It is very likely that tracks can create a self-fulfilling prophecy of behavior and belief in children and play a significant role in defining the type of person students believe themselves to be.

In their 1970 review of the literature, Findley and Bryan conclude that tracking reinforces positively the self-concept of high ability groups and reduces the self-esteem of low and average groups assigned to low tracks. This research further suggests that this educational structure does not build healthy self-concepts and desirable attitudes. In another study, Mann (1960) provides an interesting perspective of how tracking affects the self-concept of students. His research, which includes interviews with over 100 fifth graders in an American public school, calls upon each of the students to identify their specific class section. Almost all of the children in his sample responded that they were in "the best" or "the lowest" class rather than by the name of the teacher. Additionally, when asked why they were placed in that specific section, all responded by saying that they were "smarter" or "dumb" or "lazy", clearly reflecting the impact of the tracking on self-concept. Caroline Persell's (1977) analysis of tracking research concludes that tracking by ability may be detrimental to the self-concept of low and average ability students. However, she finds that it impacts positively on the self-concept of students assigned to upper tracks. These students develop very positive expectations for their performance (Oakes, 1985; Persell, 1977; Rosenthal and Jacobsen, 1968). Finally, the work of Sorenson (1969), and Page (1987) help us to understand how a change of self-confidence takes place.

Revisions of self-confidence may take place in a variety of ways. Students who are unaware that they possess upper track academic ability while grouped randomly may, upon being assigned to an upper track, become more actively aware of their academic status and incorporate this into their self-concept. Students of presumed low ability may not be as acutely aware of their status until they are publicly assigned to a low track which in turn might lead to a downward revision of self-concept.

While considerable research concludes that tracking tends to stimulate negative self-concept in lower track students, one study suggests that tracking is not associated with student self-concept (Goldberg, 1966). This study, however, was conducted in a predominately white middle class school. It is probable that the socio-economic homogeneity of the school may have impacted on the relation between self-concept and grouping. On the other hand, Sorenson (1969) speculates that the tracking of students can have a negative or positive effect. If the separation is looked upon or presented as a punishment, it is certain to have detrimental effects. However, the stigmatizing effect of the tracking can be counteracted by a change in classroom competition. Those students who are labeled as "slower students" may be able to raise their self-concept when interacting with students of similar ability. Generally, he theorizes that the stigmatizing effect will depend on the visibility of the tracking. In addition to the possibility that tracking may cause a downward revision in self-concept, some research suggests that lower tracks are structured to educate students with behavioral problems. Assignment to these classes may contribute to a downward spiral of achievement and the development of hostility, resentment and misconduct.

Misconduct and Tracking

The link between tracking and misconduct in school is difficult to establish. Essentially it rests on the presumption that students assigned to lower tracks find themselves dissatisfied with their placement. McPartland and McDill (1976) are among the first to suggest that school policy can encourage misconduct in a variety of ways. Employing self-reports these authors reveal that those students who report a greater satisfaction with school also report less truancy and misconduct. Additionally, some research suggests that assignment to a lower track may contribute to greater resentment and dissatisfaction with school eventually leading to disciplinary problems and possible withdrawal. In an early examination of tracking in American high schools, Schafer and Olexa also suggest that while a causal link between misconduct and track position is difficult to prove, assignment to a lower track does lead to frustration and rebelliousness on the part of students. In their study, 19 percent of the upper tracks compared to 70 percent of the lower track students admit to three or more school violations (Schafer, Olexa, and Polk, 1970).

If lower track students redefine their self concept as a function of track position, it is possible that this may lead to general dissatisfaction with education and the entire schooling process. Additionally, teachers may reinforce this feeling of dissatisfaction by identifying and placing value on students according to track position. Students in high upper tracks are continuously referred to as high achievers while those in lower tracks are considered slow learners. A number of other studies also suggest that assignment to lower tracks leads to misconduct, truancy and eventual withdrawal from school (Goodlad, 1984; Oakes, 1985). Finally, Goodlad's study revealed that teachers of lower track students spent more time in disciplinary measures and that lower track students were more often perceived as discipline problems. Tracking has also been known to influence the development of differential expectations on the part of teachers.

Teacher Expectations and Tracking

Research also suggests that the educational structure of tracking may influence the expectations that teachers hold for individual students. Initially, what teachers know about students very often comes from the student's track position and, in general, teachers hold lower expectations for lower track students and higher expectations for those in upper tracks (Wheelock, 1992).

Richardson (1989) found that teachers more often based their expectation for student's academic performance on track placement and not on school records. In fact, his research uncovered that when school records contradicted teachers' expectations for a student's academic performance, the teachers more often disagreed with the official record of the student.

Other studies have considered the extent to which teacher expectations influence achievement. These studies reveal that teachers hold more positive expectations for students in higher tracks and tend to convey these expectations to the students. In turn, these positive expectations seems to impact on the achievement of students (Brophy and Good, 1970; Persell, 1977; Rist, 1970; Rosenthal and Jacobson, 1968). Of sixteen studies analyzed by Persell (1977), only three do not report a positive academic gain for students for whom teachers held and verbalized high expectations. Some studies also provide an insight into exactly how the expectations are translated into grades and how differential expectations are communicated to students. For a detailed discussion of these subjects the reader is directed to Chapter 6.

There is considerable evidence to suggest that tracking may very well limit equity and excellence in schools. It is also likely that this educational practice separates students along lines of race and social class, contributing to a form of separate and not equal educational experience for many students. In light of these possibilities, many have expressed concerns about the legality of this practice in American schooling. Does tracking provide a sound strategy for dealing with the disparity in students' abilities or is it a discriminatory practice that should be banned?

THE LEGALITY OF TRACKING

The policy of segregated schooling was officially legitimized in 1896 by the U.S. Supreme Court when it ruled that "separate but equal" was consistent with the Constitution of the United States. In so doing, the Plessy decision reinforced an evolving culture of apartheid in American schools commonly referred to as Jim Crow.

The Jim Crow schools were greatly inferior to those attended by white middle-class children. They lacked even the most fundamental learning resources and in many cases, classes were taught by teachers with the most rudimentary educational skills, many of whom had not even completed the eighth grade (Irons, 2002). In general, educational differentiation was not available and these schools often taught children of different age and grade levels in the same room. If this were not bad enough, 90 percent of all Black so called "secondary" schools were actually elementary schools offering an additional year of schooling. Neither did these schools offer courses in science, art, music, literature, or foreign language. The curriculum included only the most elementary form of math and mirrored the basic skills needed for employment in the domestic and agricultural areas. Any additional education beyond this point was considered non-essential (Anderson, 1988).

In 1954, the Brown "separate but equal" ruling put a legal end to the practice of de jure segregation in the schools. The action was hailed by many as revolutionary and the first orchestrated attempt in this country to address the problem of equity in schooling. The decision also contributed to the emerging belief that education could influence opportunity and facilitate economic and social equality (Mickelson and Smith, 2004). In spite of this encouraging historical event, many continued to argue that a culture of inequality in American schooling was embedded and the reforms that slowly emerged contributed only modestly to equality of educational opportunity.

Today, in spite of the many advances, the concept of equal opportunity continues to undergo periodic setbacks. Regretfully, many argue that U.S. schools are once again becoming increasingly segregated. Some fifty years after the passage of Brown, many believe that the United States is experiencing an insidious tactic employed to maintain segregation. This tactic, tracking, employs sorting students into different levels or tracks based on their *perceived* academic ability (Welner and Oakes, 1996).

Tracking remains widespread in American schooling and has been identified as the greatest second generation threat to equality of educational opportunity (Wheelock, 1992). Many view tracking as an attempt to perpetuate the stratification system and reinforce the separation of youth along ethnic, racial and socio-economic lines. Additionally, opponents of this educational structure contend that it denies economically disadvantaged students the opportunity to achieve in the schools. They underscore research findings which call attention to tracking's impact on the affective and cognitive development of lower track students. In fact, many even contend that tracking is a subtle and insidious way of maintaining a separate but equal learning experience in the schools (Hallinan, 1995; VanderHart, 2006). So why, in spite of the mounting evidence that tracking is racially discriminatory, is this practice maintained?

Writing in the Harvard Educational Review, Welner and Oakes contend that in the wake of the progress towards school desegregation immediately following the Brown decision, Americans acted in diverse ways. Some pulled their children out of segregated schools while others called for the expanded use of ability grouping. These researchers cite the growing ranks of those opposed to the practice of tracking including the National Governors Association, the Carnegie Council for Adolescent Development, the National Education Association, and the College Board. Further, they contend that a petition to the nation's courts might provide an effective strategy in eliminating this practice, yet, they concede that the courts may be unwilling to take on this challenge.

In the past, legal actions directed against tracking have had only limited success and U.S. Courts have been reluctant to interfere in the everyday operations of the nation's public schools. However, proponents of detracking argue that by virtue of the equal protection clause of the 14th Amendment as well as the Civil Rights Act of 1964, our nation has already determined that discrimination based on race presents a danger to our society. Hence, they argue that the legality of tracking may be challenged if detracking proponents can provide *evidence of intentional discrimination which is voluntary.* However, providing voluntary intent is indeed quite difficult. Legal actions against tracking based on violations of Title VI of the 1964 Civil Rights Act must also provide evidence that the tracking has a negative impact on racial groups. In cases of this nature the school district must counter that the practice is an educational necessity in the district. Regretfully, past actions against school districts reflect a growing reluctance by the federal government to impose liability without sufficient evidence of intentional (voluntary) discrimination.

Overriding the practice of tracking will certainly not be easy. But court orders can provide an important stimulus in this effort. The legal challenge to tracking may be a possible alternative to detracking efforts but, increasingly, concerned citizens must recognize that the answer to this question rests in the hands of the key stakeholders—parents, teachers and students.

CONCLUSIONS/ IMPLICATIONS FOR EDUCATIONAL POLICY

This chapter explores the impact of within-school differences on student achievement. It is especially concerned with the educational structure of tracking and its consequences on equity and excellence in education. Early studies of tracking generally favor the practice of tracking, while more contemporary research concludes that this practice is relatively ineffective and may even be discriminatory.

Much remains to be learned about why schools choose to differentiate education according to various ability levels. Certainly, tradition and school policy play an important role in this policy decision. In the opinion of this author, tracking seems to be the program of choice primarily because it is embedded in the broader reality and culture of the school rather than because of its overall effectiveness. Like so many other school practices, it represents a well-intentioned effort on the part of parents, teachers and administrators to provide an effective educational delivery system for their student body.

Today, many Americans continue to hold strong assumptions about the nature of student differences and believe that intellectual aptitude, which also includes school success, is a product of ability and that ability is fixed and heritable. Accordingly, this assumption has contributed to the belief among numerous Americans that some children can more easily achieve success in school. Many Americans also firmly believe that most children differ appreciably in their ability to learn. Therefore, differentiated schooling (tracking) according to ability would seem to provide both equity and excellence in the educational experience. But is this assumption correct?

Public schools provide a unique opportunity for minorities and immigrants to acquire technical know-how and learn mainstream American values. However while considered fair by some, tracking has historically put in place a differentiated learning experience which has fostered elitism in education and the notion that by reason of birth, some deserve more attention and better resources than others.

This chapter suggests that tracking places most children at a distinct disadvantage. The ideological and cultural determinants of tracking, as well as the class and race influences on track assignments indicate that, well beyond its ineffectiveness, the practice reproduces inequality in a class stratified society. This view is also supported by the knowledge that recent recommendations to detrack schools have been accepted by poorer urban schools while middle-class parents have resisted the elimination of this educational structure leading some to infer the presence of underlying racism (Kohn, 1998; Wills and Serva, 1996).

Tracking is deeply embedded in the culture of the American school. It has been part of the schooling process in the United States since the end of the Civil War and is employed in some form in virtually all schools. At first, it may have provided an efficient method of assimilating immigrants into the dominant culture and at present has become a "commonsense" method of organizing diverse ability. Student placement within a specific track is also relatively permanent over the progress of a students' career and research also suggests that the academic development of lower and upper tracks becomes more sharply differentiated with each passing semester. Additionally, the pattern of sequential course taking generally locks students into a very specific sequence of opportunities, which also impacts on future educational alternatives and career choices.

Probably, the only consistent finding to evolve from the numerous studies of tracking is that this educational structure, in and of itself, has no significant effect on cognitive achievement except in cases where presumed "brighter" youth are grouped homogeneously. And in all probability, this advantage may be a function of unique processes operating within the tracks including an enriched and differentiated curriculum that upper track students receive.

Distinct patterns in allocating teachers to the various tracks may also figure significantly in the academic outcome of students. More experienced teachers with better credentials are more often assigned to teach upper tracks. In addition, teachers exhibit more positive attitudes when selected to teach in upper track classes. Thus, instead of maximizing the academic achievement of all, tracking differentiates students even more, causing them to be further apart at the end of their educational experience than they were at the beginning. Other processes operating within the tracks include an enriched curriculum, the possibility for a unique set of friendship patterns, and differential teacher expectations and interactions.

Tracking may also influence affective development. Early research fails to assess the impact of tracking on the self-concept of students. This is probably due to the fact that affective concerns were difficult to assess. Additionally, little concern existed for the impact of schooling on the urban poor at a time in our history when schooling was looked upon as a means of Americanizing foreigners. Most contemporary research suggests that tracking lowers self-concept among lower track students who are generally labeled as underachievers causing them to do worse and not better in school (Oakes, 1985; Page, 1991; Persell, 1977). In turn, this label seems to act as a self-fulfilling prophecy, which serves to lower future career aspirations. This important affective consequence may also help to explain how schools create and legitimate inequality.

Current research also finds track placements related to class and race, suggesting that the educational structure of tracking works against the concept of schooling as the great equalizer (Kershaw, 1992; Persell, 1992). Obviously, students may not be explicitly or intentionally sorted into tracks on the basis of these variables but some research is available which enables us to understand exactly how this may be accomplished.

Most schools track students according to one or a combination of the following: IQ, past grades and teacher recommendations. Regretfully, IQ is still perceived as a fixed measure of ability and a predictor of academic potential rather than a flexible indicator of a student's achievement career. While very explicit knowledge is required to answer questions on an IQ test, many social scientists agree that a student must also possess a high degree of implicit knowledge. This implicit knowledge [how to sit for an exam, or practice in problem solving], represents skills that can be learned. These skills are also not typically stressed in lower class families or in lower tracks. In view of this, lower class groups enter school at a natural disadvantage and are more readily sorted into lower tracks. Once tracked, they are also more likely to remain in the lower track and experience an even greater academic deficit over time.

When track placements are generated by teacher recommendations, it is also interesting to explore the basis upon which these recommendations are made. Some research reveals that students are often sorted on the basis of factors that are influenced by race and social class—language, dress, and behavior (Ansalone, 2003; Gouldner, 1978; Rist, 1970). Certainly, the behavior and general appearance of students are characteristics that are defined by class, race, and possibly even ethnicity and lead one to suspect that these variables significantly impact teacher expectations in some subtle ways.

Most studies also show that more learning takes place in higher tracks, even after researchers have controlled for presumed initial ability, race and socio-economic status. Often, the course content of higher tracks contains information of a more implicit nature that involves critical thinking skills, problem solving and decision-making. On the other hand, memory and rote skills are stressed in the lower tracks (Goodlad, 1984; Oakes, 1985; Pallas, 1994).

Our conclusion is, therefore, inescapable. The inequality caused by within-school differences, especially tracking, may facilitate underachievement. This being the case, the fault lies not with the cultural or genetic deficit of students but with the educational structures in our schools. Therefore, the major task that lies ahead is not to repair children but to alter and transform the atmosphere and policies of the schools.

The educational structure of tracking has evolved into a common sense management strategy for organizing students in many American schools. It is a taken-for-granted social construction of students and school organization. However, like so many other practices, well intentioned or not, it is certainly not worth the time and the trouble in light of the noted negative impact.

Policy Implications

Clearly, at issue in the tracking debate is how to enhance equity and excellence in education and, at the same time, educate a significant number of students of diverse abilities. De-tracking may not always be the answer, neither might it be possible! A solution might lie in a practical accommodation, which includes some of the following elements:

Mainstream Whenever Possible. It is likely that any organizational idea that segregates students into permanent and distinct groups based on presumed academic ability may encourage faculty to develop a kind of expectancy for their students. As they begin to expect more from some students and less from others, they also begin to make accommodations of curricula and alter their style of presentation to classes of perceived slow and better learners (Oakes, 1985). Accordingly, upper-level tracks receive curricula of more imaginative nature while students in lower tracks often receive the bare minimum (Ireson and Hallam, 1999; Oakes and Lipton, 1994). It is, therefore, not unreasonable to suggest that organizational practices, which mainstream students will be less likely to set in motion this expectancy factor. It is recommended that schools take positive actions to replace tracking with heterogeneous grouping of students whenever possible. In cases where full elimination of tracking is not possible tracking may be reduced in some subject areas or the number of ability levels can be reduced. Additionally, research has revealed that some forms of tracking may actually be less harmful and more efficient than others. These types include within-class groupings and the Joplin Plan.

Frequent Track Reassignments. Students' grade assessments should be conducted frequently in order to enhance the possibility of moving students up or down the tracking system. Track assignments should be made on the basis of students' knowledge of specific subject areas. The possibility of assigning students to a higher track will encourage them to work harder if they are dissatisfied with their placement. It may also eliminate stigma and the possibility for a student to be permanently labeled "slow" because of his/her permanent assignment to a lower track.

Positive Teacher Attitudes and Expectations. Lower-track classes must become the focus of special attention. Administrators should carefully monitor the quality of instruction in these classes. If a between-class track structure is employed, administrators and faculty must make a concerted effort to speak positively about all of the classes.

Only faculty who demonstrate a positive attitude towards lower track students should be selected to teach in these tracks. Teachers must believe that all students, regardless of track, are capable of learning. Accordingly, teachers should be provided with some reward for their service, including additional "prep" time or merit compensation.

Schools should offer periodic sensitivity sessions to teachers, alerting them to their potential for creating an "expectancy factor" which may impact students' academic achievement. Research is available suggesting that positive teacher expectations for student academic success encourage students to achieve academically (Ansalone, 2001; Brophy & Good, 1970; Rosenthal & Jacobson, 1968). Since teachers hold lower academic expectations for students assigned to lower-level tracks, this expectation may impact the achievement of these students (Oakes, 1985).

Maintaining Tracking for the Right Reasons. It is not unlikely that Administrators may feel pressure to implement or maintain a tracking structure within their schools in order to provide what parents consider acceptable curricula for their "higher ability" students. These parents may feel threatened by the social diversity present within their school and believe that achievement within the school will likewise be diverse. For them, tracking is considered a practice that will enable their children to advance at an appropriate pace with children of equal ability. At the same time, teachers, especially senior faculty, may also pressure administrators to maintain tracking so that they may have the opportunity to teach advanced or gifted classes. Additionally, many of these teachers may consider assignment to a higher-track as some form of benefit or reward and insist that teaching students of predominantly the same class is easier. Administrators, faculty and parents must become aware that if tracking is present when achievement diversity within a school is low but diversity of race and class is high, *it can almost never be defended as an appropriate academic strategy.*

Strong Commitment to Success. Schools which embark on programs of detracking must maintain a strong commitment to student equity and achievement. These same schools must support the faculty with appropriate professional development so that they may learn to work effectively with students of diverse academic backgrounds. It is also necessary to convince parents of high ability students that heterogeneous classes offer a positive learning experience and are in the best interest of their children. This may deter them from seeking another school. Proponents of detracking, Wells and Sera (1996), suggest that schools offer a number of detracking "bribes" or advantages for keeping their children in schools that are detracked. In exchange for their political "buy-in" parents of high ability students should receive assurances that the detracked school excels in one or several other "commodities" that are not necessarily available at another local school. Some of these advantages might include a well funded art or music program, excellent science curricula or smaller classes and an intensive faculty development program.

Part V

A THEORETICAL SYNTHESIS

Chapter Six

Explaining Unequal Achievement in School: A Theoretical Synthesis

There is no surer foundation for harmony than to improve the education of the common people.

Thomas Jefferson

PREVIOUS EXPLANATIONS OF UNEQUAL ACHIEVEMENT

Few issues in the sociology of education have continued to spark more controversy than the differential achievement of students from economically advantaged and disadvantaged homes. Coleman's landmark study, published over four decades ago, was among the first to underscore the strong relationship between socioeconomic status and positive academic achievement in the schools (Coleman, 1966). More recent research has also consistently revealed that the family into which a child is born is by far the single most important factor in predicting that child's overall academic success. In short, the higher the social class standing of the family, the higher the academic achievement of the child (Epps, 1995; Lareau, 1995; McLoyd, 1990). Interestingly, the relationship between social class standing and achievement remains constant regardless of how social class is measured, or which indictor of academic achievement is employed (Haveman and Wolf, 1994; Oakes, 1985). Notwithstanding the occasional exception, one thing remains clear—children from poor families do not do as well in school as do children from middle and upper class backgrounds.

But why? A number of macro-level theories have attempted to explain the cause of this perplexing problem. Macrosociological explanations of underachievement in school provide a broad-based focus on social structures that shape our society. They enable us to consider the wider spectrum and view children in schools as members of the larger social class system. This type of analysis permits us to consider how broader issues like social class, race, differential funding and organized political pressure may contribute to achievement and equity in education. Many of these macro explanations have been discussed in previous chapters and each provides some insight into the problem of unequal achievement. But, on the whole, when considered by themselves, none really provides a comprehensive explanation for underachievement or school failure. Let us, once more, briefly examine the three most popular theories in this area.

Cultural Deprivation

The Cultural deprivation model suggests that differential academic and career success is a function of students' cultural backgrounds which, in turn, also impacts on linguistic preferences and childhood experiences (Holman, 1997; Lewis, 1966). This perspective on the development of underachievement underscores how a culture of poverty can influence each and every aspect of a child's existence. As a fact of life, poorer parents are less likely to provide the extensive linguistic and cultural experiences which many consider vital to learning and academic success. Proponents of this view suggest that student learning is seriously handicapped if not totally inhibited when there is little relationship between school language and cultural patterns and the culture/language of the home.

It is also possible for some schools to unknowingly discriminate against disadvantaged students by engaging in what has been termed "cultural mismatch." Since teachers generally come from the middle class, their learning and teaching style may differ significantly from that of their students who are more likely to be from working class homes. The research of Jacqueline Jordan-Irvine is successful in identifying a number of cultural variables between African and European cultures that may have an impact on how a teacher's behavior will affect students (1991). Her research also highlights competencies that can be developed in teacher training programs to accommodate some of the unique learning styles of black students (Irvine, 1991, 2003).

In short, cultural deprivation theory contends that children of families in poverty are more likely to emerge from a home environment that lacks the intellectual stimulation and parental support capable of nurturing the development of critical thinking and intelligence. These children also lack the family mediated benefits and networking channels necessary to excel in school or later life (Bourdieu and Passeron, 1990; Dumais, 2002; Portes and Landolt, 2000).

While some of these concerns remain formidable, cultural background variables have never been isolated as prime contributors to educational deficiency and many suggest that accepting this rationale for poor academic achievement is tantamount to blaming the victims themselves. Additionally, perhaps the greatest drawback of this theory is the fact that, in spite of the handicaps noted, so many children from socially and economically disadvantaged families perform well in school!

Deficient Schools Theory

A second explanation centers on the quality of schools attended by disadvantaged students. Schools that lack the resources to motivate and educate students can have a detrimental effect on overall academic achievement. Proponents of what has been termed the "Deficient Schools Approach" suggest that only good schools with strong economic resources can remediate the differences between advantaged and disadvantaged homes. Those who advance this view affirm that schools with strong resources can contribute to student achievement well above that which can be expected based on the social and economic background of students (Weglinsky, 1997). They examine the imbalance of funding and the inferior treatments accorded to disadvantaged students attending these schools and view this as the prime factor in differential achievement. This perspective is vividly articulated by the research of Jonathon Kozol (1992) and Lisa Delpit (1995) who provide a frightening insight into this shadowy corner of American education. Their work clearly exposes the disparity in school resources and teaching strategies employed between urban and suburban schools, as well as a funding strategy that is unfairly based on the cost of local housing. Their assessment provides the core of what has been termed the "Deficient Schools Argument."

But not everyone agrees with this assessment or the impact that school resources can have on student achievement. Surprisingly, data from both the Coleman (1966) and Jencks (1972) studies suggest that equalizing funding resources for the schools would not entirely improve the academic achievement scores of disadvantaged students. Both studies conclude that family background is a more important factor than school funding. Another apparent flaw with this theory rests in the thousands of minority and disadvantaged children who attend deficient schools and continue to do well academically! Therefore, if cultural background and inferior school resources could not adequately explain the failure of disadvantaged students to succeed in school, researchers once again turned their attention to the student—this time to the heritability of intelligence.

Heritability Theory

Sir Cyril Burt (1883–1971) is credited as an early pioneer in the field of heritability and intelligence. His work with mental measurements suggests that intelligence is correlated with nature rather than nurture and that poverty is one obvious result of being less intelligent. Arthur Jensen and Richard Herrnstein are perhaps the two best known contemporary advocates of this perspective. Their controversial stance suggests that certain ethnic/racial groups suffer from severe genetic deficiencies in intelligence (Jensen, 1969; Shockley, 1972; Herrnstein and Murray, 1994) which account for their poor performance in academic and career pursuits.

The intelligence debate revolves about the meaning of intelligence and its ability to be accurately determined by IQ examinations. Obviously, proponents of a link between intelligence and heredity subscribe to the idea that IQ exams accurately measure inherited intelligence and that differential performance of racial and minority groups are valid. Jensen's notorious study concludes that identical twins reared apart differed little in their measured ability; while fraternal twins reared apart differed much more in IQ scores (Jensen, 1969). Some more recent research also confirms these findings about the possibility of a heritable component in IQ scores (Scarr and Weinberg, 1987); however the Jensen research has been the subject of great criticism. Those opposed to his conclusions argue that analysis of the four famous studies of monozygotic (identical) twins which he employed as the basis for his argument are replete with methodological flaws and as a result argue that his conclusions are in error (Fraser, 1995; Jacoby and Clauberman, 1994; Kamin, 1974). While the argument for a strong genetic link between social class and IQ or between Black White differences and IQ is particularly weak, it nonetheless continues to command the attention of many. This is especially true in light of the apparent lack of assimilation of blacks into mainstream U.S. society and the similar track record of other immigrant groups prior to their assimilation. It is also difficult to dismiss the idea that disadvantaged minorities do not perform well on such examinations since test questions may be culturally biased and deal with subjects that are not familiar to these groups. More recent research in this area also concludes that the most important factor affecting intelligence is social (Hurn, 1993). This fact seems evident when we examine a recent question on the New York State science exam which required inner-city students to select the type of surface that was best for roller-skating. The correct choice, *blacktop*, was eliminated by many inner-city children since they believed it referred to a black shirt.

TOWARD A THEORETICAL SYNTHESIS

Our initial examination of macro sociological theory examining the source of unequal achievement between students of different social origins has uncovered three seemingly interesting but inadequate explanations. As educators and citizens, it is critical for us to have a thorough understanding of *exactly* what affects achievement and school success. If it can be determined that inequality is strengthened by school policies or perhaps, some form of cultural depravity, and if we can understand how this process takes place, it may be possible to bring an end to this discouraging problem. Consequently, if it is possible for disadvantaged students to succeed in school, it will also be more difficult to discriminate against them later in life.

To arrive at a *complete* understanding of unequal achievement; our approach must contain a synthesis of both *micro and macro* sociological theory. A macro sociological approach enables us to focus on children in schools as members of the larger U.S. social class system. It permits us to understand how position in the stratification system can contribute to a student's learning trajectory and the availability of opportunity. It provides an understanding of how different values and aspirations are instilled in youth by the contemporary class structure, and what role these values play in promoting motivation and school success. On the other hand, the addition of a micro sociological approach, specifically the incorporation of interaction theory, allows us to examine how educational structures (tracking), processes (teacher expectations), and daily classroom interactions may shape academic outcomes by depressing the academic progress of disadvantaged students and facilitating success for children of the upper and middle class.

Let us now address the second of these two perspectives, the micro sociological approach, by focusing on two theories whose understanding is essential to our overall synthesis.

Symbolic Interactionism

Symbolic Interactionism, sometimes referred to as interaction theory, is concerned with micro patterns of daily, face to face interactions between people. Rather than focus on institutions or organizations, this approach examines the daily encounters of people and how they stimulate responses from each other (Blumer, 1969; Denzin, 1992). The interaction may be a *verbal* communication, a *physical* movement or even a facial expression. Each of these interactions may stimulate a response or a change in attitude on the part of another.

For example, a vibrant smile or an assuring nod from a teacher may foster increased confidence in the response of a student.

Interaction theory rests on the assumption that human beings react to subjective interpretations of the world. It can be an interesting perspective when studying underachievement in the schools since it provides us with a powerful tool in understanding how student-teacher interactions may create and even help to legitimize inequalities between children. Additionally, it focuses attention on how students learn who they are and make social comparisons necessary to develop their sense of self-concept and self-esteem.

The origins of symbolic interaction theory may be traced back to eighteenth century Scottish thinkers. These philosophers implied that people evaluate their own behavior by comparing themselves with others (Stryker, 1990). In America, several prominent social thinkers including the educator, John Dewey (1859–1952) and the sociologists, Charles Cooley (1864–1929) and George Herbert Mead (1863–1931) have contributed to the popularity of this perspective. To Symbolic Interactionists the *self* is a symbol. It is not inborn; rather, it is actively constructed by our daily interactions. It is a representation of the ideas that we have about *who we really are*.

The School as a Child's Looking Glass

Charles Horton Cooley (1864–1929) was among the first to explore the social origin of the self. His theory, *the looking glass self*, underscores the importance of daily social interactions in its development and suggests that we acquire our sense of self by seeing it *reflected* in the behaviors of others toward us and imagining what they really think of us (Cooley, 1902). This process takes place in three stages. It begins with the formation of an image of how we appear to others. Do we come across as intelligent or appear to be slow? Are we agreeable? Next, we imagine the judgment that others attach to that appearance. This also provides a clue as to how we are perceived by the broader society. Finally, our unique sense of self takes shape when we are capable of perceiving the actions and feelings of others to our own acts and thoughts. Accordingly, it is through this *looking-glass* image that we develop our sense of self (Cooley, 1902, p. 83). The looking-glass self is not necessarily a direct reflection of what others see in us, it is our imagination and subjective interpretation of what others see in us. Therefore, this perception of our self may influence us to modify our own actions. For example, if we conclude that we are amusing, we may try to enhance this characteristic and act accordingly. If we sense that we are considered too boisterous; we may modify our actions and attempt to act more conservatively. The theory of the looking-glass self underscores the importance of schools and teachers in developing the student's sense of self. But exactly, what role does the school play in this process?

Think of the school as a theater or giant stage in which the sense of self develops. In school, students begin to understand who they really are. They learn that they have an existence that is different from other students. Their interactions with peers and teachers are critical in the development of self since the reactions and comments of teachers can have a dramatic impact on how they see themselves and who they become. If students believe that teachers perceive them as being bright, they may become more energized and comfortable in the classroom. If they receive encouraging signs that foster this perception such as positive body language in the form of smiles, gestures and positive statements, it is likely that they will develop a positive self-image and a high regard for school. On the other hand, if students are the recipients of negative comments and body language relative to their academic ability and potential, this may result in a deteriorating educational experience.

Mead and Role Playing

Another theorist expressing interest in the relationship between social interaction and development of the self is George Herbert Mead (1863–1931). Mead does much to extend the overall theory of Charles Cooley and his theory places strong emphasis on the role of *play* in a child's life. Mead suggests that "play" enables children to "take on the role of the other." While playing, children assume the roles of others, which help them to understand how others feel and think (Mead, 1934). In time, the child becomes capable of understanding what "most others" think of me, hence, the *generalized other.* Mead, too, places great importance on the role of symbols and is credited with introducing the concept *symbolic interaction*—asserting that interaction between humans takes place in terms of symbols, especially language.

For the most part, the *interactionist approach*, which is so important to the development of our explanation for underachievement in the schools, is derived from the works of George Herbert Mead. This approach enables us to consider everyday social interactions that take place in the school and focus on their role in developing student self-concept. It is concerned with the process by which children begin to learn and interpret the meaning of symbols. For example, why do some children learn and accept the idea that they are academic achievers, while others construct an image of themselves as slow? Symbolic interaction underscores the part played by teachers and schools in this process and alerts us to how much of the process is subject to negotiation and interpretation.

While Mead and Cooley began with the idea that one's actions were evaluated by how people define the situation (the reality *they* attribute to it), Herbert

Blumer used the term *symbolic interaction* to describe a theoretical perspective which considers society to be composed of symbols which people use to establish meanings about a situation (Blumer, 1969). The interaction that takes place within a school may affect what and how much we learn. For example, if teachers believe that "culturally deprived" means having difficulty learning, it is likely that they will alter their interactions with children who they perceive as culturally deprived. It is also likely that these same instructors may limit the quantity and quality of the curricula that they deliver to these students, thereby restricting the students' access to knowledge and opportunity to learn. Subject matter of a higher currency value may be reserved for a "better" class. On the other hand, if an instructor believes that the class is academically gifted and greets them with encouraging smiles and affirmative nods they may participate more actively and actually learn more.

Symbolic Interaction and the Classroom

For Symbolic Interactionists, the world is composed of meaningful symbols that are an important part of how humans communicate with each other. Symbolic Interaction attempts to analyze society by understanding the subjective meanings that men and women place on these symbols. Understanding these subjective meanings enables people to act and react according to *what they believe* is true and real. Accordingly, *society is considered to be socially constructed* through the interpretation that men and women place on behaviors (Berger and Luckman, 1967). The underlying idea of the symbolic interaction approach is that people actually create the reality that they experience in their daily interactions.

This perspective is particularly interesting in the classroom since it is possible that some teachers may respond to students according to their ascribed characteristics (race, ethnicity, class, gender) and the meaning that those characteristics have for them. Clearly, this perspective shifts attention from the intrinsic ability of the student to a social reality created by teachers which is based on the meanings that they have imputed to such things as race, class, and gender.

Utilizing this approach can help us to understand the manner by which teachers and other school personnel may act toward children who possess different ascribed characteristics (race, gender, class, etc.). Accordingly, disadvantaged children may be assigned a low learning potential which might subject them to differential treatment by limiting the quantity and quality of the curriculum or the number of student/teacher interactions. In turn, this action has a direct impact on what and how students learn.

Certainly, the process of schooling should ignore a student's social origins! However, the classroom does not exist in a vacuum; it is very much influenced by the processes that impinge everyday life. The treatment of students is often impacted by issues of race, gender, and social class, or the related variables of dress, language, and diction and the meanings that teachers hold for these characteristics. Teachers are often influenced and favor students with middle-class speech, dress, and manners. Much research has uncovered that academic achievement is closely associated with students' social origins. Few, however, have attempted to clarify the role of the school in this association.

For Interactionists the school is vital to the development of the sense of self. Meanings are constructed and assigned to students based on symbols and the meanings that teachers have attached to them. Labels of "slow" or "gifted," especially if they are applied as a result of some ascribed character-istic, culturally biased exam or possibly even a different maturation rate, may cause students to internalize these labels and conform in a manner that is con-sistent with them. The resulting behavior on the part of the student only acts to reinforce the academic expectations that the teacher has for each student. It is also likely that since teachers represent strong authority figures, the label of underachiever is more likely to "stick" to students from disadvantaged families, since these families are less likely to know how to challenge the la-bel. Clearly, labeling involves a process of negotiation between parties hold-ing unequal power, and the more powerful party is considerably more influ-ential in determining the outcome (Scheff, 1968). Thus, the definition of students as "gifted," "average," or "slow" begins with these labels and fol-lows students from grade to grade. This label which often contributes to the students' performance confirms the expectations of their teachers, and the stu-dents' academic progress is recorded in all school records. Now more than ever we understand Coleman's assertion that the academic gap between ad-vantaged and disadvantaged students may be relatively small as school begins but increases significantly with each successive year of schooling (Coleman, 1966). It is likely that a self-fulfilling prophesy is created in which the ex-pectations of the teachers shape the behavior of the student that fulfills those expectations (Alexander, Entwisle, and Thompson, 1987; Brophy, 1983; Dusek, 1985). Interestingly, relying on their self-perception as non-achievers, these same students may select less challenging careers or even "give up" on improving their academic skills. Symbolic Interactionists refer to this overall shaping process as the Social Construction of Reality.

THE SOCIAL CONSTRUCTION OF REALITY

"If people define situations as real, they are real in their consequences . . ."

W. I. Thomas

A recurring theme that sheds light on the explanation of unequal achievement in the schools is the idea that human social interactions mold our perceptions of reality by the subjective meaning we ascribe to them. Discussion of this *social construction of reality* assumes that we are talking about what is "real" for specific members of the society as it is directly experienced by those members. This necessarily leads us to the question "What is reality?" Does it truly exist or can it be molded by individuals? Because these ideas are constructed by people in interaction with others, we refer to these ideas as social constructs—thus the term—social construction of reality. Symbolic interactionists suggest that we create our own reality and then proceed to exist within those definitions. Thus, in the words of W.I. Thomas "If people define situations as real, they are real in their consequences."

Defining Reality

An interesting account related by Benjamin Hoff may add clarity to our discussion. In one of his stories, Hoff describes a picturesque water well that had been dug at the side of a mountain road. Locals and travelers often commented with gratitude about the *Wonderful* Well and its ability to provide refreshment. One evening, a man approaching the Well fell into it and drowned. People heard of the accident and soon learned to avoid the *Dreadful* Well! Soon after it was learned that the man was a drunken thief and in his attempt to escape a night patrol—he slipped and fell into that *Wonderful* Well (Benjamin Hoff, 1992, *The Te of Piglet*, p.172).

What can we assume about the reality of the Well? Does its essence change, *or,* is it the perception of the well in the minds of the local resident that becomes constructed differently? Interactionists believe that people interact and respond to each other, not on the basis of objective meanings, rather on the basis of meanings *assigned* to others and their actions. Reality therefore is not fixed; it is negotiated through a process of interaction. What we believe to be true is dependent on how we see it! This social construction of reality can help us to understand human social interactions in a new light. It enables us to see how the race, gender, and social class of students is likely to impact human social experiences in a significant way. Assumptions about race, gender, and class have influenced all aspects of life including performance in school, the type of careers people pursue and the amount of money they earn.

As Peter Berger and Thomas Luckman (1967) state, humans agree on definitions of what is going on and then cooperate in order to maintain these definitions. Let us consider one interesting example. The sociologist William Chambliss (1973) observed two groups of young lawbreakers, the Saints and the Roughnecks, attending a small town high school. Both groups stretched the limits of the law, drank excessively, and committed criminal acts. One group was composed of adolescents from lower class families (Roughnecks) while the others emerged from a middle class background (Saints). Although the Saints committed more criminal acts than the Roughnecks, most of the local residents considered the Saints to be "promising" young men. By contrast, the Roughnecks were perceived to be troublemakers. Regretfully, only four of the roughnecks completed their high school program and all of them remained in constant trouble with the law. In the end, each followed blue-collar careers and two of them served time in prison. Interestingly, all of the Saints studied for advanced degrees and most entered the professions. How was it possible for the community to construct such separate realities about each of these groups?

As noted earlier, the Symbolic Interactionist perspective attaches importance to symbols. Without a doubt, social class is an important symbol which influences people's perception. The Roughnecks came from disadvantaged families and most associate trouble with this class. On the other hand, the Saints came from respectable middle class families and most expect law abiding behavior from this group. In short, most people see what they expect to see! The Saints were also socialized in middle class values and more savvy about how to win law enforcement authorities to their side. As a result, the Saints were issued warnings and entrusted to the care of their parents, while the Roughnecks met with the full vengeance of the law.

The labels that we apply to others have a significant impact on how they are perceived by others and themselves. Clearly, the Roughnecks lived up to their label. Their position in the social structure—lacking class rank and social capital—can help us to understand their sorry state. However it is when we employ a micro sociological approach to explore their daily lives and interactions that we begin to understand how their reputations closed doors of opportunity that were opened to the Saints.

While reality may be a social construct, it is likely that some groups or individuals within the society might enjoy a greater advantage in defining exactly what it is. Clearly, this raises the issue of power and everyone may not be an equal partner in this process. It is also likely that more powerful groups in society have the ability to define a situation and have others accept their definition. But what is involved in applying a new definition of reality and what is the role of negotiation in this process? In order to explore this issue, let us examine Labeling theory.

LABELING THEORY

Labeling theory emerged in the 1960s and remains an integral part of the interactionist perspective. In fact, many consider it a variation of symbolic interaction. Labeling focuses on how a new reality (a label) may be applied to a particular person and how this new identity affects that person's actions and behavior. This perspective underscores the responses of others as the most important factor in understanding how behavior is created and the label is successfully applied (Becker, 1963).

In a school environment, Labelists would be interested in how the label of "underachiever" is applied. Consequently, they would explore the interactions of teachers and students rather than focus on specific characteristics of students or the school. It is this process of interaction and the meaning that teachers and students impute to it that defines achievement or underachievement. The example that many students cheat on tests while only a few actually acquire the label of cheater provides a good example of what labelists study. In short, the labeling process examines specifically how a label is applied and exactly, how the new identity emerges. So how is this label applied?

The Process of Acquiring a Label

What is the possibility that a label will actually "stick" and what are the rules that regulate this transfer? Sociologists suggest that "power" is certainly an issue in the acquisition of a label that the less socially empowered are more likely to acquire labels (Adams, 1998). Edwin Schur was among the first to identify a three step process by which a label is successfully imposed on someone (Schur, 1971). The process includes *Stereotyping*, *Retrospective Interpretation* and *Negotiation.*

Stereotyping

The first step in acquiring a label involves the process of stereotyping. As human beings living in society, we develop preconceived notions about people, places and things. These stereotypes generally inform our everyday interactions. Some commonly held stereotypes include the belief that men are better mathematicians than women, Asian Americans have a facility in computer science and boys are better athletes than girls.

Research by Snyder and Hoffman underscores exactly how stereotypes influence our behavior. In one study, a photo of either an attractive or unattractive woman is shown to a group of college men who are informed that they will have a brief phone conversation with the woman prior to a personal introduction. After viewing the photo, the interviewer requests that they provide a description of what they expect her to be like. Viewers of an attractive photo expect an outgoing, sociable, and poised individual, while those provided with an unattractive photo anticipate an awkward and serious woman. Stereotypes influence each man's behavior since each responds with a commonly held stereotype associated with being attractive or unattractive. In turn, the women treated with warmth and humor respond in like fashion while those treated awkwardly exhibit a cold response. This experiment underscores the ability of stereotypes to influence behavior (Snyder and Hoffman, 1991).

Labelists suggest that applying a stereotype to a person is the first step in applying a label. We often define the situation by reverting to stereotypes even prior to our interaction with a person. In schools, certain ascribed characteristics of students (race, gender, social class) may send signals to teachers. In turn, teachers may associate a commonly held stereotype with each of these characteristics and attaching a stereotype becomes the first step in a process of labeling which impacts how students are treated and how they may internalize the label. Stereotypes find support in the media and are reaffirmed in daily interactions. Accordingly, the reported statement about the academic dismissal of a disadvantaged youth seems to encourage and reinforce the presumption that all disadvantaged youth will subsequently fail in school. Additionally, these stereotypes also impact on the personality and actions of the person. Stereotyping can propel mechanisms of the self-fulfilling prophesy, which are related to a second step in the labeling process.

Retrospective Interpretation. Once a stereotype has been applied, the practice of Retrospective Interpretation allows us to view our subject in an entirely new light consistent with the stereotype that we have just applied. It is a process in which we re-interpret past actions in light of the new information we now have of the person. This reinterpretation includes all knowledge of the person in question so that we may seek out subtle cues or nuances of behavior that might provide additional support for the newly applied stereotype. This rereading of the person's past, which amounts to a reconstruction of one's life-history, is central to the labeling process which is now creating a new reality about the person. But there is nothing automatic about this process since the ability to have a label imputed on someone varies with certain situational factors. The most important of these factors are power, social class, and the ability to negotiate the application of the label.

Negotiation. Negotiation, the final stage in the application of a label, involves bargaining. Research underscores the fact that members of disadvantaged classes are much more likely to be labeled. A poor black boy or member of an ethnic minority is more likely to be placed in a lower track thus denying him the opportunity to learn and eventually leading to his being labeled as "slow." Additionally, labelists suggest several ways by which the person afflicted with the new label will come to accept it. In the apparent crisis and confusion that develops while the label is being applied, the preference for consistency shapes the onlookers' general attitudes towards the subject, and also affects the individuals who are being labeled. Students come to view themselves in the same manner as they are viewed by others. They concur in the definition of their situation! In this vulnerable moment, their self-concept is changed to accept how others view them, as underachievers. *Thus, students who are told that they show little potential in school and treated accordingly will soon incorporate the label and act in a similar fashion.* In short, the process unfolds in the following manner:

1. We become aware of specific features of a person and begin to think and behave towards the person in terms of the stereotypes associated with these characteristics.
2. We reinterpret all past actions of that person in light of the new label we have applied.
3. In time, the person becomes aware of how we perceive them.
4. Those with limited ability (power) to negotiate a new reality experience a change in behavior to match our expectations.

Labeling and Tracking

Specifically, how may the labeling process play out for disadvantaged students in the schooling process?

The process of Tracking is pervasive in American schooling; approximately 80 percent of American schools are tracked (Ansalone, 2003; Oakes and Lipton, 1996). Interestingly, as an educational strategy, tracking follows cycles of popularity and suspicion and appears to be correlated with the ethnic and racial composition of the schools. Socio-economic status has also been found to influence track assignment and African-Americans and Hispanics are overrepresented in low tracks. Today tracking remains especially popular in racially and economically diverse educational systems.

The arguments for and against tracking appear in many forms. Supporters of this practice point to it as a pedagogical strategy and suggest that it improves academic achievement and student self-concept in the overall learning experience. They assert that all students make positive academic gains since the course curriculum is tailored to accommodate their level of academic ability (Ansalone, 2003; Rendon and Hope, 1996). Ironically, the same argument is employed by opponents of this process who claim that modification of the curriculum by teachers often eliminates essential course content inevitably leading to an education that denies lower track students equity and excellence, the result being that lower track students learn less because they are actually taught less.

Tracking also impacts on student teacher interactions and how teachers instruct their classes. Teachers of upper track classes more often report being challenged by the opportunity to teach upper track students. They report preparing for each class more extensively, presenting more of the curriculum and utilizing a variety of interesting techniques (Ansalone and Biafora, 2004; Rosenbaum, 1976; Oakes, 1991). Oakes reports that upper track students are more often provided with "high status knowledge" which facilitates their entry into "higher levels in the social and economic hierarchy." Teachers also stress different intellectual processes in the various tracks. Problem solving and critical thinking are common to upper track curricula, while rote and memorization skills are more commonly employed in lower tracks. This alone may account for the widening of the academic gap between students in lower and upper tracks with each year of school.

Tracks often become the subject of labeling. Very often, a student's track may initiate the construction of a new academic reality about the student's potential. What teachers know of students generally comes directly from their track assignment and lower track students are more often thought of as being "slow." As might be expected, in time, the students themselves become affected by the lower level curriculum and the newly emerging definition of their academic potential. Additionally, the differential treatment by teachers actually assists in developing new negative or positive self-concepts for these students and tracking becomes a critical factor in the social construction of failure.

In time, it is likely that both teachers and students will alter their behavior and expectations to conform to the newly created label. In turn, this becomes compounded by students who now begin to think of themselves as "slow." Additionally, this new perception may cause them to resist the extra help that may be assigned to them by concerned teachers. Soon, the ongoing tug of war may lead to a negotiated label of underachiever for the student. This reality is appreciably assisted by differential expectations that teachers hold for the academic progress of their students. But exactly how does the process of differential expectations play out? How are these expectations generated and do they really impact on the behavior of teachers? Equally important is the issue of whether or not the expectations can effect a change in the academic progress of students.

TEACHER EXPECTATIONS

By focusing on the everyday face-to-face interactions of teachers and students, the observational studies of interactionists provide exciting information enabling us to understand not only what effects schools have on different students, but why and how.

One way that labeling my influence academic achievement is by creating an "Expectancy Effect" or the possibility that teachers may develop differential expectations for the academic progress of their students. There is also considerable evidence that these expectations will eventually influence the students to behave in ways that conform to those expectations, independent of the students' actual ability. Conversely, these expectations can also have a dramatic impact on how students see themselves. It is likely that they internalize the expectations that teachers hold for them and ascend or descend the academic ladder according to the level of these expectations (Jackson, 2005; Loveless, 1999; Raffini, 1993; Rosenthal, 1995; Rubie-Davies, 2006).

Some research suggests that teachers' expectations actually influence their behavior and teaching style and also affect the academic achievement of their students (Brophy and Good, 1970; Cotton, 1989; Good and Brophy, 2003; Pellegrini and Blatchford, 2000; Rist, 1970; Jussim and Eccles, 1992). Accordingly, exploring the genesis and consequence of teacher expectations may expand our understanding of why some students succeed in school while others fail. First, let's examine how differential expectations impact on the behavior and teaching style of classroom teachers.

The Impact of Teacher Expectations on Classroom Interactions and Teaching Style

Research suggests that the "Expectancy Effect" impacts on the behavior and teaching style of classroom teachers. Observational studies suggest that teachers categorize quiet, well-dressed and respectful children as "bright and attentive." Clearly, most teachers are from middle class backgrounds and favor children who share their values and aspirations. They also find it more difficult to assign failing grades to these students (Delgado-Gaitan, 1987; Ortiz, 1988). Research reveals that teachers interact more with students from higher social classes for whom they normally hold higher academic expectations. They also offer more praise and positive encouragement to these students when they are correct (Bennett, 1986; Broko and Eisenhart 1986; Rist, 1970). Additionally, they often engage in affirming body-language with these students, smiling, eye contact, leaning forward, more so than when interacting with students who they perceive to be "slow" (Bamburg, 1994).

The expectations that teachers hold for students may also influence their teaching style. One common perception is that lower tracks are designed for students who have a hard time behaving (Oakes, 1991). Accordingly, teachers assigned to these classes stress conformity, discipline and obedience. By comparison, the course content of higher tracks involves strategies which enhance critical thinking, independent study, and problem solving—all useful in higher status careers. In one interesting study, Collins (1986) reveals how teachers employed different instructional strategies with students they perceived to be more academically competent. In his study, all children in the same class used the same basal reader; however, those perceived to be underachievers were taught to read employing a word-by-word technique with teachers providing isolated decoding clues. On the other hand, presumed achievers were taught to pay attention to clauses, comprehension, express intonation, and comment on the emotional states of characters in each story. Clearly, the existing research suggests that teachers' expectations do have an impact on their behavior and teaching style. But is it possible for these differential expectations to influence a student's academic achievement?

Teacher Expectations and Student Academic Achievement

The presence of differential teacher expectations for their students' academic performance is probably best illustrated by the research of Robert Rosenthal and Lenore Jacobson (1968). Their study focused on the possibility that within the same classroom, children from whom the teacher expected greater intellectual growth would show greater growth. The research involved providing teachers with false information about the academic potential for students in grades 1 through 6. In this landmark study, Rosenthal and Jacobson informed teachers at the Oak school, a primary school in San Francisco, that certain students in their classes had been tested for ability and would show signs of "intellectual spurting" within the next academic year. Others, who had also been tested, would show little academic promise. In reality, all of the students had been selected at random and the distinctions had absolutely no relation to ability, since the original ability tests were never graded! Clearly, Rosenthal and Jacobson's contention was that the teachers who were provided with this information would incorporate this knowledge into their subjective evaluations of the students and help to make it true. At the conclusion of the following academic year, the group that had been labeled *intellectually promising* made the most dramatic gains in academic achievement, while the others did not.

Although attempts to replicate the Rosenthal and Jacobson research have not all met with the same dramatic results as the original study, many studies have concluded that teacher expectations for students academic achievement do result in differential treatment. It is likely that the vast amount of publicity associated with this study and the fact that it is included in the curriculum of most education courses has led to some of the apparent problems of replication.

More recent examinations of how expectations influence achievement suggest that that they can and do affect achievement, attitudes towards school and learning (Bamburg, 1994; Cotton, 1989; Snyder, 1993; Turner, 2004). The Cotton report composed of forty-six studies offering research evidence on the relationship between expectations and academic achievement, finds that the presence of high teacher expectations was an essential factor in developing strong academic achievement. Another study of teacher expectations by Jussim and Eccles likewise concludes that expectations contribute to student academic achievement by 5 percent or more and argues that this accumulation over time can have a marked effect on achievement. If teacher expectations do in fact influence academic achievement, it may be important to explore how these expectations are developed.

The Genesis of Teacher Expectations

It is likely that many teachers form expectations about their students on the very first day of school and that first impressions are very often lasting ones. It is also very likely that within the classroom milieu, a number of variables influence the expectations that teachers hold for their students. If so, what do we know about the variables that may influence these expectations?

Personality Characteristics of Students and Teacher Expectations. One interesting study conducted by George Farkas suggests that certain personality characteristics of students assist teachers in developing differential expectations for their students. His study finds that these characteristics send "signals" to teachers about the academic potential of the students (Farkas, 1990). The research conducted in a large urban school district in the Southwest uncovered that students with similar test scores throughout the entire term did not necessarily complete the course with the same grade. The grades of females and Asians were appreciably higher than the grades of African Americans, Hispanics, and Whites. According to this study, those students who demonstrated "docility," "cooperation," and "interest in the subject matter" were more often identified as students with strong learning potential. The study concluded that females and Asians were more likely to display these characteristics of personality on a day-to-day basis.

In fact, in addition to the personality traits suggested by Farkas, research has revealed that certain ascribed characteristics including race and social class may also send "signals" to teachers that trigger the "expectancy factor." It is likely that differential teacher expectations for students of different races and social classes can help in understanding why children of disadvantaged families more often do poorly in schools. Let us examine the research surrounding each of these variables.

Student Social Class and Teacher Expectations. Is it possible for teacher expectations to be related to students' social class or race? In 1970, sociologist Ray Rist uncovered that teachers employed a number of seem-ingly unrelated factors including darkness of skin, body odor, dress, the ab-sence or presence of jewelry, and hair characteristics to determine the aca-demic track level of their students (Rist, 1970). The observational study followed the progress of a group of kindergarten and first-grade children in St. Louis schools. During the course of the first few days, Rist observed that teachers assigned their students to one of three academic groups based on what he perceived to be characteristics related to social class. Those stu-dents designated as most academically promising were assigned to table one, which was located in the front of the classroom and closest to the teacher's desk. Those considered less and least-academically promising were placed at tables two and three respectively. These tables were located to the side and back of the classroom. Rist also noted that students from families on welfare or unemployment or one parent households were more likely to be placed at table three, the least promising group. The most dra-matic finding uncovered by this research was the differential treatment of the three academic groups. Those assigned to the slow group were taught less frequently. They received little supportive encouragement, were criti-cized more often, and were the subject of frequent disciplinary action. On the other hand, those children who were expected to do well and who had been placed at the front of the room, received more praise and encourage-ment from the teacher, were called upon more often, and received more in-struction time and attention. In time, Rist noted the academic deterioration of the group designated as "slow." He concluded that these children became underachievers not because they could not learn but primarily because "the patterns of the classroom instruction initiated and maintained by the teacher inhibited these children from learning and from verbalizing what they had learned" (Rist, p. 42).

Interestingly, the reputations that the students developed in the Kinder-garten class followed them throughout their elementary school career. The second grade teacher used the scores provided by the kindergarten and first grade teachers to divide her class into three academic levels. The lowest level group, which she referred to as "the clowns" were provided with the least challenging readers. On the other hand, the "Tigers" and "Cardinals" (for-merly considered to be achievers in kindergarten) were provided with the most challenging texts. A clear trajectory of success or failure had been set up for these children. This study concluded that the social class standing of stu-dents was an important factor in the formulation of teacher expectations for their academic success.

It is also likely that teacher' expectations for the academic success of their students may also impact on students' self-concept. Children in one study

(Davidson and Lang, 1960) were requested to rate their teachers' attitude to them according to a list of thirty-five descriptors which included such terms as: "clever," "slow," "hard worker," and "eager to learn." An index of favorability that was computed from this list revealed that most middle and upper class children held a more positive perception of how their teachers felt toward them. This finding remained true even in cases where the students' achievement level was held constant. Once again, the research suggests that the expectations that teachers hold for students may be influenced by students' social class background.

More recently, the Baltimore Beginning School Study, a comprehensive inquiry into Baltimore City Public schools suggests a relationship between student social class and the expectations that teachers hold for them. The study concludes that children in disadvantaged schools are not only treated differently than their counterparts in middle and upper class neighborhoods, but that teachers expect children in economically disadvantaged schools to do less well academically than students in advantaged neighborhoods. At one point in the study, teachers of first grade students were requested to predict their students' academic performance at the conclusion of the next grade level. Teachers from higher socioeconomic schools expected their students to score As and Bs, while teachers in lower social class areas expected their students to perform at a C level. Interestingly, the parental expectations for their children's performance were about the same as the teachers' (Entwisle, Alexander and Olson, 1997). The study concludes that differences in teacher expectations are more often set in motion by *where* the students live rather than how they perform academically.

Students' Race and Teacher Expectations

Race may also act as a determining factor in the genesis of teacher expectations. An increasing body of research suggests that teachers often hold lower expectations for students' academic achievement if their students are from disadvantaged backgrounds (Cotton, 1989; Guskin, 1970; Ferguson, 1998; Roscigno, 1998; Tauber, 1998; Diamond and Spillane, 2004). In one of the earliest studies to document this fact, Guskin (1970) requested teachers to *listen* to tape recordings of Black and White students as they read a short paragraph. In turn, the teachers were requested to comment about the academic potential for each of these students. Of the eighty teachers in this study, all agreed that the White students possessed a greater ability to "succeed in present and future educational environments." Interestingly, both the Black and White teachers that were requested to verbalize their expectations for the future success of the students held lower overall expectations for the Black students.

Another study, conducted by Ferguson (1998) confirms that race is an important variable in the genesis of teacher expectations. In this study, teachers were requested to listen to taped responses of students and rate each response for personality, quality, academic ability, and potential. Teachers were also presented with a picture of a Black or White student, the supposed respondent. The study revealed a high correlation between the race of the student and the teacher's estimation of their academic ability and potential. Harvey and Slatin (1975) arrived at similar conclusions. This study selected ninety-six teachers from four schools in lower and upper class neighborhoods. Each of the faculty was presented with nine photos of Black pupils and nine photos of White students. The teachers were requested to evaluate what they believed to be the academic performance level of each child and whether the children came from lower, middle, or upper class families. White children were more often assigned to the upper and middle class than were the black students. Regardless of the perceived social class standing, white students were also more often expected to succeed academically, while black students were expected to fail. The teachers had no contact with the students and the study involved no opportunity for verbal exposure. Interestingly, the expectations of the teachers were made solely on the basis of the visual impression made by the photo. Clearly, there seems to be considerable evidence to suggest that a student's race impacts on teacher expectations.

The Impact of Appearance and Dress on Teacher Expectations

While some research examines the effect of race and class on the genesis of teacher expectations, some earlier studies have focused on other variables including the student's general appearance, dress, dialect and name.

Overall general appearance is usually linked to both social class and culture which once again suggests that these two variables are related to the genesis of teacher expectations. One of the earliest studies to examine the relationship between student appearance and the expectations that teachers develop about students was conducted by Clifford and Walster (1973). These researchers believed that teachers formed their expectations for students' academic success based on appearance. In this study, teachers were provided with an academic profile of students that was accompanied with a photo of an attractive or unattractive boy or girl. For the study, the scholastic record of each student was held constant. The study uncovered that the attractiveness of the student was significantly associated with the teacher's expectations of how well the child would do in school. This research suggests that physical attractiveness is significantly related to the expectations that teachers hold about students' academic potential and interest in education. The expense or

style of students' clothing and grooming habits have also been positively correlated with positive teacher expectations for their students' academic potential in studies by Brookover (1982), Cooper (1984) and Good (1987).

The research of Adams and Cohen (1974) lends further support to the work
of Clifford and Walster. The Adams and Cohen study analyzed student
teacher interactions in the classroom and revealed that the number of stu-
dent/teacher interactions was clearly influenced by the physical attractiveness
of the children. The study also uncovered a second variable that seemed to be
slightly associated with more frequent student teacher interactions: general
appearance/dress. However, it is well to mention that this research was conducted in a middle class school where all the children dressed similarly. The
researchers add that their conclusions might be different in an economically
disadvantaged area where there might be a wider range of dress diversity; in
such a case dress might be more of a factor. With respect to "attractiveness,"
the general pattern is to ascribe positive attributes to people who are considered attractive (Kenealy, Frude and Shaw, 1988). In short, these and other
studies (Conley, 2005) still strongly suggest the role that students' physical
characteristics play in the genesis of teacher expectations.

Finally and most interestingly, a student's name or dialect may also become
a factor in the development of teacher expectations. White, middle-class females continue to make up the greater part of the U.S. teaching cohort while
the school population continues to grow more and more diverse. Good's
study suggests that it is likely that certain social limitations are thrust upon a
child who carries an uncommon or difficult to pronounce name (Good, 1987).

Communicating Expectations to Students

The question of how teachers communicate their expectations to students has
been the focus of several inquiries. Some of the earliest work in this area includes the research of Brophy and Good (1970). Their observational study of
contacts and interactions in first-grade classrooms reveals that teachers employed several methods to accomplish this communication including smiles
and encouraging statements, demanding better performance and praising
those students they believed to have greater potential.

Further insight into this process is provided by Rosenthal's Four Factor theory, which suggests that teachers employ *Climate, Feedback, Input* and *Output*
in order to convey expectations. Teachers communicate expectations through
"Climate" by smiling, frowning, nodding or providing more eye contact to certain students. Communicating expectations by means of "Feedback" is accomplished by providing more cognitive information (detailed responses to
students' answers) or affective information (praise and reassurance) to stu-

dents' responses. *Input* refers to teachers who teach more to certain students thus providing them with the perception that they are important and worth the extra time and effort. Finally, *Output* as a form of communicating teachers' expectations occurs when teachers provide certain students with greater opportunity to seek clarification about class assignments (Rosenthal, 1987).

Finally, the international work of Babad and Taylor (1992) filmed the day-to-day interactions of Israeli students and teachers in order to gauge the interpretations of students to teacher behavior and expectations. In this interesting study, a group of teachers was requested to interact with students that they had previously identified as students of "high" or" low" academic potential. When another group of students was shown video clips of these interactions they were able to tell within ten seconds of viewing the clip if the teachers were responding to high or low expectation students, even though the students in the interaction were not seen. Similar results were achieved when the video clips were viewed by students in New Zealand who could not speak Hebrew. The researchers conclude that the expectations were communicated by tone and inflection of voice, and nonverbal channels including facial expressions and general body language (Babad, Bernieri and Rosenthal, 1991; Babad and Taylor, 1992).

Translating Expectations into Academic Performance

But is it possible to create intellectual competency on the part of students by simply expecting it? Rosenthal (1974) speculates that teacher expectations may cause an increase in intellectual competency *simply by expecting it*. However, when we examine the research we find that teachers who expect more of certain students actually put in process a number of factors which assist the students to succeed. This may include paying more attention to these students, employing new and more innovative teaching strategies with them, demanding more of them, approaching them in a kinder and more encouraging manner and even using unconscious facial expression and posture to encourage them. Rosenthal's research (1968) clearly underscores the different ways in which teacher expectations are transmitted to students via a variety of affirmative physical gestures and actions employed by teachers which include creating a climate of warmth and encouragement, verbalizing more praise, conducting more teaching, and calling upon certain students more frequently. In such manner, it may also be possible for teachers to communicate to their students that they expect more from them (Rosenthal and Jacobson, 1980).

Others, too, have suggested the power of expectations to create a self-fulfilling prophesy (the tendency of people to respond to and act on the basis of stereotypes and labels applied to others) as a stimulus to increased student competency (Brophy, 1986; Cardenas, 1996). Surely, "slow" and "gifted" are not innate qualities of people; rather, they are labels applied to some students by teachers. Further, once applied, certain consequences follow. Students may receive differential treatment including the possibility of being praised and encouraged more often (Bennett, 1991). Certainly, paying more attention to students might elicit greater effort from them and research reveals that teachers spend more time with those students from whom they expect more (Brophy and Good, 1970; Good & Brophy, 2003; Hallinan, 1994; Riordan, 1997). Additionally, teachers may interact more with students for whom they hold higher expectations thus causing them to be more actively involved in the class. Research also reveals that teachers who have positive expectations for students' academic performance offer more encouragements to them, call upon them regularly, and interact with them more frequently (Hallinan, 1994; Cardenas, 1996). Likewise, treating students in a more pleasant manner, evaluating them differently, expecting more of them or even utilizing different teaching modalities may lead to benefits in academic achievement for these students (Cardenas, 1996; Peng, 1974). The use of an enriched curriculum supplemented by primary sources and greater detail may also increase the opportunity-to-learn for these students (Keddie, 1971; Rendon and Hope, 1996).

Ethnomethodologists have also examined the positive effects of visual cues including eye contact, forward lean when communicating with students, affirmative head nods, and smiles on developing positive academic performance. Each of these cues was more frequently observed in upper track classes (Chaikin, Sigler, & Derlega, 1974; Gumpert, 1975; Rist, 1970; Wuthrick, 1990). Finally, students are quick to pick up these cues and the positive expectation that teachers hold for certain students may stimulate the very behavior in question as the student, too, begins to internalize it.

Here, once again, the use of micro-level observations of classroom interactions and activities can help us to uncover the different type of educational experience, which may be offered to students of different social origins, and which may help to explain success or failure in school (Cardenas, 1996; Darley and Fazio, 1980; Rosenthal and Jacobson, 1968). While material resources in schools can provide a rich atmosphere for learning, the power of positive teacher expectations—the expectancy factor—can go far in developing positive academic achievement.

Tracking and Teacher Expectations

Time and time again researchers have revealed that tracking has a definite impact on how teachers think about students. Not only has current research revealed that the greater part of what teachers know about their students comes from their assigned track but it has also uncovered that teachers generally hold lower academic expectations for students assigned to lower tracks. The research also suggests that tracks impact on the expectations that teachers hold for student achievement independently of the students' academic ability. Depending on the assigned track, these expectations are also likely to encourage teachers to provide students with different types of knowledge. High ability tracks are more likely to be taught subjects and skills that will assist them in preparing for college and professional schools. Teachers in these classes are more enthusiastic and often encourage independent study, questioning and critical thinking skills (Dauber, 1996; Wheelock, 1992). Internationally, similar results were uncovered by Boaler's analysis of six schools in England. The Boaler study revealed that tracking students created a set of expectations for the faculty that often overruled their awareness of the individual students' academic capabilities. For the most part, students assigned to the lower tracks were generally not expected to perform as well as students in the upper tracks (Boaler, 2000). Additionally, an earlier study by the same researcher found that teachers often altered their class presentations when teaching upper track students since they believed that these students were much brighter and expected them to excel (Boaler, 1997). Ireson and Hallam (1999) reported similar conclusions and suggested that tracking encouraged teachers to hold lower expectations for the academic ability of lower track students. It is also likely that the overall impact of these expectations is cumulative over the length of a student's school career. Keeping this fact in mind, it is easier for us to appreciate how tracking may impact student academic outcomes and erode student self-concept.

Tracks can easily create an expectancy factor in students and play a very significant role in determining the type of person that students believe themselves to be. Studies have uncovered that tracking is related to student self-concept and exactly how students view themselves in the hierarchy of the school (Ansalone, 2003; Hallinan, 1994; Nordman, 2001; Oakes, 1995). As we have already noted, Mann's (1960) study of 100 fifth graders assigned to various tracks makes perfectly clear the fact that these students more often identified themselves by track rather than by their teacher's name when requested to identify their class section. It is likely that students who have been assigned to lower tracks begin to define their position in the school hierarchy as low; while those placed in high tracks begin to perceive themselves as achievers. Once again, the labeling impact of a track system is apparent.

The use of educational tracking seems to stimulate a negative self-concept in students assigned to lower tracks and a more positive image for those assigned to the upper tracks. This is especially true if the tracking is viewed as some form of punishment or ranking system. It is likely that the tracking serves to further marginalize students; it identifies them as different and underachievers. It is also likely that the stigmatizing effect of the tracking will depend on the degree of visibility of the tracking.

THE PROCESS OF BECOMING AN UNDERACHIEVER

Clearly, it seems that a synthesis of macro- and micro-level sociological theories offers a far better understanding of why students succeed or fail in school. By enabling us to consider how large-scale social arrangements are structured and the effects they have on us over time, macro-level analysis permits us to examine student underachievement in relation to the broader U.S. social structure. It allows us to see and understand how issues of gender, class and race may impinge on learning, provide direction to our actions and possibly even set limits on our behavior. In schools, just as in society, people learn appropriate behavior as a result of their position in the social class structure. Macro-level theory also enables us to understand how such variables provide an advantage or disadvantage for some students within the schooling process and how these differences escalate over time. But differences in behavior are not always entirely the result of race, sex or heritable factors and these theories alone cannot offer a comprehensive explanation of why some students fail in school while others succeed.

On the other hand, Micro-level analysis, which focuses on the dynamics of interaction between teachers and students, alerts us to the interactive process involved in becoming an achiever or underachiever. It focuses on the small-scale, everyday patterns of behavior. It alerts us to the process by which people *create* the reality they encounter in their daily interactions. It explores how day-to-day interactions impact on student self-concept and how these daily encounters shape their view of the school as well as their potential for academic success within this system. For children in classrooms, the availability of praise or criticism, encouragement or ridicule will ultimately have significance far beyond the confines of the classroom. When teachers label students as "gifted" or "underachievers," it is not unreasonable to suggest that they will treat them differently. Regretfully, if teachers and other school personnel believe that one race or social class is more advantaged than another, the behaviors that follow may result in differential treatment. Thus, what occurs in the daily face-to-face interactions between teachers and students in the contemporary classroom is intimately tied to the overall organization of education in the society!

Symbolic interaction theory analyzes the socialization function of the school and the part it plays in the development of the student's self-concept. This perception that students hold of themselves is not innate; it is socially constructed by interactions with teachers and other school personnel. The resulting labeling process is key in the way children define themselves and their role in school. Previous theory has failed to take into account both of these key perspectives in explaining school failure.

A comprehensive assessment of school outcomes must also necessarily take into account the school practices and structures that control access to knowledge and the opportunity to learn. *The process of becoming an underachiever is a dynamic, often complicated and reciprocal process.* Certainly, the ways in which children learn to see themselves within the school system is an important part of this process. Interaction theory helps us to understand how a student's "reality" is created by how others act towards them and how this action is based on the meanings that certain symbols hold for them. It underscores the fact that we perceive and are perceived by others, not directly, but rather in terms of the labels that we apply to others and that others apply to us. In short, we see what we expect to see.

If, for example, a child is seen as culturally deprived and if teachers interpret this to mean that students cannot learn; it is likely that teachers will modify their actions towards these students. Accordingly, the new actions may impact on the students learning as well as their emerging sense of self. Furthermore, faced with this dilemma, the disadvantaged family often lacks the political clout (power) to negotiate a different image of their children. The result is that these children become labeled underachievers. A major element in every aspect of the drama of labeling is the imposition of the label by those legitimated to do so, and the poor or powerless are always more likely to be labeled (Becker, 1963). Further, as the label of achiever or underachiever is applied, the student begins to accept his/her status in the school environment. In turn, those students who are expected to perform well are provided with greater support and encouragement. Slowly and over time, the label of achiever or underachiever solidifies and gains momentum and the academic gap between slow and gifted students increases with each subsequent term.

Students also perceived the manner by which they are treated and make a corresponding adjustment in self-concept. Students treated as gifted begin to think of themselves as achievers and work harder, while slower students who perceive their position in the school hierarchy as the bottom become further discouraged, leading to even poorer performance. In sum, both students and teachers accommodated their behavior to fit the expectation that has been created and tactfully applied to each student.

Equally important is the manner by which teachers construct reality about the nature of their students. Very often this reality is influenced by the expectations that they hold for their students' academic progress, which is often influenced by ascribed characteristics including race, class, and ethnicity. Clearly, these expectations influence student outcomes, especially as students learn to adapt themselves to schools based on how they respond to the expectations of their teachers.

Finally, educational structures and practices including testing, tracking, and special education programs are intended to assist in the education of underachievers. Regretfully, research reveals that these strategies do little more than separate students while denying many the Opportunity-to-Learn. They further marginalize and relegate certain students to learn less and less with each subsequent term.

While it is true that some disadvantaged students manage to escape the dire circumstances and do well, countless others fail and their numbers are ever increasing. Clearly, education is not working as it should. If our analysis is correct, it calls for a radical overhaul of some of the time-honored and cherished educational ideas and structures within the schools. Only by such a dramatic transformation can we ever hope to effect change!

Part VI

CONCLUSIONS AND DISCUSSION

Chapter Seven

Where Do We Go From Here: Discussion and Policy Implications

One day a captain named Jonathan captured a Pelican on an island in the
Far East.

This Pelican laid an egg from which came a Pelican, astonishingly like the
first.

In turn, this second Pelican laid an egg, from which came another, who did
the same thing.

This thing can go on for ever, if you don't make an omelet . . . .

Robert Desnos, *Chantefables, Chantefleurs*

SOLVING THE PROBLEM OF UNEQUAL ACHIEVEMENT

Throughout this book I have attempted to examine the conditions leading to
unequal achievement and lack of equity in our schools. Hundreds of studies
have been cited. In light of this research, it is now time for me to summarize
the findings into some coherent plan of action.

In my opinion, one of the most important functions of schooling is to assure that every student has an equal opportunity to succeed. Increasingly, success in school is a forerunner of success in life. But for many, schools fail in
this respect. In fact, by not providing students with an access to knowledge
and an equal opportunity to learn, they often restrict the career trajectory of
disadvantaged populations. In turn, they perpetuate mediocrity, facilitate inequality and contribute to unequal achievement. Schools must do better!

The focus of this book is unequal achievement. For decades, in their attempts
to understand this problem, educators have focused only on the characteristics of
children or schools. Rarely have they considered the important day to day interactions of children and teachers within classrooms or the educational structures

187

and practices that help to shape student self-concept and self-efficacy. Only more recently have we focused on the possibility that failure, including unequal achievement in schools, may be a social construction! This book is an attempt to call upon the wealth of macro and micro research to bring about a truly comprehensive understanding of this problem. Each has so much to offer.

Sociological research on the macro-level examines the problem of underachievement by directing our attention to its links with social class, racial, and gender group membership. Specifically, it explores how membership in these groups can influence students' educational opportunity and future life chances. By reminding us that race and class often determine the schools that children attend or the opportunities available to them, it permits us to understand how the broad social structure may dictate the presence or absence of opportunity. Certainly, if we are to understand and address the problem of unequal achievement, it is imperative that we develop a strategy to respond to each of these limiting factors.

But race, gender, and class, as we have seen, may also play a role in creating the initial expectations that teachers hold for their students' academic success. Children interact with teachers, counselors and other students on a daily basis. Micro-level research permits us to observe the details of these daily interactions. It also enables us to observe the intersection of class, race and gender with educational structures and practices and how this may impinge on academic achievement. By focusing on these interactions, it enables us to realize the power that teacher expectations, biased testing and educational tracking have on how students construct a reality of who they are as students and learners. Clearly, our strategy to respond to unequal achievement must also consider these factors. In sum, a comprehensive understanding of underachievement necessitates a micro and macro sociological perspective.

This chapter attempts to consider both approaches in attempting to create an effective strategy to combat underachievement. First, we turn our attention to schools. By examining the Effective Schools Research, we identify some correlates of effective schools and suggest policy initiatives to effect a change in the contemporary status quo. Recognizing the importance of family, we define effective schools in much the same manner as Coleman—as those which make reliance on family and social origin less important (Coleman, 1966, p. 71). Next, recognizing the importance of positive student self-concept to strong academic achievement, we discuss specific ways in which schools can significantly improve academic achievement through changes in policy and practice that impact negatively on student self-concept and self-efficacy. Hopefully, these policy changes will help to create a level playing field for ALL students. Finally, the role of family and government in raising the level of student achievement is discussed.

Clearly, it is my hope that this dialogue will not only inform but stimulate the development of new strategies that will benefit all children in a democratic society, regardless of their social origin! Let us begin. If schools are partly at fault in the problem of underachievement, what can be done to make them more effective?

WHAT CAN SCHOOLS DO? EFFECTIVE SCHOOLS RESEARCH

The desire among educators to identify the characteristics of effective schools flourished immediately following the Coleman research of the late 1960s. The inescapable conclusion from this controversial study credited the determinants of school performance to factors outside of the school. Coleman underscored family as one of the few significant factors in students' school success. Home experiences followed by composition of the school's student body explained considerably more of the variance in school achievement than did the actual facilities of the school. Schools, the report asserted, could do little to impact the success of students from disadvantaged families. As would be imagined, the academic community vigorously challenged the conclusions of this report, and to this day, some still refuse to accept many of its conclusions.

Utilizing the most sophisticated research tools and designs, a number of prominent educators and social scientists began what eventually became a national pastime—an attempt to identify specific characteristics of successful schools. Researchers made every attempt to identify their absence or presence in schools considered unsuccessful in similar social class areas where children were falling behind. Many researchers considered this to be the birth of what eventually became known as "effective schools research."

The effective schools movement gained new momentum to the point of becoming a national obsession in the 1980s with the publication of the Presidential Blue Ribbon Report, *A Nation at Risk.* This assessment of the nation's schools underscored the need to make educational outcomes more equitable by improving the achievement of disadvantaged students in order to enhance the nation's ability to compete in the economic sector. The report identified a new urgency in the struggle to create effective schools and recommended a comprehensive reconstruction of American education for the sole purpose of enhancing equity and excellence. To many, the Commission's report was yet another call for reform of the nation's troubled school system.

Since that time, hundreds of position papers, in Europe and the United States, have sought to identify correlates of successful schools. In so doing, they were also asserting and validating that schools *can and do* make a difference. As the list of completed projects increased, a number of "effective correlates" surfaced. Recent replication of much of this research confirms the existence of several characteristics of effective schools. Recognizing that schools can make some difference in unequal achievement, this chapter will focus on some of the more important recommendations surfacing from this body of research. First, let us begin with a definition of what we mean by an effective school.

Defining Effective Schools

Clearly, our definition of an effective school is important in determining what characteristics make it effective. Many define effective schools as those which improve the overall academic achievement of *all* students. However, since it is undeniable that academic achievement is influenced by home background variables and that schools are usually composed of students from diverse socio-economic backgrounds, in order to be effective, schools must also strive to diminish the differences between students' homes. If they fail to do so, one must assume that the end result will be social reproduction and the perpetuation of inequality. Therefore, by lessening the impact of the home and social origin and making the conditional probabilities less conditional, the effectiveness of the school is enhanced (Coleman, 1966). Accordingly, our position remains that schools are effective only insofar as they facilitate academic quality for *all* students and reduce the dependence of students' opportunities upon their social origins. In this way, disadvantaged students may enjoy educational equity and have the opportunity to excel academically. In this regard, effective schools are those which do not promote inequality by perpetuating the dominant stratification system. They provide excellence, equity, access to knowledge and an equal opportunity-to-learn for all students.

Correlates of Effective Schools

Michael Rutter's research of British schools, *Fifteen Thousand Hours,* provides us with one of the most interesting studies in effective schools research. It offers valuable insights into what constitutes an effective school. His unusual title refers to the amount of time that students spend in British schools from entry to final graduation. The study examines the quantity and quality of student-teacher interaction by interviewing students and teachers about their experiences in school and finally, comparing student admission data with achievement test scores at graduation. It was conducted in twelve inner-city London schools over a period of three years.

The Report argues that schools are essentially unequal; some draw their students from economically disadvantaged homes while others are primarily composed of students from privileged families. It concludes that the overall effectiveness of schools cannot be judged in terms of graduating students, but rather in terms of the individual gains made by each student. Interestingly, the report finds that physical facilities have little impact on student academic achievement, behavior or attendance rates. Rather, achievement seems to be significantly influenced by the everyday interactions between teachers and students. School characteristics that impact on academic achievement include a positive teacher attitude, effective teaching, high teacher expectations for student success, active student involvement in the learning process and a disciplined environment.

The one inescapable conclusion that may be drawn from the present theoretical synthesis is that students learn better when their teachers know them as individuals, express concern for their progress and expect them to do well. Regretfully, U.S. society does not expect children from disadvantaged families to succeed in school. These children are often identified as low achievers by their teachers and this label usually sets in motion a self-fulfilling prophesy of low expectations and results. In order to better understand the dynamics of expectations and results, educational sociologists employing an interactionist perspective focus on the details of interaction among teachers and students and how they impact on student outcomes. Since children spend a considerable portion of their early life in school, a significant part of their social development and self-image begins to take shape in this educational environment. The conclusions emerging from *Fifteen Thousand Hours* underscore the importance of examining the daily interactions of students and teachers. It also provides the basis for much of the research conducted during the next few decades.

Without a doubt, some of the characteristics of effective schools seem to be nothing more than common sense. Still, many schools fail to actively support these attributes and promoting them is often compromised in favor of other routine problems within the school. Some of the other more commonly agreed upon correlates of the effective schools research which should be explored in an effort to improve the achievement of all students include the following:

A Clearly Articulated School Mission. Effective schools have a clearly articulated mission statement. This statement informs all sectors of the educational environment including academic programs and budget. In addition to its presence, the school mission must also be understood and accepted by the entire school staff as reflecting a commitment to the educational goals and procedures of the school. By means of this academic vision for all children within the school, both teachers and administrators share a commitment to instructional priorities, assessment practices and academic outcomes. Additionally, these goals must be articulated for each grade level and for each class within the grade. Likewise, a shared commitment to accountability is likewise essential.

Strong Administrative Leadership. Effective school research also identifies the Principal as a strong instructional leader who understands the school mission and applies the characteristics of instructional effectiveness. Schools that are effective are characterized by strong administrators who communicate the mission of the school to staff, parents and students. The Principal acts as an instructional leader and applies the characteristics of instructional effectiveness in the overall management of the academic and extra-curricular programs.

A Safe and Orderly Environment. Especially in contemporary society, teaching and learning require security. It is essential for the school climate to be conducive to teaching and learning. Effective schools are safe harbors where children can learn and teachers can teach. They are orderly and disciplined environments in which children and teachers feel secure.

A Positive and Encouraging School Climate. The appearance of the classroom—the sense of order and discipline that it transmits, as well as the persistent encouragement of the teacher with students who may be experiencing difficulty—will help to develop a solid foundation for positive student outcomes. Schools which stress academic achievement, praise students for good work and encourage faculty to interact with all students are often more effective than schools which do not (Good, 1987; Tauber, 1998).

Standards and Policies which Stress the Importance of High Academic Achievement. The superior performance of students in effective schools is not always due to better students but to higher standards and the refusal on the part of the school administration to "dumb down" the curriculum (Coleman & Hoffer, 1987).

Rethink the System of Rewards. Good grades which are considered the reward for good work are often treated as a scarce resource. A competitive reward system employing this philosophy runs the danger of creating and labeling more "losers" than winners. While the fear of grade inflation is understandable, a limit on the number of high grades may also dampen student motivation to succeed.

Strong Home-School Relations. There is growing evidence of the value of parental involvement in the school for student academic success. Effective schools encourage parental involvement in their children's education. They also make parents aware of the school mission and provide them with the opportunity to play an important part in assisting the school to achieve that mission. Research has underscored the importance of parental involvement in the school and its relationship to cognitive achievement.

Staff Who Demonstrate High Self-Efficacy. The staff must be equal to the task. Faculty in effective schools assume responsibility for student performance and must demonstrate by word and deed that they can effect change in students (Cotton, 2001; Murphy et al., 1982; Rubie-Davies, 2006).

Employing a Team Approach. Effective schools employ a team approach. Considered one of the best teachers in America, Jamie Escalante took on a class of underachievers in an East Los Angeles economically disadvantaged area with the hope of reversing their downward progress in mathematics. Escalante's students now rank fourth in the nation among students who have taken and passed the Advanced Placement SAT Calculus exam. How was this possible?

Escalante's approach stressed self-efficacy. Students were made to believe in themselves and in their unique ability to learn. His unusual strategy included instituting a team approach to learning. One of his motivational techniques included wearing specially designed caps and jackets—like those worn by a sports team. Additionally, parents and students were requested to sign a contract that required them to participate in a summer program and attend periodic practice (study) sessions that were as intense as any sports team (Escalante, 1990). Interestingly, the spirit d'corps generated by the enthusiastic program and the generation of positive expectations for the success of each of the students factored considerably in their success.

The formation and communication of positive expectations for students is often done unconsciously. In some cases, teachers view the differential treatment as appropriate because they are dealing with students at different ability levels. Effective schools advocate in-service training programs to help teachers develop a team approach to learning and realize the importance of maintaining positive expectations for their students. Such training is particularly important in under-achieving schools or those which employ tracking structures.

Changes to School Policy and Practice that Impact on Student Self-concept and Self-efficacy

A number of additional modifications to school practice and policy which directly impact on the development of student self-concept and self-efficacy are now recommended.

The Development of a Culture of High Expectations for Student Success

Symbolic interactionists have routinely found that teacher expectations can be especially significant in determining what and how well students learn.

Schools routinely place academically oriented labels (gifted, slow, talented, etc.) on their students. Students who have been identified as troublemakers or con artists find it especially difficult to rid themselves of these labels while those considered "gifted" accrue many benefits both real and perceived because of the imposition of these labels. The available research suggests that a *self-fulfilling prophesy* occurs when teachers who expect their students to succeed are actually motivated to work and interact with them more often to ensure that they do. In effect, their positive expectations and predictions about future academic progress help shape students actions and actually empower them to succeed. On the other hand, as research reveals, teachers often interact less with those whom they expect to fail and in time, these students arrive at the anticipated negative outcome. Clearly, teachers' expectations for a student's ability can help shape and create the anticipated result.

Our theoretical synthesis also suggests that it is likely that certain student social characteristics can trigger the formation of these labels. Research has uncovered that often these expectations and predictions can be related to students' race, ethnicity, social class, gender, and even religion. A close look at future demographic trends suggests that the schools of the future will be composed of a much greater proportion of students from racial, ethnic and religious minorities. In fact, it is anticipated that minority membership will make up approximately one-third of the student population in the near future. On the other hand, only about 5 percent of the teaching force will be members of minority groups (United States Department of Education, 2001). Teachers need to be made aware of the power contained in these labels, how they influence student achievement and the social characteristics of students which often inspire their development!

The presence of positive expectations for student achievement is high on the list of factors which are essential in developing a positive learning environment in the schools. Teachers must believe that all students are capable of learning, and by utilizing positive teacher expectations for academic success, encourage students to succeed. High expectations are a critical correlate of effective schools since they affect student self-concept, academic achievement and other school outcomes. With this thought in mind, lower track classes must become the focus of special attention. Administrators should carefully monitor the progress and quality of the curricula presented to these classes. If tracking must be maintained, then both teachers and administrators must make a special effort to speak positively about these classes and students. Additionally, only those teachers who demonstrate a positive attitude should be selected to teach in lower tracks. Regardless of track, teachers must believe that all students are capable of learning. Accordingly, lower track teachers should be provided with some reward for their services, including additional "prep" time and or merit compensation. Schools should also offer periodic sensitivity workshops to train teachers about the problems inherent in developing and expressing negative expectations. They should be alerted to the possibility of creating an "expectancy effect" which may impact student achievement. A climate of high expectations for student academic success must be an important part of the school culture. One important means of eliminating the possibility of creating labels is to mainstream whenever possible.

Mainstream Whenever Possible/Lessen the Reliance on Tracking

Throughout this book, I have attempted to make clear that children, especially those from poor families, are consistently disadvantaged by an educational practice that is pervasive in American schooling. I have consistently argued that tracking may influence students' academic outcomes in a number of ways but especially via its influence on the expectations that teachers hold for the success of their students. Additionally, teachers communicate these positive or negative expectations to their students in a variety of ways which may affect student academic outcomes. In schools where tracking must be maintained, a more gradual modification of the tracking policy may be desirable. This might include reducing the number of tracks in the school or eliminating tracking in some of the subject areas. Additionally, both teachers and administrators must make a concerted effort to speak positively about the different tracks.

As discussed earlier, tracking refers to a number of different organizational arrangements within and between classes with the overall purpose of facilitating student instruction and enhancing strong academic achievement (Slavin, 1987). As we have noted earlier, it is likely that certain types of tracking structures may produce greater inequality while others may be more academically advantageous or at least less harmful to student self-concept (Gamoran, 1992; Slavin, 1986). Clearly, tracking has an influence on student learning and development. However, some forms may be less detrimental than others. When tracking must be part of the organizational structure of the school, schools should employ those tracking structures which have been reported as having the least negative impact on student self-concept. We have already examined some of the different kinds of tracking structures and the reported student outcome for each (Chapter 5). Let us review some of our results.

Between-class Grouping, Setting and Within-class Groupings

Between–class grouping refers to the separation of students into self-contained classes based on perceived ability for instructional purposes. Most teachers continue to utilize this plan since it enables them to manage more easily the wide range of academic diversity among their students (Ansalone and Biafora, 2004). This plan has the greatest potential to set in motion a labeling process which facilitates a teacher's ability to identify students as slow or bright based almost exclusively on the student's track level (Oakes, 1997). It also has the greatest potential for enabling teachers to modify the content of their classes as well as their approach to instruction based on the perceived ability level of their classes (Entwisle et al. 1997; Oakes and Wells, 1998). In so doing, many students, obviously those assigned to lower track, are denied access to knowledge and an equal opportunity-to-learn. Without a doubt, between-class tracking also results in the greatest stigma to tracked students simply because it clearly identifies students as slow or fast learners. It should be the first form of tracking structure to be eliminated. A second type of grouping that is common in schools is setting.

Setting, another popular type of tracking, assigns students to "homerooms" of diverse academic ability for a portion of the school day and then reassigns them on the basis of perceived ability to two or three tracked subject area classes. When setting is employed there is also less probability that a student will be assigned a label of gifted or slow.

When re-grouping is practiced for the sole purpose of reading instruction, it may be referred to as the Joplin Plan. Like setting, it is likely that the plan minimizes the negative impact and stigma of exclusive assignment to a class of low-achievers. Yet another type of tracking structure that is employed in U.S. schools is Within-class grouping.

Within-class grouping entails assigning students to one of a number of smaller ability-level groups in order to facilitate instruction. The prime advantage is that it allows teachers to present a lesson to the entire class and then divide the class into previously designated groups based on presumed ability of the student. Once again, this type of tracking structure eliminates some of the potential for stigma associated with separating students into entirely different, permanent and identifiable tracks.

Since tracking is often embedded in the very culture of the school, a radical transition to detracking may not always be the very best strategy if a reduction in tracking is the goal.

A solution may lie in a practical accommodation which lessens the schools' reliance on tracking. It is likely that any educational practice that segregates students into permanent and distinct groups based on presumed ability can encourage instructors to develop "expectancy" for their students. As faculty begin to expect more from some students and less from others, they may also make accommodations to the curricula and alter their manner of presentation in classes perceived to be *slow* or *fast* learners. Inevitably, upper tracks will receive more imaginative presentations and enriched curricula while those in the lower tracks will be denied the opportunity-to-learn. Therefore, in cases where tracking cannot be eliminated, every attempt should be made to put in place the type of tracking structure that does not distinctly and permanently identify students as members of groups that are "slow" or "fast" learners. Within-class groupings, Setting and the Joplin Plan seem to be the least harmful types of organizational plans. Ideally, mainstreaming students, whenever and wherever possible, should be the general policy which is followed in the schools.

Monitor Students and Teachers Regularly

In any school, student grade assessment should be conducted frequently. This is especially necessary in schools that employ a tracking system to provide students with the opportunity to change tracks. Additionally, in schools that employ tracking, assignment to a specific track should be made on the basis of a student's knowledge of a specific subject matter rather than on perceived overall knowledge. Assigning students to a higher track may also encourage students to work harder. It may also eliminate the possibility that a student will be labeled "slow" because of his/her assignment to a lower track.

Schools should resist the practice of assigning their most senior personnel or most qualified teachers to upper tracks. Neither should teachers be assigned to an upper track as some form of reward. Permanent assignment of teachers to any one track should be avoided.

Provide Learning Opportunities for Teachers to Develop New Teaching Strategies

There is little evidence to support the claim that tracking or any form of ability grouping improves academic achievement for all groups of students. In all likelihood, the desire to provide each group of students with a learning experience on par with their academic potential inadvertently leads to the development of a differential curriculum. It is also likely that a change to heterogeneous classes may create some pedagogical difficulties. Therefore, attempts to detrack the schools must also be accompanied by the development of creative learning environments that successfully engage students of all ability levels and eliminate many of the pitfalls of tracking or at least modify some of its negative effects. Unfortunately, most teachers lack the expertise and teaching strategies required to do so.

The elimination of tracking is a radical proposal and one which must be accompanied by strong teacher education programs that can improve the overall quality of teaching and facilitate the learning process. Without a doubt, it will require a dramatic reconstruction of instructional practice. The new strategies must enable teachers to instruct classes of diverse learners and allow for differences among children without relegating them to low status curriculum or lower tracks. A variety of methodologies, including team teaching, multigrade classrooms, cooperative learning and the utilization of learning styles, are examples of such practices. For example, cooperative learning strategies especially designed for bilingual classrooms and the adoption of a learning-styles approach have led to dramatic achievement gains and in many instances have reversed the high dropout rates in schools.

Cooperative Learning

Cooperative learning refers to a unique teaching methodology in which students assist each other in the learning process. The roots of this pedagogical technique can be traced back to Greek and Roman schools (Socratic Learning) which emphasized questioning and discourse among students. This discovery based approach to learning emphasizes the generation of knowledge, rather than the transmission of information. As a type of collaborative learning, it enables teachers to act as guides in the learning process, set the class agenda and direct students in the research process. Within the structure of small groups, students learn by mastering a subject, and explaining it to others in the group. Clearly, this form of delivery system is better suited for small groups of students who are more active in their approach to learning (Millis and Cottell, 1997).

High levels of success are reported when cooperative learning groups are kept small, generally no larger than three to five members. The small group approach helps to encourage full participation and avoid the "sleeper effect." Often, teachers beginning to work with cooperative learning permit their students to select their own group. However, the greatest potential for success is realized when teachers assure a heterogeneous mix of students within the group—a balanced mix of ethnic, racial, high/ low ability, female/male students. Students may work on any assignments they would ordinarily complete on their own. They may brainstorm, discuss a problem or formulate concepts from the facts they have generated. As a team member, each student is responsible for learning and assisting other group members to learn.

The research literature on cooperative learning suggests that it promotes student learning, increases retention of the subject matter (since students are actively involved in the learning process), assists in the development of oral and social skills, and promotes self-esteem. Another interesting advantage of this learning strategy is that it seems to improve one's appreciation of racial and ethnic diversity since the cooperative learning groups are generally composed of heterogeneous rather than homogeneous groups (Thousand, 1994).

Cooperative Learning is based on the idea that students who have the opportunity to work collaboratively will learn quickly, efficiently and experience a greater retention of the subject matter. One popular type of cooperative learning, Jigsaw, entails assigning students to small heterogeneous groups with the tasks to be learned also divided into as many sections as there are students. Members of different teams who have the same topic form "expert groups" and study together. In time, each student returns to their original group and teaches that section of the assignment to the other teammates. This procedure especially increases the possibility that all students will interact freely and learn from each other. For example, a unit on FDR might include three groups of students of three students each. One student in each group might research the highlights of his first, second, or third term as president. All of the students exploring his first term might form an expert group and explore this aspect of his presidency in detail. Finally, each member of the expert group will return to their initial group to explain and report their findings to the other students (Johnson and Johnson, 2001).

Elements of Cooperative Learning

Some of the learning strategies that are employed with cooperative learning and help to make it a successful learning strategy include:

Positive Interdependence—the general awareness that the group is linked and that each member's efforts and cooperation are essential for the group to be successful. Each student makes a special contribution to the finished product and, in sum, the work of one impacts all!

Faces to Face Interaction—teammates provide each other with effective assistance, encouragement, the exchange of resources and feedback to improve performance.

Individual Accountability—there is no free ride when Cooperative Learning is employed. Each individual student is accountable and assumes responsibility for his/her portion of the project. This aspect of cooperative learning is enhanced by having students teach what they have learned to others in the group.

Interpersonal/Small Group Skills—each member of the group gets to know and trust each other, communicates effectively, supports each other and resolves conflicts constructively.

Group Processing—teammates are encouraged to reflect often on how well the group is operating and what procedures should be maintained or improved (Johnson and Johnson, 2001).

As a learning strategy, cooperative learning enables all students to participate actively in the learning process. At times, teachers, too, become learners. Students become vested in their own learning and learn to gain from each other's efforts.

Modality Theory (Learning Style)

Another interesting teaching methodology is referred to as Modality theory or Learning Styles. Perhaps the most widely used and comprehensive application of learning style is the one developed by Ken and Rita Dunn. Learning style refers to the very different ways that students retain and process difficult information. Each individual has a unique learning style and proponents of this perspective suggest that one's style evolves from developmental and heritable factors. Since it is composed of biologically and developmentally determined personal characteristics, the same type of teaching strategy may be effective for one student but not for another.

In order to identify a person's learning style, it is necessary to look at what is most likely to initiate and maintain concentration, respond to one's natural processing style and generate long term memory. Teachers cannot identify correctly all the elements of learning style, some elements may not be observable. But for the most part, many of the most significant elements of style have been isolated (Dunn, Dunn, & Perrin, 1994). Clearly, research underscores the fact that one's preferred learning style guides the way we learn. Research suggests that teaching students according to their unique style will maximize their learning ability (Dunn and Dunn, 1993). Students who are aware of their learning style may be able to improve their academic achievement by utilizing instructional strategies that complement their style. This approach also suggests that when a mismatch occurs between a student's learning style and a teacher's instructional style; students may become bored and inattentive, and eventually do poorly in class. Instructors should attempt a number of instructional strategies in order to eliminate this possibility and reach the greatest number of students (Feldman and Henriques, 1995).

According to a popular learning style theory (Dunn and Dunn, 1993), a student's learning preference is determined by examining five stimuli groups that are capable of influencing a person's ability to learn.

The five stimuli groups include:

- ENVIRONMENTAL—students' sensitivity to light, sound and temperature
- SOCIOLOGICAL—students' preference for learning alone or with others
- PHYSIOLOGICAL—the need for food/drink or mobility while learning
- PSYCHOLOGICAL—the need for a global or analytic style of presentation
- EMOTIONAL—the amount of motivation, persistence and structure required by students during the learning process.

Learning style may be assessed by the Learning Style Inventory (LSI) for students in grades 3 to 12 and the Productivity Environmental Preference Survey (PEPS) for adults (Dunn and Dunn, 1994). Interestingly, research suggests that a student's academic achievement improves when the teacher's instructional method matches a student's learning style (Dunn and Griggs, 2000).

Direct Instruction/Increased Wait Time

Finally, effective teaching and delivery of subject matter is also important to student success. Research suggests that the use of "direct instruction" in teaching may also be helpful in increasing levels of student achievement and bolster student self-confidence. This type of teaching generally involves the use of teacher directed instruction that proceeds in small steps. It begins with a review of relevant previous learning. It presents new material in small steps and periodically injects questions to check for understanding. Finally, it supervises and monitors independent student seat work cautiously and provides weekly review of what has been learned (Cooper, 1999; Stahl and Haynes, 1996).

Another way to enhance learning and engage all students within the class is to ask appropriate questions. Questioning skills remain an important part of an effective teaching strategy. Research suggests that a longer wait time after posing a question significantly improves student participation and learning. When students have adequate time to consider a response they often do just that—think! Questions that encourage students to think and work with several ideas at the same time are also more effective in developing thinking skills than responses that require a verbatim recall of facts (Chuska, 1995; Glazer, 1999).

Undoubtedly, many of these changes will require the cooperation and blessing of teacher unions. Additionally, policy makers and local governing boards will be required to make the necessary investments in teacher education and provide the willingness to cut class size to accommodate the new teaching methodologies. Finally, local policies will also need to provide the necessary incentives to attract and retain high-quality teachers in the schools. This will be most critical in schools located in economically disadvantaged areas. One incentive might provide bonus pay for teachers in these critical areas while some other "perks" might include lower student-teacher ratios, more free time for planning and additional financial resources for special equipment and materials.

Develop and Implement New Types of Assessment

Recent research has pointed to the presence of multiple intelligences and the probability that many cognitive processes go unmeasured. One such example would be the Multiple Intelligences theory of Dr. Howard Gardner. Multiple Intelligences theory argues that individuals possess several different types of "intelligences." In the past, the idea of intelligence was perceived as unitary. For the most part, it was believed that a score on an IQ exam could accurately convey the person's intelligence level. In his now classic work, *Frames of Mind* (1983), Gardner debates this belief and argues that individuals exhibit varying levels of different intelligences which contribute to their cognitive profile. Regretfully, today's schools focus most of their attention on only two types of intelligence—linguistic and mathematical. But Gardner contends that they must also learn to recognize and measure other types of intelligence. The remaining six types of intelligence which he has identified include: Spatial, Body-Kinesthetic, Interpersonal, Intrapersonal, Musical and Naturalistic intelligence.

The Gardner Theory of Multiple Intelligences proposes major changes in the ways our schools are run. It argues that teachers must teach in a wide variety of ways using art, music, cooperative learning, role play, multimedia, to name just a few. Further, it suggests that other types of expertise be included under the banner of what we consider to be intelligence. If American schooling is to succeed, new types of assessments that measure and reveal what causes students to think rather than what test score they achieved will be required in the immediate future. This new type of assessment will undoubtedly improve the educational environment by providing insights into mental processes and provide strategies for overcoming deficiencies.

Provide an Equal Opportunity-to-Learn for All Students

Most Americans assume that the curriculum in any grade is relatively fixed with only slight variations for all students in that grade. But do all students within a school have the same opportunity to learn the same course content? Are variations between tracks issues of pace, presentation style or course content? Are some students presented with a curriculum that is more highly valued and leads to greater educational and career opportunity? Essentially, these are some of the issues that threaten equity in American schooling.

Opportunity to learn is defined as the percentage of the intended curriculum that is made available to students. Since teachers' expectations influence presentation, it is likely that lower tracks may contain less of the intended curriculum for the course. Thus the quantity of the course content implemented in lower track classes may seriously handicap those students by not providing an equal opportunity to learn.

The research literature reveals that tracking encourages the development of a differentiated curriculum and often restricts this opportunity to learn. Children of advantaged families are often provided with a curriculum content that may be more "high currency" or "high-status." On the other hand, lower track classes are offered a curriculum that is less relevant. Learning to draw conclusions, critical thinking and problem solving are commonplace in upper track classrooms (Boaler, 2000; Gamoran, 1990; Oakes, 1990; Riordan, 1997). Certainly, all students must be provided with an opportunity to learn. They cannot be expected to learn unless they are provided with access to educationally and socially relevant topics, and one of the more serious disadvantages of tracking is that it restricts this access to knowledge.

Change the Basic Assumptions about Learning

Minor changes in the educational system alone will not solve the problems of American education. If all children are to succeed, it will be necessary for educators to periodically question and examine the assumptions that underscore the status quo of American schools. This status quo is deeply imbedded in the ideological and cultural assumptions relative to the nature of ability, intelligence and equity. Fundamental changes in our perception of ability and equity must precede these changes.

American conceptions of ability and equity date back to the turn of the last century and often confound any attempt to introduce change in the schools. Regretfully, they often hamper serious attempts to provide access to knowledge and opportunity to learn for all students. Some time ago, a distortion of the biological theories of Darwin permitted Americans to scientifically categorize disadvantaged immigrants as socially and morally inferior human beings. It permitted a rationalization and justification of their poverty and educational underachievement. Today, Americans continue to hold strong assumptions about student differences in academic ability and subscribe to the belief that intellectual aptitude, including success in school, is a product of ability and that ability is fixed and heritable (Oakes, 1990; Welner, 1999; Wells and Oakes, 1998). These assumptions suggest that educational differentiation for students of diverse ability may best serve their needs. Accordingly, this has led Americans to believe that some children can achieve more easily than others. Additionally, since most Americans believe that most children differ in their ability to learn, differentiated schooling or tracking according to ability would seem to provide both excellence and equity in schooling. In the past, public schools were looked upon as places where immigrants and the disadvantaged were provided with the opportunity to learn occupationally related skills commensurate with their abilities. The schools taught the mainstream values and attributes required in everyday living. Today, schooling, originally employed to Americanize the immigrants, now continues to sort students into class related careers and occupations.

Many still believe that a differentiated education that restricts access to some types of knowledge for certain groups is perhaps the best means to prepare less-able students for their position in the job market, while enabling advantaged children access to careers in the professions. However, while considered fair and equitable by many, this perception has permitted a type of differentiated learning experience which has led to a form of educational elitism and the notion that some children because of their birthright deserve better schools with better resources and better teachers. In turn, this belief has severely restricted access to education to some segments of the society. This philosophy of education must be replaced with the underlying belief that all children have the potential to learn. All children must be looked upon and treated as equally capable but differently motivated. In this way, both family and school can assume more of the responsibility in providing the necessary incentives to learn. A unique egalitarian educational philosophy of providing all the children with all of the course content may go far in achieving equity and excellence in classrooms. Regretfully, many of the educational beliefs relative to intelligence, as a fixed quantity remain in effect to this day. Clearly, this perception must be changed!

Education in America has been extolled as an avenue of upward mobility. Yet it is generally acknowledged that social class related hierarchies prevail in American schooling and that social origin remains a prime factor in school success (Jencks, 1993; Persell, 1992). Clearly, schools are not presently moving towards equity and excellence, and yet the overall perception persists that schools are meritocracies in which all children have an equal opportunity to realize their potential. But if schools are to succeed, there must be an equitable distribution of resources and all students should have an equal access to quality learning. A meritocratic system necessitates a level playing field! It necessitates the distribution of resources, full access to quality learning for all students and a curriculum that is relevant to all students. But the current system provides an appreciable advantage to the economically advantaged and fair treatment is not currently available to all. Our educational philosophy and actions must match our articulated intention that education should serve as a leveling factor in society. The ethos of egocentrism and greed must be replaced with a moral mandate of the Golden Rule, a social ethic of social reciprocity which is based on considering others as being as valuable as ourselves (Brantlinger, 2003). Educators and policy makers should not manufacture debilitating roles for children by constructing differentiating educational policies and practices (Oakes, et al. 2000). But in order to accomplish this difficult philosophical transformation it will be necessary for middle class parents to be convinced that their children will also benefit if equity in schooling is improved and if schools become responsible to the community and not to special interest groups.

A recent study undertaken by the U.S. Department of Education, The Condition of Education, 2001, underscores the disturbing gaps and inequities in educational access and academic performance among various ethnic, racial, and socioeconomic groups. Further, it suggests that these gaps exist early in a student's career and increase over time! The purpose of this chapter was to suggest ways by which schools can be made more effective for all of the children they serve. My aim was to describe current issues and outline new policy initiatives and practices that might inspire a renaissance in thought about ways to improve schools for a broad range of students. This goal can only be achieved if we let go of some of our time-honored and class-based assumptions about education. Neither can it be achieved without a sincere and genuine desire for change.

WHAT CAN FAMILIES DO?

There are a number of commonsense approaches that families may take to improve the achievement of their students. Unquestionably, an increasing body or research suggests that parental involvement, in almost any form, impacts favorably on student academic achievement. This is especially true if the involvement begins at the elementary level. For the most part, researchers define parental involvement as participating actively in the educational experience of children. This involvement may take a variety of forms including demonstrating interest in school related activities, assisting children with homework, participating in school functions or maintaining an open channel of communication (access) with one's children.

Clearly, there is one thing that families can do. Parents must do more parenting! They must become intimately involved in the education of their children. They must communicate with their children on a daily basis in order to convey a strong sense of parental attitudes and values towards learning. This type of involvement not only provides the child with the social capital needed to succeed but it also conveys to the child that the parent is aware of and concerned with what is happening in the school. It is important that parents monitor more, exert more pressure and establish open channels of communication with their children and their children's teachers. Obviously, two parent families are at an advantage since it is possible for them to do more parenting. The presence of two parents within the home makes it considerably easier for the child to obtain emotional support, assistance with homework activities and grow intellectually as a result of interacting with two adults. Thus, parental involvement is often a function of family structure. Parental presence and involvement are paramount to the academic success of their children.

It is also becoming increasingly apparent that achieving students generally come from families that hold high expectations for them. It is important for parents to set high standards in relation to their children's academic progress. Parents of achieving students expect more and communicate this expectation to their children. Additionally, they also teach their children the behavior required to achieve these expectations. While all students may have the desire to succeed, only a select few may be aware of how to play the role of a student and demonstrate the behaviors that will lead to academic success. On the first day of school, those students arriving without this knowledge, including the acceptable speech pattern and appropriate dress, will most likely be assigned to a slower class and fall behind the middle-class peers the longer they remain in school.

Parents should also monitor closely the impact of peers, peer subcultures and the media on the social development of their children. In the absence of parental supervision, the young increasingly turn to one another for social cues and strategies to solve perceived and real problems. The so-called "peer group effect" can often have a negative impact on achievement and school related activities.

Finally, it is important for parents to realize that students' academic outcomes will vary considerably not only as a result of attending different schools but as a result of the policies and practices that occur within the same school. Parents must learn that differences within schools are of as much importance to the education of their children as are differences between schools. Within-school resources including more effective teachers, curricula, and tracking practices may be differentially allocated by class, race, and gender. In cases where the perceived disparity seems unjust, parents should approach school representatives for an explanation. They should insist that their children are placed in the correct track or if possible, work for the elimination of tracking.

WHAT CAN GOVERNMENTS DO?

The government, too, has an obligation to work for equity and excellence in schools. Governments should employ a wide range of approaches in order to raise the overall level of achievement, especially among disadvantaged populations. As a starting point, so much more should be done to recognize the burdens faced by teachers and schools that register large numbers of disadvantaged students. Traditionally, students facing multiple needs require teachers and administrators to dialogue often with social service agencies. It is likely that the considerable amount of time spent liaising with police and social services will considerably take away from the time devoted to students.

Further ways of assisting these teachers and schools should be considered. Perhaps some reduction in class size or extra compensation should be provided for teachers within these schools. Identifying the needs of these schools and providing additional resources may go far in reducing underachievement. Finally, change is about structural reform and government may be best able to support such change. Funding for increased research in the sociology of education or providing financial support for detracking programs may contribute to many desirable academic outcomes.

CONCLUSION

By utilizing the resources provided by macro and micro research, we arrive at a better understanding of the causes and possible solutions for underachievement in the schools. Each has so much to contribute to our understanding of this national enigma.

Macro sociology enables us to understand how variables like culture and social class shape and mold the lives of students. Understanding and appreciating exactly how social characteristics influence behavior is essential if we are to understand why students succeed or fail. This perspective allows us to investigate how culture and social class are related and how each affects academic outcomes. It provides an appreciation of how academic opportunity is facilitated or denied for students depending on social class and family membership. On the other hand, a macro approach often falls short in its ability to explain why so many of these students continue to succeed in spite of the odds. To this end, micro sociology permits us to examine another ingredient in the mix of school success or failure. From time to time, all children, especially economically disadvantaged children, may have some difficulty in learning. Often this is compounded by their position within the social structure. By providing an in-depth look into the social interactions that shape their self-concepts, micro sociological theory provides us with the tools and understanding to realize exactly how being Black or disadvantaged within society can facilitate a social construction of failure. It provides the opportunity to look closely at face-to-face interactions with teachers and other school officials and understand how students often take cues about their ability and intelligence from these encounters. It enables us to examine how teachers react to students' culture, language, and social class and begin to formulate expectations for their academic success. Finally, it allows us to understand how these expectations are communicated to students and how they may, in turn, help to create a new social construction of reality for each student.

Finally, our conclusion is inescapable; unequal achievement in school is in large part, a social construction. But it is a social construction which is facilitated by student attributes including gender, race, ethnicity and socioeconomic status, as well as by the educational structures and policies employed by schools. It is likely that student-teacher interactions colored by student attributes and educational structures within the schools set in motion a social construction, which may actually facilitate academic success or failure. Because of this undeniable fact, educational practitioners and policy makers must continue to investigate school policies and perceptions relative to student abilities, to understand how they may be related to student achievement. Informed by this knowledge, they must strive to see the power inherent in schooling and vigorously explore avenues for change.

Glossary

abilities—the capacity to perform a particular act.

ability grouping—the practice of organizing students into classes on the basis of academic ability.

achievement test—an exam that is intended to measure what students have actually learned rather than their potential.

"acting white"—slang term used by Black students as a derogatory description of other Black students who decide to perform well in classes—equating good grades with "whiteness."

ad valorem property taxes—taxes placed by the local government on the "value" of real estate owned in order to support the local schools.

age cohort—a group of people born during the same time period.

ascribed characteristics—individual characteristics acquired at birth, such as sex and race.

assimilation—the act of an outsider (minority) joining a dominant group and losing their difference by conforming to its standards and expectations.

between-class grouping—a type of tracking that separates students into self-contained classes for the purpose of instruction on the basis of perceived academic ability.

between-school effects—any differences between two or more schools that may affect academic achievement within the schools.

Brown decision (*Brown v. Board of Education*)—Supreme Court case which resulted in the desegregation of public schools in the United States, stating that separate but equal is inherently unequal.

busing—the act of transporting students to achieve a balance in race and equity in schools.

The Catholic School Effect—the term used to describe the "special advantage" in outcomes that seems to result when students attend Catholic schools, particularly in the form of higher academic achievement.

charter schools—public schools founded by parents, teachers or administrators and managed by private parties operating under a special agreement from the state—for the purpose of providing innovative learning environments with fewer bureaucratic regulations.

climate—one of the four communicative factors in Rosenthal's Four Factor theory. Communicating through "climate" is usually done through body language, such as "smiling, frowning, or nodding."

code of power—anything that may give an advantage to someone to succeed.

cognitive skills—mental abilities that are used during the attempt to gain knowledge (abstract thinking skills).

cohort—a group of individuals that share a common characteristic.

The Coleman Study—Equality of Educational Opportunity-1966. Federally funded study originally intended to document that unequal academic achievement by students of different social origins was the result of unequal educational opportunity caused, in part, by unequal funding of the schools. In fact, the study uncovered that there was little relationship between school quality and academic achievement.

common schools—publicly supported general schools, proposed by Horace Mann in 1837—a school for all the people.

compensatory education—school programs funded by the federal government that provide additional education to compensate for disadvantages resulting from poverty.

compulsory education—school attendance mandated by law based on the belief that education benefits all of the people.

Conflict Perspective—The approach states that schools often perpetuate inequalities related to class, race, and gender as some attempt to maintain their positions of dominance in society.

cooperative learning—a teaching methodology in which students assist each other in the learning process.

correlation—the degree of relationship between two variables.

Correspondence Principle—the belief that the social organization of the classroom mirrors the social organization of work.

creeping credentialism—the term used to describe the rise in the amount of education an individual requires in order to be considered qualified for even a menial job.

cultural capital—a person's knowledge base which generally includes general knowledge, patterns of speech, manners and skills.

cultural deficiency—the belief that some cultures have characteristics that may translate into disadvantages over another cultures' characteristics.

cultural depravity—the belief that some students are raised in homes which lack a rich and stimulating environment.

cultural difference—the belief that a culture may be at odds (different but not deficient) with the dominant white culture, and not necessarily lacking in any way.

culture of poverty—a term first used by Oscar Lewis which describes a culture in which members hold low expectations for their educational and career success and also believe that fate or luck controls one's destiny.

dame schools—early primary schools in New England towns in which women [usually widows] taught children of the poor in their own homes.

de facto segregation—the occurrence of race separation that is not sponsored or intended by the law.

detracking—the act of removing tracking from educational institutions.

differential educational opportunity—opportunity which differs according to one's social origin.

differential expectations—the difference in anticipated output among students, usually of students in one track compared to another track.

direct instruction—involves the use of teacher directed instruction that proceeds in small steps. It begins with a review of relevant previous learning and presents new material in small increments while periodically injecting questions to check for understanding. Finally, it supervises and monitors independent student work cautiously and provides weekly reviews of what has been learned.

dumbed down—slang term used to describe the act of making a curriculum more simple.

economic capital—control over cash and assets.

economic segregation—the separation of individuals by class, particularly by communities.

education—the process of learning over the course of one's life.

educational achievement—the amount of education one absorbs, measured by grades.

educational attainment—the number of years of formal education.

educational deflation—the term used to describe the result of high school diplomas and college degrees losing value due to the number of individuals receiving them.

educational sociologists—sociologists who focus on the educational system.

effective school movement—term used to describe the national obsession which peaked in the 1980's which attempted to identify characteristics of effective schools.

effective schools—schools which are able to both improve the overall academic achievement of all their students, and diminish the differences between homes of differing socio-economic background.

egalitarianism—the belief that all people are equal.

embodied cultural capital—socially learned traits of culture which are transmitted generally through the family and the socialization process.

equity—the quality of being fair or treating equally.

ethnicity—term used to denote a group (ethnic group) sharing a common and distinctive culture, religion, language.

eugenics—early twentieth century movement concerned with mating and heredity as a strategy for improving society.

Eurocentrism—considering Europe and Europeans as the focal point to world culture, history, and economics.

expectancy effect—the development of expectations for the academic progress of students, which may or may not be actually caused by the students' abilities.

family structure—the composition of a family, such as nuclear families consisting of a mother, father, and children, or extended families, consisting of a nuclear family and grandparents, aunts, uncles, cousins, or single parent homes.

faucet theory—the belief that under-privileged students do not have the opportunity to learn during the summer months when school is not in session, essentially "turning off their flow of knowledge". This theory is intended to explain the discrepancy between lower-socioeconomic and higher socioeconomic individuals' educational achievement.

feedback—One of the four communicative factors in Rosenthal's Four Factor theory. Communicating through "feedback" usually involves either cognitive information or affective information.

feminism—the doctrine advocating rights of women equal to those of men.

feminist theory—attempts to identify exactly how norms, institutions and expectations both control and limit a woman's behavior.

functional illiteracy—term used to describe the number of individuals who are unable to read and write enough to function in society.

functionalism—A perspective which views society as being made up of interrelated components.

functionalist perspective—the belief that each structure in society has a function that contributes to the welfare and stability of the whole.

gender—expectations about members of each sex that are socially learned.

gender bias—a distortion of information that is related to gender.

gender equity—equality among all people, regardless of sex.

gender roles—the positions one assumes in society based on his or her sex.

generalized other—what most others think of us.

genetic hereditability—traits that are passed on through chromosomes from adults to offspring.

Head Start program—a national program that promotes school readiness by enhancing the social and cognitive development of children by providing educational, health, nutritional, and social services.

heritability theory—theory which adheres to the belief that characteristics, such as intelligence and ability, have a basis in genetics.

heterogeneous—a group comprised of differing individuals.

hidden curriculum—lessons, values, et cetera which are taught as a means to undermine the education one receives, such as teaching punctionality, respect and acceptance to children of the economically disadvantaged.

high culture—products of culture which are believed to be of the best class, such as classical music and art, as opposed to "low culture," which may include country or rap music.

home schooling—a form of education in which students are taught at their place of residence by a parent as opposed to a government run facility.

Input—one of the four communicative factors in Rosenthal's Four Factor theory. Communicating through "input" usually involves teachers teaching more to certain students thus providing them with the perception that they are important.

institutionalized capital—recognition of the advantage a person holds in the form of academic credentials which often guarantees a certain monetary value in recognition of a certain level of achievement.

IQ Deficit Theory—the theory which attributes the lack of educational ability to a lack of intelligence on the part of the individual.

Jencks' Study—a study by Christopher Jencks which reexamined the data collected by Coleman and determined that "academic outcomes are much more influenced by poverty and social class rather than schools. It also concluded that family background is the most important variable in school success or failure.

jigsaw—a cooperative learning technique which entails assigning students to small heterogeneous groups with tasks to be learned also divided into as many sections as there are students. Members of different teams who have the same topic form 'expert groups' and study together. In time, each student returns to their original group and teaches that section of the assignment to the other teammates.

labeling—the process by which individuals or groups are assigned traits or characteristics by others that may or may not be accurate. Labeling theory examines how these assigned characteristics impact behavior.

latent functions—unintended [or] unstated goals or consequences of some phenomenon.

liberal feminism—a perspective which attempts to achieve equality in all areas of life and to transform traditional beliefs and attitudes about femininity and masculinity. It strives to transform the understanding of male and female roles in all sectors of society and insert choice rather than biology as the determining factor of what men and women do.

life-chances—the opportunities enjoyed by individuals as members of a certain class.

looking-glass self—a theory by Charles Horton Cooley in which people begin to see themselves as others see them.

macro-Sociology—the study of large-scale social phenomenon.

magnet schools—schools [that] attempt to attract white students to predominately minority schools. They are public schools with high academic standards and a specialized curriculum.

manifest functions—intended [or] stated goals or consequences of some phenomenon.

meritocracy—a system in which a person's abilities or achievements are used to determine status.

micro-Sociology—the study of small systems of interaction among people, such as an individual's daily interaction.

modality theory—otherwise known as learning styles refers to the very different ways students retain and process difficult information.

Monitorial Schools—schools in which one teacher assisted by several bright students [monitors] taught large groups of students—developed by Joseph Lancester and Andrew Bell.

A Nation at Risk—A national report of the early 1980s—it warned of a "rising tide in mediocrity" in education and revealed that verbal and math scores were on a dramatic decline and that functional illiteracy was dramatically increasing in the United States.

negotiation—the third and final step in Edwin Schur's process of labeling.

No Child Left Behind (NCLB)—legislation which is intended to close the achievement gap between students by utilizing accountability, flexibility, and school choice.

objectified capital—cultural items or goods which are owned and can be transmitted physically, i.e., paintings and sculpture.

opportunity-to-learn—the percentage of the intended curriculum that is actually made available to students.

output—one of the four communicative factors in Rosenthal's Four Factor theory. Communicating through "output" usually involves teachers providing certain students with greater opportunity to seek clarification about class assignments.

overt curriculum—the plan which outlines the educational experience of all students in a school.

parochial schools—denominational schools—usually Roman Catholic.

patriarchy—a form of social organization in which the [male] exerts the supreme authority.

per-capita spending—the amount of money spent per individual.

positive interdependence—the awareness that a group is linked and that each member's efforts and cooperation are essential for the group to be successful.

Protestant Ethic—the belief that hard word and denial will lead to salvation.

Pygmalion Effect—a slang term used to describe the act of one individual's outward impressions that elicit a positive result or change in another individual.

Quality of Schools Argument—the belief that some schools themselves are inferior to other schools based on the amount of funding received.

race—persons related by common descent or heredity.

racial segregation—the separation of individuals by race.

radical feminism—the belief that total separation from men and the development of a women's culture is necessary to gain equity between the sexes.

remedial instruction—the teaching intended to improve one's skill.

reproduction of consciousness—the perpetuation and reproduction of values/ideologies of dominant societal groups.

resource dilution model—theory which suggests that the intellectual development of children depends on family resources and that larger families generally tend to dilute resources because of their larger size.

school choice—permitting parents to decide where their children attend schools.

schooling—the process by which young members of a society acquire values and skills in formal educational institutions.

self-concept—how an individual sees him or herself.

self-efficacy—the ability of an individual to motivate him or herself to perform in a desired fashion.

self-esteem—the impression that one has of self.

self-fulfilling prophesy—the tendency of people to respond to and act on the basis of stereotypes and labels applied to others.

setting—a type of tracking which separates students by ability for only some subjects.

sibship size—term used to describe the number of siblings in a family.

single-gender schools—schools which are separated by sex, such as an all-boys school or an all-girls school.

"sleeper effect"—term used to describe the resulting lack of participation of certain students when separated into groups.

social capital—a type of currency that develops as a result of relationships between persons.

social construction—a belief or idea that is created by society.

Social Darwinism—a social philosophy that stresses perfection of society through a natural, evolutionary process—the theory of biological evolution applied to society.

social engineering—changing or manipulating a group to function in a particular way in society.

social integration—the inclusion of an individual or group of individuals into society.

socialization—a continuing process whereby an individual acquires a personal identity and learns the norms, values, behavior, and social skills of a group.

social promotion—the policy of automatically promoting students who have not satisfied the requirements for the lower grade.

social transmission—the transfer of information, values, mores, et cetera from individuals in society to other individuals in the same society.

socialist feminism—form of Feminism which believes that gender equity can only be achieved if we transform the social system, since gender oppression is a consequence of a patriarchal capitalistic system.

socioeconomic status (SES)—a position that one holds in society based on their income (mainly) and social standing.

standardized tests—exams given that are graded with consistency among students, not taking into consideration any individual characteristics or qualities within particular groups or individuals.

stereotyping—an oversimplified belief about some group that is used to categorize all members of that group.

Symbolic Interaction theory– a perspective which suggests that people act toward other things and other persons because of the meanings that they attach to them.

"teach to the test"—slang term used to describe the act of educators teaching only the material that they knows will be on a given exam.

tracking—the separation of students by ability and curriculum.

underachievement—the act of not performing to the assumed ability of an individual.

unequal achievement—the term used to describe the discrepancy between the academic performance of individuals, usually between differing socioeconomic groups or races.

values-oriented education—a curriculum which focuses not simply on the typical school subjects, but morality as well.

voucher system—a system in which parents are given "vouchers" or certificates which may be used to send their children to private schools.

within-class grouping—grouping within classes in which students are assigned to one of a number of smaller ability-level groups in order to facilitate instruction.

Bibliography

Aarum, Richard and Irenee Beattie. *The Structure of Schooling*. New York: McGraw Hill, 1999.

Aarum, Richard and Michael Hout. "The Transition from School to Work in the United States." Pp. 471–510, *Criminology* 37, no. 3 (1999): 515–540.

Abadiz, Helen. "Ability Grouping Effects on Academic Achievement and Self-Esteem: Who Performs in the Long Run as Expected." *Journal of Educational Research* 79, no. 1 (1985): 36–40.

Achilles, Charles, Patrick Egelson, and Paula Harmon. "Using Research Results on Class Size to Improve Achievement Outcomes." *Research in the Schools* 2, no. 22 (1995): 22–30.

Adams, Gerald and Allan Cohen. "Children's Physical and Interpersonal Characteristics that Effect Student Teacher Interactions." *Journal of Experimental Education* 43, no. 1 (1974): 1–5.

Adams-Price, Carolyn E., ed. *Creativity and Successful Aging: Theoretical and Empirical Approaches*. New York: Spring Publishing Company, 1998.

Ainsworth-Darnell, James, and Douglas Downey. "Assessing the Oppositional Culture Explanation for Racial/Ethnic Differences in School Performance." *American Sociological Review* 63 (1998): 536–553.

Alexander, Karl, and Doris Entwisle. "Achievement in the First Two Years of School." *Monograph of the Society for Research in Child Development* 53, no. 2 (1988): 1–139.

Alexander, Karl, and Doris Entwisle. "Educational Tracking in the Early Years." Pp. 83–113 in *Generating Social Stratification*, edited by Alan Kerckhoff. New York: Westview Press, 1996.

Alexander, Karl, Doris Entwisle, and Susan Dauber. *On the Success of Failure*. New York: Cambridge University Press, 1994.

Alexander, Karl, Doris Entwisle, and Maxine Thompson. "School Performance, Status Relations and the Structure of Sentiment." *American Sociological Review* 52 (Oct 1987): 665–682.

Alexander, Karl, and Edward McDill. "Selection and Allocation within Schools." *American Sociological Review* 41, no. 6 (Dec 1976): 963–980.

Alexander, Karl, Cornelius Riordan, James Fennessey, and Aaron Pallas. "Social Background, Academic Resources and College Graduation." *American Journal of Education* 90 (1982): 315–333.

Allington, Richard. "The Reading Provided Readers of Different Abilities." *Elementary School Journal* 83 (1983): 548–559.

Amato, Paul and Alan Booth. *A Generation at Risk: Growing up in an Era of Family Upheaval.* Cambridge, MA: Harvard University Press, 1997.

Amato, Paul, and Bruce Keith. "Parental Divorce and Adult Well-being." *Journal of Marriage and the Family* 53 (1991): 43–58.

American Association of University Women Educational Foundation. *How Schools Shortchange Girls.* Washington, D.C.: AAUW/NEA, 1992.

———. *Gender Gaps: Where Schools Still Fail Our Children.* Washington, D.C.: AAUW/NEA, 1998.

Anderson, James. *The Education of Blacks in the South.* Chapel Hill, NC: University of North Carolina Press, 1988.

Ansalone, George and Frank Biafora. "Elementary School Teachers' Perceptions to the Educational Structure of Tracking." *Education* 125, no. 2 (2004): 249–259.

Ansalone, George. "Keeping on Track: A Reassessment of Tracking in the Schools." *Race Gender and Class* 7, no. 3 (2000): 1–25.

———. "Schooling, Tracking and Inequality." *Journal of Children and Poverty* 7, no. 1 (2001): 33–47.

———. "Poverty, Tracking and the Social Construction of Failure." *Journal of Children and Poverty* 9, no. 1 (2003): 3–21.

———. "Tracking: A Return to Jim Crow." *Race, Gender, and Class* 13, no. 1–2 (2006): 144–153.

Arnold, Anita. "Designing Classrooms with Students in Mind." *English Journal 82,* no. 2. (1993): 81–83.

Ayres, Leonard. *Laggards in Our Schools.* New York: Charities Publication Committee, 1909.

Babad, Elisha, Frank Berneiri, and Robert Rosenthal. "Students as Judges of Teachers' Verbal and Nonverbal Behavior." *American Educational Research Journal* 28 (1991): 211–234.

Babad, Elisha and Paul Taylor. "Transparency of Teacher Expectations across Language, Cultural Boundaries." *Journal of Educational Research* 86 (1992): 120–125.

Baker, Amy and Lauren Solden. "Parent Involvement in Children's Education: A Critical Assessment of the Knowledge Base." Paper presented at the annual meeting of the American Educational Research Association, Chicago, IL, 1997.

Baker, David and David Stevenson. "Mother's Strategies for Children's School Achievement." *Sociology of Education* 59 (1986): 156–166.

Ballantine, Jeanne. "Getting Involved in Our Children's Education." *Childhood Education* 75 (1999): 170–171.

Bamburg, Jerry. *Raising Expectations to Improve Student Learning.* Oak Brook, IL: North Regional Educational Laboratory, 1994.

Bankston, Carl and Min Zhou. "The Ethnic Church, Ethnic Identity, and Social Adjustment of Vietnamese Adolescents." *Review of Religious Research* 38, no. 1 (1996): 18–37.

Baratz, Sheryl and Joan Baratz. "Early Childhood Intervention: The Social Science Base of Institutional Racism." *Harvard Educational Review* 40 (1970): 29–50.

Barr, Rebecca and Robert Dreeben. *How Schools Work.* Chicago: Chicago University Press, 1983.

Barthelmess, Harriet and Philip Boyer. "An Evaluation of Ability Grouping." *Journal of Educational Research* 26 (1932): 284–294.

Becker, Howard. *Outsiders.* New York: Free Press, 1963.

Beeghley, Leonard. *The Structure of Social Stratification in the United States.* Boston: Allyn & Bacon, 2008.

Bennett, Kenneth. "A Study of Reading Ability Groups" (Ph. D. dissertation, University of Cincinnati, 1986).

Bennett, William, Willard Fair, and Chester Finn. "A Nation Still at Risk." Pp. 177–183 *Taking Sides 13th Ed.*, edited by James Noll. Guilford, CT: McGraw Hill Dushkin, 2006.

Berger, Peter and Thomas Luckman. *The Social Construction of Reality.* Garden City, NY: Anchor Books, 1967.

Betts, Julian and Jamie Shkolnik. "The Effects of Ability Grouping on Student Achievement and Resource Allocation." *Economics of Education Review* 19 (2000): 1–15.

Bianchi, Suzanne and Lynne Casper. *American Families Resilient After Fifty Years of Change.* Washington, DC: Population Reference Bureau, 2001.

Biblarz, Timothy and Greg Gottainer. "Family Structure and Children's Success: A Comparison of Widowed and Divorced Single-Mother Families." *Journal of Marriage and the Family* 62 (2000): 533–548.

Blake, Judith. "Family Size and Achievement." *Studies in Demographics 3.* Berkeley, CA: University of California Press Doc # 201554, 1989.

Blumer, Herbert. *Symbolic Interactionism.* Englewood Cliffs, NJ: Prentice Hall, 1969.

Boaler, Jo. "Setting, Social Class and the Survival of the Quickest." *British Educational Research Journal* 23, no. 5 (1997): 575–595.

Boaler, Jo, Dylan William, and Margaret Brown. "Students Experiences of Ability Grouping: Disaffection, Polarization, and the Construction of Failure." *British Educational Research Journal* 26, no. 5 (2000): 631–648.

Boocock, Sarane. *An Introduction to the Sociology of Learning.* New York: Houghton Mifflin, 1980.

Borko, Hilda and Margaret Eisenhart. "Students' Conceptions of Reading and Their Reading Experience in School." *The Elementary School Journal* 86 (1986): 589–612.

Borland, Melvin and Roy Howse. "An Examination of the Effects of Elementary School Size on Student Academic Achievement." *International Review of Education* 49, no. 5 (2003): 463–474.

Borman, Geoffrey. "A Reassessment of the Coleman Data." Presentation at the Annual Meeting of the Educational Research Association, Washington, DC, 2005.

——. "Early Reading Skills and the Social Composition of the School." In *Educational and Instructional Consequences of High-poverty Schooling* edited by Michael Ross, George Bohrnstedt, and Francis Hemphill. Washington, DC: National Center for Education Statistics, U.S. Department of Education, 2007.

Bouchard, Thomas, and Matt McGue. "Genetic and Environmental Differences on Human Psychological Differences." *Journal of Neurobiology* 54, no. 1 (2003): 4–45.

Bourdieu, Pierre. *Distinction: A Social Critique of the Judgment of Taste.* Cambridge, MA: Harvard University Press, 1984.

——. "Forms of Capital." Pp. 241–258 in *The Handbook of Theory and the Research for the Sociology of Education*, edited by John G. Richardson. Westport, CT: Greenwood Press, 1986.

——. *The Logic of Practice.* Stanford, CA: Stanford University Press, 1993.

Bourdieu, Pierre and Jean Claude Passeron. *The Inheritors.* Chicago: University of Chicago Press, 1979.

——. *Reproduction in Education, Society and Culture.* New York: Sage Publications, 1990.

——. *Reproduction in Education, Society, and Culture.* London: Sage, 1977.

Bowles, Samuel and Herbert Gintis. *Schooling in Capitalist America.* New York: Basic Books, 1976.

Bracey, Gerald. *High States Testing.* Center for Educational Research, Analysis and Innovation. School of Education, University of Wisconsin. 2000. http://www.asu.edu/edu/eps/epru/documents/cerai-0032.htm#_ednrefee (accessed prior to 2008).

Bradley, Robert and Robert Corwyn. "Socio-economic Status and Child Development." *Annual Review of Psychology* 53 (2002): 371–399.

Brantlinger, Ellen. *Dividing Classes.* New York: Routledge Falmer, 2003.

Bronfenbrenner, Urie. *Two Worlds of Childhood.* New York: Simon & Schuster, 1972.

Brookover, Wilbur. *Creating Effective Schools.* Holmes Beach, FL: Learning Publication, Inc., 1982.

Brooks, Charlotte. "Some Approaches to Teaching English as a Second Language." Pp. 516–517 in *The Disadvantaged Learner*, edited by Staten Webster. San Francisco, CA: Chandler, 1966.

Brooks, Nancy, Ella Bruno, and Tracy Burns. "Reinforcing Student Motivation through Parental Interaction." Thesis (1997), St. Xavier University. Eric Document ED 411074.

Brophy, Jere. "Research on the Self-Fulfilling Prophesy and Teacher Expectations." *Journal of Educational Psychology* 75 (1983): 631–661.

——. *On Motivating Students.* East Lansing, MI: Institute for Research on Teaching, Michigan State University, 1986. Eric document ED 276724.

Brophy, Jere, and Thomas Good. "Teachers' Communication of Differential Expectations for Children's Classroom Performance." *Journal of Educational Psychology* 60 (1970): 365–374.

Brutsaert, Herman. "Coeducation and Gender Identity Formation." *British Journal of Sociology of Education* 20 (1999): 343–353.

Burt, Cyril. "The Genetic Determination of Intelligence." *British Journal of Psychology* 27 (1966): 175–190.

Carbonaro, William. "Tracking Student Effort and Academic Achievement." *Sociology of Education* 78 (2005): 27–49.

Cardenas, Jose. "Ending the Crisis in the K-12 System." Pp. 51–70 in *Educating a New Majority*, edited by Laura Rendon and Richard Hope. San Francisco: Jossey-Bass Publishers, 1996.

Carey, Nancy, Laurie Lewis and Elizabeth Farris. "Parental Involvement in Children's Education." *National Center for Education Studies*. Washington, DC: U.S. Gov. Printing Office, 1998. 20402–9328.

Carnoy, Martin, Rebecca Jacobsen, Lawrence Mishel and Richard Rothstein. *The Charter School Dust Up: Examining the Evidence on Enrollment and Achievement.* Washington, DC: Economic Policy Institute, 2005.

Cazden, Courtney, Vera John, and Dell Hymes. *Functions of Language in the Classroom.* New York: Teachers College Press, 1974.

Chambliss, William. "The Saints and the Roughnecks." *Society* 22 (November 1973): 24–31.

Chapman, Paul. *Schools as Sorters*. New York: NYU Press, 1988.

Charkin, Aaron, Ellen Sigler, and Valerian Derlega. "Nonverbal Mediators of Teacher Expectancy Effects." *Journal of Personality and Social Psychology* 30 (1974): 144–149.

Chubb, John, and Terry Moe. *Politics, Markets and America's Schools*. Washington DC: Brookings Institute, 1990.

Chuska, Kenneth. *Improving Classroom Questions*. Bloomington, IN: Phi Delta Kappa, 1995.

Cipriani-Sklar, Rosemary. "A Quantitative and Qualitative Examination of the Influence of the Normative and Perceived Social Environments of a Coeducational Public School Vs. a Single Sex Catholic School." (Ph.D. dissertation, St. John's University, 1996).

Clifford, Margaret, and Elaine Walster. "The Effect of Physical Attractiveness on Teacher Expectations." *Sociology of Education* 45 (1973): 248–258.

Cloud, John, and Jodie Morse. "Home Sweet School." *Time* (August 27, 2001): 46–54.

Coleman, James. *Equality of Educational Opportunity*. Washington, DC: U.S. Government Printing Office, 1966.

———. "Social Capital in the Creation of Human Capital." *American Journal of Sociology* 94, Supplement (1988): S95–S120.

———. *Equality and Achievement in Education*. Boulder, CO: Westview Press, 1990.

———. *Foundations of Social Theory*. Cambridge, MA: Belknap Press, 1990.

Coleman, James, and Thomas Hoffer. *Public and Private High Schools*. New York: Basic Books, 1987.

Coleman, James, Thomas Hoffer, and Sally Kilgore. High School Achievement. New York: Basic Books, 1982.

College Board, 2007. "Mean SAT Scores of College Bound Seniors, 1967–2007." http://www.collegeboard.com/prod_downloads/about/news_info/cbsenior/yr2007/tables/2.pdf (accessed May 22, 2008).

College Board. 2001. "College Bound Seniors Are the Largest and Most Diverse Group in History." *College Board News.* http://www.collegeboard.com/pres/senior01 (accessed August 28, 2008).

Collins, James. "Differential Instruction in Reading Groups." Pp. 138–165 in *Social Construction of Literacy*, edited by Jenny Cook-Gumperz. New York: Cambridge University Press, 1986.

Collins, Patricia, and Margaret Andersen, eds. *Race, Class and Gender*. 5th ed. Belmont, CA: Wadsworth Publishing, 2004.

Collins, Randall. *The Credential Society*. New York: Academic Press, 1979.

Conant, James. *The Comprehensive High School*. New York: McGraw Hill, 1967.

———. The American High School. New York: McGraw Hill, 1959.

Conley, Dalton. *Being Black, Living in the Red*. Berkeley, CA: University of California Press, 1999.

Conley, Millicent. "A Study of the Impact of Teacher Expectations, Staff Development for Teachers, and Mastery Learning on Student Achievement" Ph.D. dissertation, University of Chicago, 2005.

Cook, Philip, and Jens Ludwig. "Weighing the Burden of Acting White: Are There Race Differences in Attitudes Toward Education." *Journal of Policy Analysis and Management* 16 (1997): 411–429.

Cook, Roger. *A Study of the Results of Homogeneous Grouping*. National Society for Study of Education 23 (1924).

Cookson, Peter, and Caroline Persell. *Preparing for Power: America's Elite Boarding Schools*. New York: Basic Books, 1985.

Cooley, Charles. *Human Nature and the Social Order*. New Brunswick, NJ: Transaction, 1902, 83.

Cooper, Harris, and David Tom. "Teacher Expectation Research." *Elementary School Journal* 85, (1884): 77–89.

Cooper, James. Classroom Teaching Skills. Boston: Houghton Mifflin, 1999.

Cotton, Kathleen. *Expectations and Student Outcomes*. Washington, DC: Office of Educational Research and Improvement, U.S. Dept of Education Contract, 1989.

———. The School Practices that Matter Most. Alexandria, VA: Association for Supervision and Curriculum Development, 2001.

———. Teacher Practices that Matter Most. Northwest Regional Educational Laboratory.

Cotton, Kathleen, and Karen Wikelund. "Parental involvement in education." School Improvement Research Series #6. Portland, OR: Northwest Regional Education Laboratory, 2001.

Crane, Jonathan. "Effects of Home Environment, SES, and Maternal Test Scores on Math Achievement." *Journal of Educational Research* 89, (1996): 305–314.

Crosnoe, Robert. "Academic Orientation and Parental Involvement During High School." *Sociology of Education* 74, no. 3 (2001): 210–230.

Dale, Reginald. *Mixed or Single Sex Schools? Volume III: Attainment, Attitudes and Overview*. London: Routledge & Kegan Paul, 1974.

Daly, Peter. "Science Course Participation and Achievement in Single Sex and Coeducational Schools." *Evaluation and Research in Education* 9, no. 2 (1995): 91–98.

Dar, Yehezkel, and Nura Resh. "Classroom Intellectual Composition and Academic Achievement." *American Educational Research Journal* 23 (1986): 357–374.

Darley, John, and Russell Fazio. "Expectancy Confirmation Processes Arising in Social Interaction Sequences." *American Psychologist* 35 (1980): 867–881.

Darling-Hammond, Linda, and Joslyn Green. "Teacher Quality and Equality." Pp.
237–258 in *Access to Knowledge: An Agenda for Our Nation's Schools*, edited by
John Goodlad and Pamela Keating. New York: College Board Publications, 1990.

Dauber, Susan, Karl Alexander, and Doris Entwisle. "Tracking and Transitions
Through Middle Grades." *Sociology of Education* 69, no. 4 (1996): 290–307.

Dauber, Susan, and Joyce Epstein. "Parent Attitudes and Practices of Involvement in
Inner-city Elementary and Middle Schools." Pp. 53–72 in *Families and Schools in
a Pluralistic Society*, edited by Nancy Chavkin. Albany: State University of New
York Press, 1993.

Davidson, Helen, and Gerhard Lang. "Children's Perception of Their Teachers' Feelings Toward Them." *Journal of Experimental Education* 29 (1960): 107–118.

Davis, James, Tom Smith, and Peter Marsden. *General Social Surveys: Cumulative
Codebook*. Chicago: National Opinion Research Center, 2005.

DeGraff, Nan, Paul DeGraff, and Gerbert Kraaykamp. "Parental Cultural Capital and
Educational Attainment in the Netherlands." *Sociology of Education* 73, no. 2
(2000): 92–110.

Deidrich, Francis. "Comparisons of Sociometric Patterns of 6th Grade Students in
Two School Systems." *Journal of Educational Research* 26 (1964): 284–296.

Delgado-Gaitan, Concha. "The Value of Conformity." *Anthropology and Education
Quarterly* 19 (1988): 354–382.

Delpit, Lisa. *Other People's Children*. New York: The New Press, 1995.

DeMarrais, Kathleen. *The Way Schools Work*. New York: Longmans, 1991.

Denzin, Norman. *Symbolic Interactions*. Cambridge, MA: Blackwell, 1992.

Deslandes, Rollande, Egide Royer, Daniel Turcotte, and Richard Bertrand. "School
Achievement at the Secondary Level: Influence of Parenting Style and Involvement." *McGill Journal of Education* 32, no. 3 (1997): 197–207.

Dewey, John. *Experience and Education*. New York: McMillan, 1938.

DiMaggio, Paul, and John Mohr. "Cultural Capital, Educational Attainment and Marital Selection." *American Journal of Sociology* 90, no. 6 (1985): 1231–1261.

DiMaggio, Paul. Cultural Capital and School Success. *American Sociological Review*
47 (1982): 189–201.

Diamond, John, and James Spillane. "Teachers' Expectations and Sense of Responsibility for Student Learning: Importance of Race, Class and Organizational Habi-
tus." *Journal of Anthropology and Educational Quarterly* (2004): 123–45.

Donahuem, Michael, and Peter Benson. "Religion and the Well-being of Adolescents." *The Journal of Social Issues* 51, (1995): 145–160.

Downey, Douglas. "When Bigger is Not Better: Family Size, Parental Resources and
Children's Educational Performance." *American Sociological Review* 60, (1995):
746–71.

Dreeban, Robert, and Rebecca Bar. "Classroom Composition and the Designs of Instruction." *Sociology of Education* 61 (1988): 129–142.

Drummond, Kathryn, and Deborah Stipek. "Low Income Parents' Belief About Their
Role in Children's Learning." *Elementary School Journal* 104, no. 3 (2004):
197–213.

DuBois, David, Robert Felner, Henry Meares, and Marion Krier. "Prospective Investigation of the Effects of Socioeconomic Disadvantage, Life Stress and Social Adjustment on Early Adolescent Adjustment." *Journal of Abnormal Psychology* 103 (1994): 511–522.

Dumais, Susan. "Cultural Capital, Gender and School Success." *Sociology of Education* 75, no. 1 (2002): 44–68.

Duncan, Greg, Jeanne Brooks-Gunn, W. Jean Yeung, and Judith Smith. "How Much Does Childhood Poverty Affect the Life-Chances of Children?" *American Sociological Review* 63, (1998): 406–423.

Dunn, Rita, and Kenneth Dunn. *Teaching Elementary Students through Their Individual Learning Styles*. Boston: Allyn & Bacon, 1993.

Dunn, Rita, and Shirley Griggs. *Practical Approaches to Using Learning Styles in Higher Education*. Westport, CT: Bergin & Garvey, 2000.

Dunn, Rita, Kenneth Dunn, and Janet Perrin. *Teaching Young Children through Their Individual Learning Styles*. Boston: Allyn & Bacon, 1994.

Dunn, Rita, and Kenneth Dunn. *Teaching Students through Their Individual Learning Styles*. Needham Heights, MA: Allyn & Bacon, 1993.

Durkheim, Emile. *Education and Sociology*. (trans. Sherwood Fox). New York: Free Press, 1956.

Dusek, Jerome. *Teacher Expectancies*. Hillsdale, NJ: Erlbaum, 1985.

Emmison, Michael, and John Frow. "Information Technology as Cultural Capital." *Australian University Research* 41, no. 1 (1998): 41–45.

Entwisle, Doris. *Children, Schools and Inequality*. Boulder, CO: Westview Press, 1997.

Entwisle, Doris, Karl Alexander, and Linda Olson. "The Nature of Schooling." Pp. 207–217 in *The Structure of Schooling,* edited by Richard Arum & Irenee Beattie. Mountain View, CA: Mayfield Publishing, 2000.

Entwisle, Doris, Karl Alexander, and Linda Olson. *Children, Schools and Inequality*. Boulder, CO: West View Press, 1997.

Epps, Edgar. "Race, Class and Educational Opportunity." *Sociological Forum* 10, no. 4, (1995): 593–608.

Epstein, Joyce, Lucretia Coates, Karen Salinas, Mavis Sanders, and Beth Simon. *School, Family and Community Partnerships*. Thousand Oaks, CA: Corwin Press, 1997.

Epstein, Joyce, and Steven Sheldon. "Improving Student Attendance through Parental Involvement." *Journal of Educational Research* 94 (2001): 185–196.

Epstein, Joyce, and M. G. Sanders. *School, Family and Community Partnerships*. Thousand Oaks, CA: Corwin Press, 2002.

Erickson, Frederick. "School Literacy, Reasoning and Civility." *Review of Educational Research* 54 (1984): 525–546.

Escalante, Jaime. "Escalante Math Program." *Journal of Negro Education* 59, no. 3 (1990): 407–423.

Esposito, Dominick. "Homogeneous and Heterogeneous Ability Grouping." *Review of Educational Research* 43, (1973): 163–179.

Evans, William, and Robert Schwab. "Finish High School and Starting College: Do Catholic Schools Make a Difference?" *Quarterly Journal of Economics* 110, (1995): 947–974.

Falconer, Renee, and Deborah Byrnes. "When Good Intentions Are Not Enough." *Journal of Research in Childhood Education* 17, no. 2 (2003): 188.

Farkas, George, Robert Grobe, Daniel Sheehan, and Yuan Shuan. "Cultural Resources and School Success." *American Sociological Review* 55, (February 1990): 127–142.

Feldman, Richard, Eunice Henriques. "Learning and Teaching Styles in Foreign Language Education." *Foreign Language Annals* 28, no. 1 (1995): 21–31.

Ferguson, Ronald. "Teachers' Perceptions and Expectations and the Black-White Test Score Gap," Pp. 273–317 in *The Black-White Test Score Gap,* edited by Christopher Jencks and Meredith Phillips. Washington, DC: Brookings Institute, 1998.

Figlio, David, and Marianne Page. "School Choice and the Distributional Effects of Ability Tracking." *Journal of Urban Economics* 51, (2001): 497–514.

Findley, Warren, and Miriam Bryan. *Ability Grouping: Status, Impact and Alternatives.* Athens, GA: Center for Educational Improvement, 1970.

Finn, Jeremy, and Charles Achilles. "Tennessee's Class Size Study: Findings, Implications, Misconceptions." *Educational Evaluation and Policy Analysis* 21, no. 2 (1999): 97–109.

Finn, Jeremy, and Donald Rock. "Academic Success Among Students at Risk for School Failure." *Journal of Applied Psychology* 82, (1997): 221–234.

Firestone, William and Sheila Rosenblum. "Building Commitment in Urban High Schools." *Educational Evaluation and Policy Analysis* 10, (1988): 285–299.

Ford, Laurie and Debbie Amaral. 2006. "Research on Parent Involvement: Where we've Been and Where We Need to Go." *BC Educational Leadership Research,* (March 2006).

Fowler, William. "What Do We Know about School Size?" Paper presented at the Annual Meeting of the American Educational Research Association, San Francisco, CA, April 20–24, 1992.

Francis, Becky. "Lads, Lasses and Labor." *British Journal of Sociology of Education* 20 (1999): 355–373.

Fraser, Steven. *The Bell Curve Wars: Race, Intelligence and the Future of America.* New York: Basic Books, 1995.

Gallup, Jr., George. "Education: The Perspectives in Detail." Public Agenda Online, 2000.

Gallup Poll. "Gallup Poll of Public Attitudes toward Public Schools." *New York Times,* August 23, 1991, A15.

Galton, Francis. 1914. *Hereditary Genius.* London: Macmillan 1869/1914.

Gamoran, Adam. "The consequences of track-related instructional differences for student achievement." Paper presented at the American Educational Research Association Boston, MA, 1990.

———. "Access to Excellence: Assignments to Honors English Class." *Educational Evaluation and Policy Analysis* 14, (1992): 185–220.

———. "The Variable Effect of High School Tracking." *American Sociological Review* 57, (1992): 812–827.

Gamoran, Adam, and William Carbonaro. "High school English: A national Portrait." *High School Journal* 86 (2003): 1–13.

Gamoran, Adam, and Robert Mare. "Secondary School Tracking and Educational Inequality." *American Journal of Sociology* 94, no. 5 (1989): 1146–1183.

Gamoran, Adam, Martin Nystrand, Mark Berends, and Paul LePore. "An Organizational Analysis of the Effects of Ability Grouping." *American Educational Research Journal* 32 (1995): 687–715.

Gamoran, Adam, Walter Secada, and Cora Marrett. "The Organizational Context of Teaching and Learning." Pp. 37–63 in *Handbook of Sociology of Education*, edited by Maureen Hallinan. New York: Kluwer Academic Plenum, 2000.

Gamoran, Adam, and Matthew Weinstein. "Differentiation and Opportunity in Restructed Schools." *American Journal of Education* 106, no. 3 (1998): 385–343.

Gardner, Howard. *Frames of Mind*. New York; Basic Books, 1993/1999.

George, Paul. "Tracking and Ability Grouping." *Middle School Journal* 20, no. 1 (1988): 21–28.

George, Paul, and William Alexander. *The Exemplary Middle School*. Belmont, CA: Wadsworth/Thomson, 2003.

Gilbert, Dennis. *The American Class Structure in an Age of Growing Inequality*. Belmont, CA: Wadsworth, 2003.

Ginorino, Angela, and Michelle Huston. *Yes, We Can*. Washington, DC: American Association of University Women, 2000.

Glass, Gene, and Mary Smith. *Meta-analysis of Research on the Relationship of Class Size and Achievement*. San Francisco: Far West Laboratory for Educational Research and Development, 1978.

Glazer, Susan. "Using KWL Folders." *Teaching K-8.* (January 1999): 106–109.

Goldberg, Miriam. "The Effects of Ability Grouping." New York: Columbia University Press, 1966.

Good, Thomas. "Two Decades of Research on Teacher Expectations." *Journal of Teacher Education* 38, no. 4 (1987): 32–47.

Good, Thomas, and Jere Brophy. *Looking in Classrooms*. Boston: Allyn & Bacon, 2003.

Goodlad, John. *A Place Called School*. New York: McGraw Hill, 1984.

Gould, Stephen. *The Mismeasure of Man*. New York: W.W. Norton, 1981.

Gouldner, Helen. *Teachers' Pets, Troublemakers and Nobodies*. Westport, CT: Greenwood Press, 1978.

Gracey, Harry. "Kindergarten as Boot Camp." Pp. 390–404 in *Down to Earth Sociology, 7th Edition*, edited by James Henslin. New York: Free Press, 1972.

Grant, Linda and James Rothenberg. "The Social Enhancement of Ability Differences." *Elementary School Journal* 87 (1986): 29–50.

Greeley, A. 1982. *Catholic High Schools and Minority Achievement*. New Brunswick, NJ: Transaction.

Griffith, James. "Test of a Model of the Organizational Antecedents of Parent Involvement and Satisfaction with Public Education." *Human Relations* 49, no. 12 (1996): 1549–1571.

Grissmer, David, Ann Flanagan and Stephanie Williamson. "Why Did the Black-White Score Gap Narrow in 1970's and 1980's?" Pp. 182–226 in *The Black–White Test Score Gap*, edited by Christopher Jencks and Meredith Phillips. Washington, DC: Brookings Institute, 1998.

Gumpert, Edgar and Joel Spring. *The Superschool and the Superstate*. New York: Wiley, 1975.

Guo, Guang and Leah VanWey. "Sibship Size and Intellectual Development." *American Sociological Review* 64, no. 2 (1999): 169–187.

Guskin, Alan. *A Social Psychology of Education.* Reading, MA: Addison Wesley, 1970.

Gutek, Gerald. *Historical and Philosophical Foundations of Education.* Upper Saddle River, NJ: Merrill/Prentice Hall, 2001.

——. *Philosophical and Ideological Voices in Education.* New York: Pearson Publishing, 2004.

Hallinan, Maureen. "Tracking: From Theory to Practice." *Sociology of Education* 67, no. 2 (1994): 79–84.

——. "School Differences in Tracking Structure and Track Assignment." *Journal of Research on Adolescence* 1, no. 3 (1991): 251–275.

——. "Tracking and Detracking Practices." Pp. 38–55 in *Transforming Schools*, edited by Peter Cookson and Barbara Sheider. New York: Garland Press, 1995.

——. "Track Mobility in Secondary Schools." *Social Forces* 74 (1996): 983–1002.

——. *Ability Grouping and Student Learning.* Washington, DC: Brookings Papers on Educational Policy, 2003.

Hara, Steven, and Daniel Burke. "Parent involvement: The Key to Improved Student Achievement." *School Community Journal* 8, (1998): 9–10.

Harris, Richard, and Juanita Firestone. "Changes in Predictors of Gender Role Ideologies in Women." *Sex Roles* 98 (1998): 239–52.

Hart, Betty, and Todd Risley. *Meaningful Differences in Everyday Parenting and Intellectual Development.* Baltimore, MD: P. Brookers, 1995.

Harvey, Dale, and Slatin, Gerald. "The Relationship Between Child's SES and Teacher Expectations." *Social Forces* 54 (1975): 140–159.

Hastings, Nigel. "Seats of Learning." *Support for Learning* 10, no. 1 (1995): 8–11.

Haveman, Robert, and Barbara Wolfe. *Succeeding Generations.* New York: Russell Sage, 1994.

Hawthorne, Susan. "In Defense of Separatism." Pp. 312–318 in *Reader in Feminist Knowledge*, edited by Sneja Gunew. New York: Routledge & Kegan Paul, 1991.

Headden, Susan. "The Hispanic Dropout Mystery." Pp. 220–231 in *Troubled Times*, edited by Robert Lauer and Jeanette Lauer. London: Oxford Press, 2000.

Heath, Shirley. *Ways with Words.* New York: Cambridge University Press, 1983.

Heathers, Glen. "Grouping." Pp. 33 in *Encyclopedia of Educational Research,* edited by Robert Ebels. New York: Macmillan, 1969.

Hedges, Larry, Richard Laine, and Rob Greenwald. "An Exchange Part I: Does money matter?" *Educational Researcher* 23, no. 3 (April 1994): 5–14.

Hedges, Larry, and Amy Nowell. *Black-White test score convergence since 1965.* Washington DC: Brookings Institute Press, 1998.

Heffernan, Erin. "All Female Education." Unpublished Masters Thesis, Dominican College of San Rafael, San Rafael, California, 1996.

Hellinger, Daniel, and Dennis Judd. *The Democratic Façade.* Pacific Grove, CA: Brooks/ Cole, 1991.

Henderson, Anne, and Nancy Berla. *A New Generation of Evidence.* Washington, DC: National Committee for Citizens in Education, 1994.

Herrnstein, Richard, and Charles Murray. *The Bell Curve.* New York: Free Press, 1994.

——. *IQ in the Meritocracy.* Boston: Little Brown, 1973.

Hess, Robert, Virginia Shipman, and David Jackson. "Some New Dimensions in Providing Equal Educational Opportunity." *Journal of Negro Education* 34, (1965): 220–231.

Hetherton, E. Mavis, Kathleen Camara, and David Featherman. "Achievement and Intellectual Functioning of Children in One-parent Households." Pp. 208–284 in *Achievement and Achievement Motives,* edited by Janet Pence. San Francisco, CA: W. H. Freeman, 1983.

Heyneman, Stephen, and William Loxley, "Influences on Academic Achievement across High and Low Income Countries." *Sociology of Education* 55 (January 1982): 13–21.

Heynes, Barbara. "Social Selection and Stratification within Schools." *American Journal of Sociology* 79 (1974): 89–102.

Higher Education Research Institute. *The American Freshman: National Norms.* Los Angeles, CA: University of California, 2007.

Hill, Nancy, and Lorraine Taylor. "Parental School Involvement and Children's Academic Achievement." *Current Directions in Psychological Science* 13, no. 4 (2004): 161–165.

Holman, Linda. "Working Effectively with Hispanic Immigrant Families." *Phi Delta Kappa* 78, no. 8 (1997): 647–649.

Hunt, John. "The Psychological Basis for Using Pre-school Environment as an Antidote for Cultural Deprivation." *Merrill-Palmer Quarterly* 10, (1964): 236.

Hurn, Christopher. *The Limits and Possibilities of Schooling.* Boston: Allyn & Bacon, 1993.

Huston, Aletha. "Children in Poverty." Social Policy Report, Society for Research in child Development 8, no. 2 (1994): 1–15.

Hyman, Herbert, and Charles Wright. *Education's Lasting Influence on Values.* Chicago: University of Chicago Press, 1979.

Illich, Ivan. "Vernacular Values and Education." *Teachers College Record,* 81 (Fall 1979): 31–75.

Institut National d'Etudes Demographiques. Enquete nationale sur le niveau Intellectuel des Enfants d'age Scolaire. Cahier No. 64. Paris: Presses Universitaires de France, 1973.

Ireson, Judith, and Susan Hallam. "Raising Standards: Is Ability Grouping the Answer." *Oxford Review of Education* 25, no. 3 (1999): 344–360.

Irmischer, Katherine. "School size." *Eric Digest* 113, July 1997. EDO-EA-97-5.

Irons, Peter. *Jim Crow's Children.* New York: Viking Press, 2002.

Irvine, Jacqueline. *Black Students and School Failure.* New York: Praeger, 1991.

——. Educating Teachers for Diversity. New York: Teachers College, 2003.

Jackson, Carolyn, and Ian Smith. "Poles Apart: An Exploration of Single-sex and Mixed Sex Educational Environments." *Educational Studies* 26 (2006): 409–422.

Jackson, Mary. *An Investigation of the Relationship Between Teacher Expectations and Student Achievement.* Michigan: Wayne State University, 2005. Publication Number: AAT 3196206.

Jacoby, Russell, and Naomi Clauberman, eds. *The Bell Curve Debate.* New York: Times Books, 1994.

Jasinski, Jana. "Beyond High School: An Examination of Hispanic Educational Attainment." *Social Science Quarterly* 81 (2000): 276–301.

Jencks, Christopher. *Inequality.* New York: Basic Books, 1972.

————. *Rethinking Social Policy, Race, Policy and the Underclass*. New York: Harper Collins, 1993.

Jencks, Christopher, and Meredith Philips, eds. *The Black-White Test Score Gap*. Washington, DC: The Brookings Institution Press, 1998.

Jensen, Arthur. "How Much Can We Boost IQ and Scholastic Achievement?" *Harvard Educational Review* 39 (1969): 1–23.

Jeynes, William. *Divorce, Family Structure and Academic Success*. Binghamton, NY: Hayworth Press, 2002.

————. 2005. "Effects of Parental Involvement and Family Structure on Academic Achievement." *Marriage and Family Review* 37, no. 3 (2005): 99–116.

Johnson, David, and Roger Johnson. Cooperative Learning, 2001. http://www.clcrc .com/pages/cl.html (accessed March 2008).

————. An Overview of Cooperative Learning. 2001. http://www.clcrc.com/pages/ overviewpaper.html (accessed March 2008).

Jones, Vincent, and William McCall. "Application of Two Techniques in Evaluating Policies Dealing with Bright Children." *Teachers College Record* 27, 1926.

Juel-Nielsen, Niels. "Individual and Environment." *Acta Psychiatra et Neurologica Scandinavica* 56 (1965): 471–479.

Jussim, Lee and Jacquelyn Eccles. "Teacher Expectations II: Construction and Reflection of Student Achievement." *Journal of Personality and Social Psychology* 63, no. 6 (1992): 947–961.

Kamin, L. J. *Science and Politics of IQ*. Potomac, MD: Erlbaum Associates, 1974.

Karcher, Michael. "The Cycle of Violence and Disconnection among Rural Middle School Students: Teacher Disconnection as a Consequence of Violence." *Journal of School Violence* 1 (2002): 35–39.

Katz, Michael. *Class, Bureaucracy and Schools*. New York: Praeger Press, 1975.

Keddie, N. "Classroom Knowledge." Pp. 133–160 in *Knowledge and Control*, edited by Michael F.D. Young. London: Collier, McMillan, 1971.

Keith, Timothy, and Ellis Page. "Do Catholic High Schools Improve Minority Student Achievement?" *American Educational Research Journal* 22, no. 3 (1985): 337–349.

Kemp, Alice. *Women's Work: Devalued and Degraded*. Englewood Cliffs, NJ: Prentice Hall, 1994.

Kenealy, Pamela, Neil Frude, and William Shaw. "Influences of Children's Physical Attractiveness on Teacher Expectations." *Journal of Social Psychology* 128, no. 3 (1988): 373–383.

Kershaw, Terry. "The Effects of Educational Tracking on the Social Mobility of African Americans." *Journal of Black Studies* 23, no. 1 (1992): 152–169.

Keysar, Ariel, and Barry Kosmin. "The Impact of Religious Identification on Differences in Educational Attainment among Women." *Journal for the Scientific Study of Religion* 34 (1995): 49–62.

Khmelkov, Vladimir, and Maureen Hallinan. "New developments in teacher education in the U.S." Pp. 31–50 in *Educating the Educators*, edited by Sam Drudge and Elizabeth Oldham. Ireland: Cardinal Press, 2000.

Kingston, Paul. "The Unfulfilled Promise of Cultural Capital Theory." *Sociology of Education* (Extra Issue 2001): 88–99.

Kingston, Paul, Ryan Hubbard, Brent Lapp, Paul Schroeder, and Julia Wilson. "Why Education Matters." *Sociology of Education* 76, no. 1 (2003): 55–70.

Kohn, Alfie. "How Privileged Parents are Undermining School Reform." *Phi Delta Kappa*, 79 (1998): 8–16.

Koret Task Force. *Are We Still at Risk?* Hoover Institute: Stanford University Public Policy Research, 2003.

Kozol, Jonathan. *Savage Inequalities*. New York: Perennial, 1992.

———. *Shame of the Nation*. New York: Random House, 2005.

Kulik Chen-Lin. "Effects of Ability Grouping on Secondary School Students." *American Educational Research Journal* 19 (1982): 415–428.

Labov, William. "The Logic of Non-standard English." Pp. 201–240 in *Language in the Inner-city*. Philadelphia: University of Pennsylvania Press, 1972.

Lareau, Annette. "Assessing Parent Involvement in Schooling." Pp. 57–66 in *Family School Links*, edited by Alan Booth and Judith Dunn. Hillsdale, NJ: Lawrence Erlbaum, 1995.

Lee, Jaekyung. "Racial and Ethnic Achievement Gap Trends." *Educational Researcher* 31, no. 1 (2000): 3–12.

Lee, Valerie, and David Burkam. *Inequality at the Starting Gate*. Washington, DC: Economic Policy Institute, 2002.

Lee, Valerie, and Anthony Byrak. "Curriculum Tracking as Mediating the Social Distribution of High School Achievement." *Sociology of Education* 61, no. 2 (1988): 78–94.

Lenski, Gerhard. *The Religious Factor*. New York: Doubleday, 1961.

LePore, Paul, and John Warren. "A Comparison of Single-sex and Coeducational Catholic Secondary Schooling." *American Educational Research Journal* 34 (1997): 485–511.

Levine, Donald, and Mary Jo Bane. (Eds). *The Inequality Controversy*. New York: Basic Books, 1975.

Lewis, Oscar. "The Culture of Poverty." *Scientific American* 215 (1966): 19–25.

Lily, W. F. "Now or Later: Issues Related to Early Education." Pp. in *Early Childhood and Family Education*. New York: Harcourt Brace and Jovanovich, 1990.

Lindsay, Paul. "High School Size: Participation in Activities, and Young Adult Social Participation." *Educational Evaluation and Policy* 6 (1984): 73–84.

Losen, David, and Kevin Welner. "Racial Inequality in Special Education." Pp. in *Racial Inequality in Education*, edited by David Losen and Gary Orfield. Cambridge, MA, 2002.

Loveless, Tom. *The Tracking Wars*. Washington, DC: Brookings Institution Press, 1999.

Lucas, Samuel. *Tracking Inequality*. New York: Teacher's College Press, 1999.

MacFarlane, Audrey. "Racial Education Values." *America* 17, no. 9 (1994): 10–12.

Maier, Peter, Alex Molnar, Stephen Percy, Phillip Smith, and John Zahorik. "First Year Results of the Student Achievement Guarantee in Education Program." Milwaukee: University of Wisconsin, Center for Urban Initiatives and Research, 1997.

Majoribanks, Kevin. "Academic Achievement: Social Class and Social Class Correlates." in *Environments for Learning*, edited by Kevin Majoribanks. Windsor, Berks: NFER Publishing, 1974.

Mann, Maxine. "What Does Ability Grouping Do to Self-Concept?" *Childhood Education*, 36 (1960): 356–361.

Marger, Martin. *Social Inequality.* Boston: McGraw Hill, 2002.

Marsh, Herbert, and Kenneth Rowe. "The Effects of Single-sex and Mixed-sex Mathematics Classes within a Coeducational School." *Australian Journal of Education* 40, (1996): 147–162.

Marshall, Susan. *Splintered Sisterhood.* Madison, WI: University of Wisconsin Press, 1997.

Marx, Karl, and Friedrich Engels. *Economic and Philosophical Manuscripts.* Translated and edited by Tom Bottomore. New York: McGraw Hill, 1844/1963.

Mawdsley, Ralph. "Homeschools and the law." *ELA Notes* 35, no. 2 (2000): 4–5.

McClelland, David, et al. "Religious and Other Sources of Parental Attitudes towards Independence Training." Pp. 389–400 in *Studies in Motivation*, edited by David McClelland. New York: Appleton Century Crofts, 1955.

McDill, Edward, Gary Natriello, and Aaron Pallas. "A Population at Risk." Pp. 106–147 in *School dropouts: Patterns and Policies*, edited by Gary Natriello. New York: Teachers College, 1986.

McEwin, Kenneth, Thomas Dickinson, and D. Jenkins. *America's Middle Schools in the Next Century.* Westerville, OH: National Middle School Association, 2003.

McLanahan, Sarah, and Gary Sandefur. *Growing Up with a Single Parent.* Cambridge: Harvard University Press, 1994.

McLeod, Douglas, Benjamin Detenber, and William Eveland. "Behind the Third Person Effect," *Journal of Communication* 51, no. 4 (2001): 678–695.

McLoyd, Vonnie. "The Impact of Economic Hardship on Black Families and Children." *Child Development* 61 (1990): 311–346.

McPartland, James, and Edward McDill. *The Unique Role of Schools in Causes of Youth Crime.* Johns Hopkins University. Center for the Social Organization of Schools, 1976.

Mead, George. *Mind, Self and Society.* Chicago: University of Chicago Press, 1934.

Menaghan, Elizabeth. "Intergenerational Costs of Parental Stressors." *Journal of Health and Social Behavior* 38, (1997): 72–86.

Menaghan, Elizabeth, and Toby Parcel. "Stability and Change in Children's Home Environments: The Results of Parental Occupational Experiences." Presented at the Society for Research in Child Development meeting, Seattle, WA, April 1991.

Meyer, John. "The Effects of Education as an Institution." *American Journal of Sociology* 83 (1977): 55–77.

Mickelson, Roslyn. "Why Does Jane Read and Write So Well?" Pp. 326–337 in *Structure of Schooling*, edited by Richard Arum & Irenee Beattie. London: Mayfield Publishing Co, 2000.

Mickelson, Roslyn, and Stephen Smith. "Can Education Eliminate Race, Class and Gender?" Pp. 361–370 in *Race, Class, Gender,* edited by Margaret Anderson. New York: Wadsworth Press, 2004.

Miedel, Wendy, and Arthur Reynolds. "Parental Involvement in Early Intervention for Disadvantaged Children." *Journal of School Psychology* 37, no. 4 (1999): 379–390.

Miller, Lamar, Ed. *Brown Plus Thirty: Perspectives on Desegregation.* New York: New York University, Metropolitan Center for Educational Research, 1986.

Millis, Barbara, and Philip Cottell. *Cooperative Learning for Higher Education.* Phoenix: American Council on Education/Oryx Press, 1977.

Mitrsomwang, Suparvadee, and Willis Hawley. *Cultural Adaptation and the Effect of Family Values and Behaviors on Academic Achievement.* Final Report to the Office of Educational Research and Improvement of the U.S. Department of Education, Grant R, 1993. 117E 00045.

Molnar, Alex, Philip Smith, John Zahorik, Amanda Palmer, Anke Halbach, and Karen Ehrle. "Evaluating the Sage Program." *Educational Evaluation and Policy Analysis* 21, no. 2 (1999): 99–110.

Morse, Jodie. "A Victory for Vouchers." *Time* July 8, 2002: 32–34.

Morgan, David and Duane Alwin. "When Less is More: School Size and Social Participation. *Social Psychology Quarterly* 43 (1980): 241–253.

Morris, Valarie. An Evaluation of Student Achievement in a Primary Plan. Dissertation Abstracts (1969), 293809-A. University microfilms (69-7352).

Mortimore, Peter and Peter Blatchford. "The Issue of Class Size for Young children in Schools: What can we Learn from Research?" *Oxford Review of Education* 20, no. 4 (1994): 411–428.

Morton, Samuel. *Crania Americana.* Philadelphia: J. Dobson, 1839.

Moses, Paul. "A Study of Inter-class Ability Grouping on Achievement in Reading." *Dissertation Abstracts* 26 (1966), 4342.

Mostellar, Frederick. "The Tennessee Study of Class Size in Early School Grades." *Future of Children* 5, no. 2 (1995): 113–117.

———. Sustained inquiry in education. *Harvard Educational Review* 66, no. 4 (1996): 797–842.

Moyer, Edward. "A Study of the Effects of Classification by Intelligence Tests." In *The Twenty-Third Yearbook of the National Society for the Study of Education, Part I: Report of the Society's Committee on the Education of Gifted Children,* edited by Guy Whipple. 1924.

Moynihan, Daniel. *The Negro Family: The Case for National Action.* Washington, DC: U.S. Department of Labor, 1965.

Muijs, Daniel. "Predictors of Academic Achievement." *British Journal of Educational Psychology* 67, no. 3 (1997): 263–277.

Mulkey, Lynn, Robert Crain, and Alexander Harrington. "One Parent Households and Achievement." *Sociology of Education* 65 (1992): 48–55.

Muller, Chandra. "Gender Differences in Parental Involvement." *Sociology of Education* 71 (1998): 336–356.

Muller, Chandra, and Christopher Ellison. "Religious Involvement, Social Capital and Adolescent Academic Progress." *Sociological Focus* 34, no. 2 (2001): 155–183.

Murphy, Joseph, Marsha Weil, Philip Hallinger, and Alexis Mittman. "Translating High Expectations into School Policies and Classroom Practices." *Educational Leadership* 40 (1982): 22–26.

National Center for Education Statistics. *Indicators of School Crime and safety.* Washington, DC: U.S. Department of Education, 2006.

National Center for Education Statistics. Dropout rates in the U.S., 1999. http://nces.ed.gov/ (Accessed prior to May 2008).

National Center for Education Statistics. *High School and Beyond Study.* 1992.

National Center for Education Statistics. *The Conditions of Education.* Washington, DC: U.S. Department of Education, 1999.

National Commission on Excellence in Education. *A Nation at Risk.* U.S. Department of Education. U.S. Government Printing Office, Washington, DC, 1983.

National Education Association, Per Capita Expenditures report, 2003. *National Society for the Study of Education.* 23.

Neal, Derek. "The Effect of Catholic Secondary School on Educational Attainment." *Journal of Labor Economics* 15 (January 1997): 98–123.

——. "What Have We Learned about the Benefit of Private Schooling?" *Economic Policy Review* 4, no. 1 (1998): 79–86.

Newman, Horatio, Frank Freeman, and Karl Holzinger. *Twins: A Study of Heredity and Environment.* Chicago: University of Chicago Press, 1937.

Nieto, Sonia. *Affirming Diversity.* White Plains, NY: Longmans, 1996.

Noguera, Pedro, and Antwi Akom. "The Significance of Race in the Racial Achievement Gap in Academic Achievement." In *Motion Magazine* June 19, 2000.

Nolan, T. "The Effects of Ability Grouping." (Ph.D. Dissertation, University of Colorado, Boulder Press, 1985).

Nordman, Nancy. "The Marginalization of Students with Learning Disabilities as a Function of School Philosophy and Practice." *Journal of Moral Education* 30, no. 3 (2001): 273–286.

Nowell, Amy, and Larry Hedges. "Trends in Gender Differences in Academic Achievement." *Sex Roles: Journal of Research,* (July 1998): 1–3.

Oakes, Jeannie. *Keeping Track: How Schools Structure Inequality.* New Haven, CT: Yale University Press, 1985.

——. "Tracking in Secondary Schools." *Educational Psychologist* 22, no. 2 (1987): 129–153.

——. *Multiplying inequalities.* Santa Monica: CA: Rand, 1991.

——. Two cities' Tracking and Within-School Segregation. *Teachers College Record* 96 (1995): 681–690.

——. "Detracking." *Teacher's College Record* 98 (1997): 483–510.

Oakes, Jeannie, and Amy Wells. "Detracking for High Student Achievement." *Educational Leadership* 55, no. 38 (1998): 41–48.

Oakes, Jeannie, and Martin Lipton. "Tracking and Ability Grouping: A Structural Barrier to Achieving." Pp. 187–205 in *Access to Knowledge*, edited by Pamela Keating. New York: College Board, 1994.

——. "Developing Alternatives to Tracking and Grading." Pp. 168–200 in *Educating a New Majority,* edited by Laura Rendon and Richard Hope. San Francisco: Jossey-Bass Publishers, 1996.

Oakes, Jeannie, Karen Quartz, Steve Ryan, and Martin Lipton. *Becoming Good American Schools.* San Francisco: Jossey Bass, 2000.

Oliver, Melvin, and Thomas Shapiro. *Black Wealth, White Wealth.* New York: Rutledge, 1995.

Orr, Amy. "Black-White Differences in Achievement: The Importance of Wealth." *Sociology of Education* 76, no. 4 (2003): 281–304.

Ortiz, Flora. "Hispanic-American Experiences in the Classroom." Pp. 63–87 in *Race, Class, and Gender in American Education,* edited by LoisWeis. Albany: State University of New York Press, 1988.

Page, Ellis, and Gary Grandon. "Family Configuration and Academic Ability." *American Educational Research Journal* 16 (1979): 257–272.

Page, Reba. *Lower Track Classrooms.* New York: Teachers College Press, 1991.

———. *Lower Track Classes at College Prep High Schools.* Spindler, 1987.

Pallas, Aaron. "Ability Group Effects: Instructional, Social or institutional?" *Sociology of Education* 67, no. 1 (1994): 27–46.

Parcel, Toby, and Mikaela Dufur. "Capital at Home and at School." *Social Forces* 79 (2001): 881–912.

Parcel, Toby, and Laura Geschwender. "Explaining Disadvantage in Verbal Facility among Young Children." *Social Forces* 73, no. 3 (1995): 841–874.

Passeron, Jean Claude, and Pierre Bourdieu. *Reproduction in Education, Society and Culture.* London: Sage, 1977.

Pellegrini, Anthony, and Peter Blatchford. *The Child at School: Interactions with Peers and Teachers.* London: Arnold, 2000.

Peng, Samuel. "Expectations, Instructional Behavior and Pupil Achievement." Ph.D. dissertation, University of NY at Buffalo, 1974.

Persell, Caroline. *Education and Inequality.* New York: Free Press, 1977.

———. Understanding Society. New York: Harper and Row, 1990.

———. "Differential Asset Conversion: Class and Gender Pathways to Selective Colleges." *Sociology of Education* 65, no. 3 (1992): 208–225.

Peterson, Richard. "Understanding Audience Segmentation." *Poetics* 21 (1992): 243–58.

Phillips, Meredith. "Sibship size and academic achievement: What we now know and what we still need to know: Comment on Gue & VanWey." *American Sociological Review* 64, no. 2 (1999): 188–192.

Phillips, Steven, Michael Smith, and Joseph Witted. *Parents and Schools: Staff Report to the Study Commission on Quality of Education in Milwaukee Schools.* Milwaukee, WI: Milwaukee Schools, 1985.

Piestrup, Ann. Black dialect interference and accommodation in first grade. Berkeley, CA: Language behavior research laboratory. Monograph, no. 4, 1973.

Plewis, Ian. "Underachievement: A Case of Conceptual Confusion." *British Educational Research Journal* 17, no. 4 (1991): 377–385.

Plowden Report. Children and Their Primary Schools: A Report of the Central Advisory Council for Education (England). London: Her Majesty's Stationery Office. Population Investigation Committee and the Scottish Council for Research in Education, 1949.

Portes, Alejandro, and Patricia Landolt. "Social Capital: Promise and Pitfalls of Its Role and Development." *Journal of Latin American Studies* 32 (2000): 529–547.

Powell, Brian, and Lala Steelman. "The Educational Benefits of Being Spaced Out: Sibship Size Intensity and Educational Progress." *American Sociological Review* 58 (1993): 367–381.

Provus, Malcolm. "Ability Grouping in Arithmetic." *Elementary School Journal* 64, (1960): 387–392.

Pulliam, John, and James Van Patten. *History of Education in America*. Upper Saddle River, NJ: Merrill/Prentice Hall, 2003.

Pulliam, John. *The History of Education in America*. New York: Prentice Hall, 1999.

Putnam, Robert. *Bowling Alone*. New York: Simon & Schuster, 2000.

Raffini, James. *Winners without Losers: Structures and Strategies for Improving Student Motivation*. Needham Heights, MA: Allyn and Bacon, 1993. ED 362 952.

Rainwater, Lee. *Behind Ghetto Walls*. Chicago: Aldine, 1970.

Raley, R. Kelly, Michelle Frisco, and Elizabeth Wildsmith. "Maternal Cohabitation and Educational Success." *Sociology of Education* 78, no. 2 (2005): 144–164.

Ray, Brian. *Strengths of Their Own: Homeschoolers across America*. Salem, OR: National Home Education Research Institute, 1997.

Reed, William. "After Four Decades, Segregation Prevails." New York: *New York Beacon*, 1995.

Reglin, Gary. "Ability Grouping." *Illinois School Review* (1992): 43–47.

Regnerus, Mark. "Shaping Schooling Success." *Journal for the Scientific Study of Religion* 39 (2000): 363–370.

Regnerus, Mark, and Glen Elder. "Staying on Track in School: Religious Influences in High and Low Risk Settings." *Journal for the Scientific Study of Religion* 42, no. 4 (2003): 633–649.

Rendon, Laura, and Richard Hope, eds. *Educating a New Majority*. San Francisco: Jossey Bass, 1996.

Richardson, Virginia. *School Children at Risk*. New York: Falmer Press, 1989.

Riordan, Cornelius. *Girls and Boys in School: Together or Separate?* New York: Teachers' College Press, 1990.

———. Single-gender schools. *Research in Sociology of Education and Socialization* 10, (1994): 177–205.

———. *Equality and Achievement*. New York: Longman Press, 1997.

Ripley, Aamanda, and Sonja Stephoe. "Time Is on Our Side." *Vermont Education Report* 5 (20), 2005.

Rist, Ray. "Student Social Class and Teacher Expectations: The Self-fulfilling Prophesy in Ghetto Education." *Harvard Educational Review* 40 (1970): 411–451.

Robinson, Glen. "Synthesis of Research on the Effects of Class Size." *Educational Leadership* 47, no. 7 (1990): 80–90.

Robinson, Glen, and James Wittlebols. *Class Size Research*. Arlington, VA: Educational Research Service, 1986.

Rohwedder, Cecilie. "London Parents Scramble for Edge in Preschool Wars." *Wall Street Journal*, February 12, 2007, 1(A).

Roscigno, Vincent. "Race and the Production of Educational Disadvantage." *Social Forces* 76 (1998): 1033–1060.

Rose, Lowell, and Alec Gallup. "The 36th Annual Phi Betta Kappa Poll of the Public's Attitude Towards the Public Schools." *Phi Delta Kappa* 86, no. 1 (2004): 41–58.

———. "The 31st Annual Phi Delta Kappa/Gallup Poll of the Public's Attitudes Toward Public Schools." *Phi Delta Kappa* (September 1999): 41–56.

Rosenbaum, James. *Making Inequality*. New York: Wiley, 1976.

——. (1980). Social implications of educational grouping. In *Review of Research in Education*. Washington, DC: American Educational Research Association.

Rosenbaum, James, and Amy Binder. "Do Employers Really Need More Educated Youth?" *Sociology of Education* 70 (January 1997): 69–85.

Rosenthal, Robert. "The Pygmalian Effect Lives." *Psychology Today* 12 (September 1974): 56–63.

——. "Critiquing Pygmalion." *Current Directions in Psychological Science 4*, (1995): 171.

——. *Productivity and the Self-fulfilling Prophesy*. Carlsbad, CA: CRM Films, 1987.

Rosenthal, Robert, and Lenore Jacobson. *Pygmalian in the Classroom*. New York: Holt, Rinehart and Winston, 1968.

Rothman, Stanley. "The Politics of Catholic Parochial Schools: An Historical and Comparative Analysis." *The Journal of Politics* 25, no. 1 (1963): 49–71.

Rouse, Cecilia. "Low Income Students and College Attendance." *Social Science Quarterly* 85 (December 2004): 1299–1317.

Rubie-Davies, Christine. "Teacher Expectations and Student Self-perception." *Psychology in Schools* 45, no. 5 (2006): 537–551.

Rubie-Davies, Christine, John Hattie, and Richard Hamilton. "Expecting the Best for Students." *British Journal of Educational Psychology*. Leicester 76, no. 3 (2006): 429–45.

Rutter, Michael. *Fifteen Thousand Hours*. Cambridge: Harvard University Press, 1979.

Sadker, Myra, and David Sadker. *Failing at Fairness: How Our Schools Cheat Girls*. New York: Charles Scribner and Sons, 1994.

——. *Teachers, Schools, and Society*. New York: Random House, 1988.

Sampson, Robert, and John Laub. "The Role of Schools, Peers and Siblings." Pp. 99–102 in *Crime in the Making*. Cambridge, MA: Harvard University Press, 1993.

Sanders, William. "Private Schools and Public School Achievement." *The Journal of Human Resources* 34, no. 4 (1999): 697–709.

Sanders, William, and Anthony Krautmann. "Catholic Schools, Dropout Rates and Educational Attainment." *Economic Inquiry* 23 (1995): 217–233.

Sarcona-Navarra, M. "The Effects of Parental Involvement on Achievement and Motivation in Science for High School Students." (Ph.D. dissertation, St John's University, New York, 2007).

Scarr-Salapatek, Sandra, and Richard Weinberg. "When Black Children Grow Up in White Homes." *Psychology Today* 9 (1975): 80–82.

Scarr, Sandra, and Richard Weinberg. "The Influence of Family Background on Intellectual Attainment." *American Sociological Review* 43 (October 1978): 674–692.

Schafer, Walter. *Tracking and Opportunity*. Scranton, PA: Chandler, 1971.

Schafer, Walter, Carol Olexa and Kenneth Polk. "Programmed for Social Class." *Transaction* 7 (1970): 39–63.

Scheff, Thomas. *Being Mentally Ill*. Chicago: Aldine, 1966.

Scheurich, James, and Michael Imber. "Educational Reform Can Reproduce Societal Inequalities." *Educational Administration Quarterly* 27, no. 3 (1991): 297–320.

Schur, Edwin. *Labeling Deviant Behavior.* New York: Harper and Row, 1971.

Shakeshaft, Carol. "A Gender at Risk." *Phi Delta Kappa* 67 (1986): 449–506.

Shields, James. *Monozygote Twins Brought Up Apart and Brought Up Together.* London: Oxford University Press, 1962.

Shockley, William. "Dysgenics, Geneticity, Raceology: A Challenge to the Intellectual Responsibility of Educators." *Phi Delta Kappan* (1972): 297–307.

———. "Variance of Caucasian Admixture in Negro Populations, Pigmentation Variability and IQ." Proceedings of the national Academy of Sciences, USA, 1973. 70, 2180a.

———. *Shockley on Eugenics and Race.* Washington, DC: Scott-Townsend Publishers, 1992.

Singh, Kusum, Claire Vaught and Ethel Mitchell. "Single Sex Classes and Academic Achievement in Two Inner City Schools." *Journal of Negro Education* 67, no. 2 (1998): 157–167.

Sirin, Selcuk. "Socioeconomic Status and Academic Achievement: A Meta-Analytic Review of Research." *Review of Educational Research* 75, no. 3 (2005): 417–453.

Slavin, Robert. "Achievement Effects of Ability Grouping." *Review of Educational Research* 60 (1990): 471–499.

———. "Best Evidence Synthesis: An Alternative to Meta-analytic and Traditional Reviews." *Educational Researcher* 15, no. 9 (1986): 5–11.

———. Ability grouping and student achievement. *Review of Educational Research* 57, no. 3 (1987): 293–336.

———. "Ability Grouping in the Middle Grades: Achievement Effects and Alternatives." *The Elementary School Journal* 93, no. 5 (1993): 535–552.

———. "Best Evidence Synthesis: An Alternative to Meta-analytic and Traditional Reviews." *Educational Researcher* 15, no. 9 (1986): 5–11.

———. "Achievement Effects of Substantial Reductions in Class Size." Pp. 247–257 in *School and Classroom Organization*, edited by Robert Slavin. Hillside, NJ: Erlbaum, 1989.

Slavin, Robert, and Nancy Karweit. "Effects of Whole Class and Ability Group Instruction on Math Achievement." *American Educational Research Journal* 22, no. 3 (1985): 351–367.

Smith, Page. *Killing the Spirit.* New York: Viking Penguin, 1990.

Snyder, Mark. "Self-fulfilling Stereotypes." Pp. 153–160 in *Down to Earth Sociology*, edited by James Henslin. New York: Free Press, 1993.

Snyder, Thomas, and Charlene Hoffman. *Digest of Education.* Washington, DC: National Center for Education Statistics, 1991.

Sorensen, Aage. "Organizational Differentiation of Students and Educational Opportunity." Baltimore, MD: Center for the Study of Social Organization of Schools, 1969.

Southwest Educational Laboratory. *Building Support for Better Schools.* Austin, TX: Southwest Educational Development Laboratory, 2002. http://www.sedl.org/pubs/family27/building_support.pdf (accessed Prior to November 26, 2005).

Stahl, Steven, and David Haynes. *Instructional Models in Reading.* Mahwah, NJ: Erlbaum, 1996.

Stanton-Salazar, Ricardo, and Sanford Dornbush. "Social Capital and the Reproduction of Inequality." *Sociology of Education* 68 (1995): 12.

Statistical Abstract of the United States. U.S. Bureau of the Census. Washington, DC:U.S. Government Printing Office, 1999.

Stein, Annie. "Strategies of Failure." *Harvard Educational Review* 41 (1971): 158–204.

Strum, Charles. "Schools, Tracks and Democracy." *New York Times*, April 1, 1993, 1(B).

Stryker, S. Symbolic Interactionism: Themes and variations. In M. Rosenberg and R. Turner eds. *Social Psychology*. New Brunswick, NJ: Transaction, 1990.

Stumpf, Heinrich. "Gender Differences in Tests of Cognitive Ability." *Learning and Individual Differences* 7 (1995): 275–288.

Sullivan, Alice. "Cultural Capital and Educational Attainment." *Sociology* 35, no. 4 (2001): 893–912.

Tardiff, T., E. Hoff, and B. Laursen. "Socio-economic Status and Parenting." Pp. 156–171 in *Handbook of Parenting, Vol. 2*, edited by Marc Bornstein. Mahwah, NJ: Erlbaum, 2002.

Tauber, Robert. "Good or bad: What teachers expect for students they generally get." Washington, DC: Eric Clearinghouse on Teaching and Teacher Education, 1998. Eric ED 426985.

Taylor, H. "Intelligence." *Encyclopedia of Sociology*, edited by Edgar Borgatta and Marie Borgatta. New York: Macmillan, 1996.

Tedin, Kent and Gregory Weiher. "Racial/Ethnic Diversity and Academic Quality as Components of School Choice." *Journal of Politics* 66 (2004): 1109–1134.

Thio, Alex. *Deviant Behavior*. Boston: Allyn & Bacon, 2001.

Thompson, Godfrey. The Trend of Scottish Intelligence. London: University of London Press Ltd, 1967.

Thompson, Maxine, Karl Alexander and Doris Entwisle. "Household Composition, Parental Expectations and Academic Achievement." *Social Forces* 67, no. 2 (1988): 424–436.

Thousand, Jacqueline, Richard Villa and Ann Nevin. *Creativity and Collaborative Learning*. Baltimore: Brooks Press, 1994.

Turner, Julianne and Helen Patrick. "Motivational Influences on Student Participation in Classroom Learning Activities." *Teachers College Record* 106, no. 9 (2004): 1759–1785.

U.S. Bureau of the Census. American Community Survey. Washington, DC: Government Printing Office, 2006.

——. *Educational Attainment in the United States*. Washington, DC: U.S. Government Printing Office, 2004.

——. *Statistical Abstract of the United States*. Washington, DC: U.S. Government Printing Office, 2000.

U.S. Department of Education, National Center for Education Statistics. *The Condition of Education 2006*. Washington, DC: U.S. Government Printing Office, 2006.

——. National Commission on Excellence in Education. *A Nation at Risk: Imperatives for Educational Reform*. Washington, DC: Government Printing Office, 1983.

——. *Digest of Educational Statistics*. Washington, DC: Government Printing Office, 2003.

——. National Center for Education Statistics. National Assessment of Adult Literacy. Washington, DC: Institute for Education Sciences, 2003

——. *The Condition of Education, 2001*. Washington DC: Government Printing Office, 2001.

Valentine, Charles. *Culture and Poverty*. Chicago, IL: University of Chicago Press, 1968.

VanderHart, Peter. "Why Do Some Schools Group by Ability?" *American Journal of Economics and Sociology* 65, no. 2 (2006): 436–462.

Vanfossen, Beth, James Jones and Joan Spade. "Curriculum, Tracking and Status Maintenance." *Sociology of Education* 60, no. 2 (1987): 104–122.

Vang, Christopher. "Minority Students Are Far from Academic Success and Still At-Risk in Public Schools." *Multicultural Education* 12, no. 4 (2005): 9–15.

Villas-Boas, Adelina. "The Effects of Parental Involvement in Homework on Student Achievement in Portugal and Luxembourg." *Childhood Education* 74 (1998): 367–371.

Wade, Nicholas. "IQ and Heredity." *Science* 194 (November 26, 1976): 916–919.

Walberg, Herbert and Kevin Majoribanks. "Family, Environment and Cognitive Achievement." *Review of Educational Research* 46, no. 4 (1988): 527–551.

Wallace, John and David Williams. "Religion and Adolecscent Health-compromising Behavior." Pp. 444–468 in *Health Risks and Developmental Transitions During Adolescence,* edited by John Schulenberg, Jennifer Maggs and Klaus Hurrelmann. Cambridge, U.K.: Cambridge University Press, 1997.

Wallerstein, Judith and Julia Lewis. "The Long-term Impact of Divorce on Children." *Family and Conciliation Reports Review* 36 (1998): 368–383.

Wallis, Claudia and Sonja Steptoe. "How to Fix No Child Left Behind." *Time* (June 4, 2007): 34–41.

Warrington, Molly and Mike Younger. "Single Sex Classes and Equal Opportunity for Boys and Girls." *Oxford Review of Education* 27 (2001): 339–356.

Wax, Murray and Rosalie Wax. "Cultural Deprivation as an Educational Ideology." Pp. 127 in *The Culture of Poverty: A Critique,* edited by E. Leacock. New York: Simon and Schuster, 1971, p. 127.

Weber, Max. *The Protestant Ethic and the Spirit of Capitalism,* trans. Talcot Parsons (New York: Charles Scribner & Sons, 1954).

Webster, Staten, ed. *The Disadvantaged Learner*. San Francisco: Chandler, 516–517.

Wells, Amy and Robert Crain. *Stepping Over the Color Line.* New Haven, CT: Yale University Press, 1997.

Wells, Amy and Irene Sera. "The Politics of Culture: Understanding Local Political Resistance to Detracking in Racially Mixed Schools." *Harvard Educational Review* 66, no. 1 (1996).

——. "Liability Grouping." *Harvard Educational Review* 66, no. 1 (1996): 95–119.

Wells, Amy and Jeannie Oakes. "Tracking, Detracking and the Politics of Educational Reform." Pp. 158–180 in *Emerging Issues in the Sociology of Education*, edited by Carlos Torres. Albany, NY: Suny Press, 1998.

Welner, Kevin. "They Retard What They Cannot Repel: Examining the Role Teachers Sometimes Play in Subverting Equity-Minded Reforms." *Journal of Negro Education* 68, no. 2 (1999): 200–212.

———. "Liability Grouping: The New Susceptibility of School Tracking to Legal Challenges." *Harvard Educational Review* 66, no. 3 (1996): 451–470.

Welner, Kevin and Jeannie Oakes. "The New Susceptibility of School Tracking Systems to Legal Challenges." *Harvard Educational Review* 66, no. 3 (1996): 451–70.

Weglinsky, Harold. "How Money Matters: The Effect of School District Spending on Academic Achievement." *The Sociology of Education* 70 (July 1997): 221–237.

West, Anne and Hazel Pennell. *Underachievement in Schools*. New York: Routledge Falmer, 2003.

Wheelock, Anne. *Crossing the Tracks*. New York: Norton Press, 1992.

Wilson, Alan. "Residential Segregation of Social Classes and Aspirations of High School Boys." *American Sociological Review* 24 (1959): 836–845.

Wilson, Bruce and Thomas Corcoran. *Successful Secondary Schools*. New York: Falmer, 1988.

Word, Elizabeth, John Johnson and Helen Bain. *Student/Teacher Achievement Ratio (STAR): Tennessee's K-3 Class Size Study.* Nashville, TN: Tennessee Department of Education, 1990.

Wuthrick, Marjorie. "Blue Jays Win! Crows Go Down in Defeat." *Phi Delta Kappa* 71, no. 7 (1990): 553–557.

Wyndham Harold. *Ability Grouping: Recent Developments*. Melbourne: M.U.P., 1934.

Yair, Gad. "Educational Battlefields in America." *Sociology of Education* 73 (2000): 247–269.

Yang, Min, Harvey Goldstein, Rumana Omar, Rebecca Turner and Simon Thompson. "Meta-analysis Using Multilevel Models with an Application to the Study of Class Size Effects." *Journal of the Royal Statistical Society*, Series C, 49 (2000): 1–14.

Young, Deidra and Barry Fraser. "Sex Differences in Science Achievement." (1992) (ERIC Document Reproductive Service No. 356 947).

Young, Michael. *Knowledge and Control*. London: Collier Macmillan, 1971.

Zill, Nicholas. *Family Change and Student Achievement.* Hillsdale, NJ: Booth and Dunn, 1996.

Index